SUSTAINABLE FASHION

SUSTAINABLE FASHION

Past, Present, and Future

JENNIFER FARLEY GORDON AND COLLEEN HILL

BLOOMSBURY

LONDON • NEW DELHI • NEW YORK • SYDNEY

Bloomsbury Academic

An imprint of Bloomsbury Publishing Plc

50 Bedford Square	1385 Broadway
London	New York
WC1B 3DP	NY 10018
UK	USA

www.bloomsbury.com

Bloomsbury is a registered trade mark of Bloomsbury Publishing Plc

First published 2015

© Jennifer Farley Gordon and Colleen Hill, 2015

Jennifer Farley Gordon and Colleen Hill have asserted their right under the Copyright, Designs and Patents Act, 1988, to be identified as Authors of this work.

British Library Cataloguing-in-Publication Data

A catalogue record for this book is available from the British Library.

ISBN HB: 978-0-8578-5184-0
PB: 978-08578-5185-7
ePDF: 978-08578-5186-4
ePub: 978-0-8578-5187-1

Library of Congress Cataloging-in-Publication Data

Farley, Jennifer.
Sustainable fashion : past, present, and future / Jennifer Farley and Colleen Hill.
pages cm
ISBN 978-0-85785-185-7 (paperback)– ISBN 978-0-85785-184-0 (hardback)– ISBN 978-0-85785-186-4 (epdf)
I. Hill, Colleen, 1982- II. Title.
TT507.F295 2015
746.9'2–dc23
2014013549

Typeset by Fakenham Prepress Solutions, Fakenham, Norfolk NR21 8NN
Printed and bound in India

For our families, with love.

CONTENTS

LIST OF ILLUSTRATIONS

Plate Section

1a. Reticule, ivory silk with multicolor embroidery.

1b. An image from Greenpeace's "Toxic Glamour" fashion shoot in China, as part of their larger, on-going Detox campaign.

2. Man's patchwork dressing gown made from crazy quilt, multicolor patchwork and black moiré.

3. Installation shot from *Eco-Fashion: Going Green*. Maison Martin Margiela, sweaters made from socks, army green wool.

4. Adrian, suit, tan, grey, blue and red wool.

5. Evening dress, multicolor printed paper and pink ostrich feathers.

6. Installation shot from *Eco-Fashion: Going Green*. Organic by John Patrick, ensemble, hand-painted white organic cotton mesh, purple silk.

7. Dress, orange rayon/cotton blend, multicolored floral cotton.

8. Giorgio di Sant'Angelo, halter dress, yellow, green and purple polyester knit.

9. Installation shot from *Eco-Fashion: Going Green*. Left: Dress and pelerine, green, yellow, and red roller-printed cotton, c. 1821, England. Right: Dress, aubergine jacquard patterned silk.

10. Dress, purple and black striped silk taffeta.

11. Two-piece day dress, green silk faille, chenille.

12. Isoude (Kate Brierley), *Eirene* evening gown, coral tussah silk, Mabe pearl shell.

13. Morris & Co. (William Morris), *Bird and Anemone*, furnishing fabric, indigo-discharged and block-printed cotton.

14. Sophie, dress and sweater set, black silk twill with discharge floral print, cashmere.

15. Yoshiki Hishinuma, dress, heat-transfer printed polyester tulle.

16. Costello Tagliapietra, dress, polyester peau de soie.

Chapter One

Chapter Two

Chapter Six

ACKNOWLEDGMENTS

The idea for this book began as an exhibition entitled *Eco-Fashion: Going Green,* which was on view at The Museum at FIT (MFIT) in 2010. We express our heartfelt gratitude to all of our colleagues at MFIT, especially Dr. Valerie Steele, director and chief curator, Patricia Mears, deputy director, and Fred Dennis, senior curator, for their guidance through every phase of this project. We also extend our appreciation to the Museum's photographer, Eileen Costa, to Thomas Synnamon, for his assistance in preparing objects for photography, and to our conservators Ann Coppinger, Marjorie Jonas and Nicole Bloomfield. Thanks also to MFIT editor Julian Clark, whose assistance with writing text for the *Eco-Fashion* exhibition proved invaluable to this publication as well.

Sustainable fashion is a topic close to our hearts, and we are thrilled to have met so many people who share our enthusiasm. Many thanks to Adam Baruchowitz, Bob Bland, Kate Brierley, Naomi Gross, Leanne Mai-ly Hilgart and John Patrick for providing such insightful interviews on their work. There are also a number of sustainable fashion designers who provided clothing for the *Eco-Fashion* exhibition, and whose work has also been included in this publication: Natalie Chanin, Rebecca Earley, Ali Hewson, Peter ngwersen, Stella McCartney, Carlos Miele, Sarah Ratty, Per Åge Sivertsen, and Yeohlee Teng. We are in awe of the talent that these designers possess, and we also have tremendous respect for their principles.

For the generous use of images, we thank Greenpeace; Yeohlee, Leanne Mai-ly Hilgart and Gregory Vaughan; the Kheel Center at Cornell University; the New York Public Library; Jane Thylan and the Fashion Institute of Technology|SUNY, Gladys Marcus Library, Department of Special Collections. The staff of the latter—Karen Cannell, April Calahan, and Juliet Jacobson—also provided invaluable assistance with research.

At Bloomsbury Academic Publishers, we extend our gratitude to our commissioning editor, Anna Wright, who helped us take the first steps toward making this book a reality. We are also grateful to Hannah Crump, Chloe Darke and Abbie Sharman, for their kind assistance and input on *Sustainable Fashion: Past, Present and Future.*

INTRODUCTION

Sustainable Fashion: Past, Present and Future is the first book to concentrate on the history of the relationship between the fashion industry and the environment. As examinations of eco-friendly materials and techniques—and the fashion labels that embrace them—are essential to furthering knowledge of sustainable fashion, it has become the subject of numerous publications over the course of the last decade. Yet most of these publications have focused primarily on contemporary examples of sustainability. Those that have investigated the past have typically looked back no further than the 1960s, linking sustainable fashion initiatives to the birth of the environmental movement. A deeper understanding of the past is crucial to our grasp of the present.

This book is organized around more than 60 examples of fashion and textiles from the eighteenth century to the present. Each object is discussed with regards to its materials and/or methods of production, as well as its larger significance to fashion's past. Through a discussion of the exploitation of human labor, animals and the environment, readers will gain knowledge of long-standing negative production practices within the fashion industry—and the urgency of incorporating sustainability into contemporary fashion will be made apparent. In contrast, certain positive practices—many of which have long been abandoned by most designers and manufacturers—offer possible solutions for fashion's future.

What is sustainable fashion?

The general definition of sustainability refers to an ecological system that is designed to maintain balance, meaning that no more should be taken from the environment than can be renewed. The term sustainable fashion is typically used to encompass a scope of fashion production or design methods that are environmentally and/or ethically conscious—but it does not have a standard definition. "Sustainable" is often used interchangeably with other words, such as "eco," "green" and "organic." A general absence of environmental standards within the fashion industry adds to the confusion. Because the definition of sustainable fashion is subject to interpretation, even those working within the field have differing opinions on best (or most important) practices.

It is nearly impossible for the fashion industry to be truly sustainable. Fashion is guided by a cycle of style change, in which the old is rapidly replaced by the new. Some design theorists, therefore, feel that sustainable fashion is inherently paradoxical, as sustainability cannot fit easily within such a system of planned obsolescence. As Sandy Black, author of *Eco-Chic: The Fashion Paradox*, notes: "at all stages of design and production decision-making there are trade-offs to be made, reconciling fashion and style with available materials, costs and time constraints."[1] Although there are a number of obstacles facing those who seek to implement environmentally friendly practices, awareness of the ways in which fashion may be produced, disseminated and discarded allows designers, manufacturers and consumers to make informed choices.

Why is sustainable fashion important?

Human impact on the environment has been a source of intense emotion and debate for nearly five decades. As pollution spreads and natural resources diminish, many people are becoming increasingly conscious of the adverse effects on their health and well-being. Current initiatives by various industries to stop, lessen and repair the damage being done to the environment are not merely conscientious—they are crucial.

The fashion industry has received no small measure of criticism for its environmentally destructive practices. Each stage of the clothing production cycle—from the cultivation of raw fibers to the shipment of the finished garment—has harmful consequences, and the rapid pace of the fashion cycle only compounds the problem. Also, the value of clothing has changed—and not, as advocates of sustainable fashion would argue, for the better. Once a revered commodity, fashion is now all too often considered disposable.

The fashion industry employs over forty million people, making it one of the largest industries in the world—as well as one of the planet's biggest polluters. As the consequences of human impact on the environment continue to excite passions and stir controversy, the fashion industry is coming under increasingly intense scrutiny. Accordingly, sustainable fashion is a growing subject of interest to a wide range of people, including environmentalists, fashion students and conscientious consumers.

The increasing speed of the fashion cycle is significantly changing the way that clothing is valued. For example, because of the prevailing trend for disposable "fast fashion," many of today's inexpensive fashions are discarded after being worn just a handful of times. The fast fashion cycle has become so established that many wonder whether it is fundamentally possible to change patterns of consumption. In contrast, "slow fashion" could provide considerable benefit to the environment. However, altering the way we consume fashion may not be without negative ramifications: across the globe, millions of livelihoods depend upon the constancy of change in fashion. These challenges, many of which have existed for over a century, will not be easily or quickly solved.

When did the sustainable fashion movement begin?

Many scholars believe that the roots of the sustainable fashion movement can be traced back to the 1960s and 1970s, in correspondence to rising concerns over the environment. Yet issues surrounding topics such as labor relations, animal rights and the mass production of clothing have long been subjects of discourse. Designers today face problems that date at least as far back as the nineteenth century—when technological developments resulted in quickly produced but inferior textiles, for example. Mechanization and mass production have escalated into the manufacture of cheap, disposable clothing that has become all too common in the industry.

Problems related to fashion production escalated throughout the twentieth century. By the 1940s, a number of designers were experimenting with synthetic fibers, many of which will take hundreds of years to biodegrade. "Natural" fibers, especially cotton, were grown using large amounts of chemical fertilizer and pesticides, polluting both soil and water supplies. Despite ethical concerns, animal products, especially furs, became increasingly fashionable luxury commodities. Throughout the United States, garment workers' unions formed to promote fair wages and healthy work environments. This has prompted a reactionary response of outsourcing of production to third-world countries, where workers are paid very little and labor conditions are often dangerous.

The need for significant change in fashion production was established by the 1960s. Often viewed as the foundation of the environmentalist movement, Rachel Carson's book *Silent Spring* (1962) specifically referenced the use of pesticides in fiber growth, as well as the damage caused by fabric finishes. By the end of the decade, the "natural" look of the hippies was associated with environmentalism. Several elements of their clothing choices—earth tones, hemp fabric and patchwork, for example—were considered prototypes for some of today's sustainable fashions. Many of today's chic styles, however, are a far cry from their earthy 1970s counterparts.

As environmental problems—and their possible solutions—have evolved, so has sustainable fashion. Today, there are a number of ways to "go green." While the choice of organic fabrics seems an obvious method, others, including 'investment' purchases of high-quality, long-lasting goods, are perceived as a way to slow consumerism. No matter the approach, the challenge for designers is to provide sustainable fashions that are affordable, diverse and accessible—and to do so without compromising aesthetic value. However difficult that may be, sustainable fashion provides opportunities for new, creative approaches to design, and industry experts feel optimistic about its future. A 2012 consumer study found that of over 6,000 people surveyed, two-thirds were aware of the importance of ethical fashion.[2] Once viewed as a trend, sustainable fashion today is widely considered an influential part of the environmentalist movement. This book will examine and discuss fashion's relationship with the environment—past, present, and future.

Collecting and exhibiting sustainable fashion

This publication was inspired by an exhibition that was held at The Museum at The Fashion Institute of Technology in 2010, co-curated by the authors. The exhibition, entitled *Eco-Fashion: Going Green,* featured over one hundred examples of clothing, accessories and textiles from the eighteenth century to the present. The objects were arranged chronologically in the Fashion and Textile History Gallery, a space devoted to the exhibition of material from the Museum's permanent collections.

Two ensembles that were featured in an earlier exhibition, entitled *Fashion & Politics*, inspired the idea for a show on sustainable fashion. *Fashion & Politics* explored the various ways in which fashion has raised political, social and environmental awareness. A hand-painted dress by the American fashion designer Kate Brierley underscored her mission to produce quality garments that eschew mass production, while an ensemble by the Danish sustainable fashion label Noir, made from organic cotton and by-product leather, blended luxury with sustainability.

The desire to further explore the importance of sustainable fashion led to the development of *Eco-Fashion: Going Green*, which opened one year later. With an increase of press and publications regarding the sustainable fashion industry, as well as a growing number of sustainable clothing lines, we thought it was the perfect time to organize an exhibition on the subject. Although other exhibitions devoted to sustainable fashion had been organized prior to the opening of *Eco-Fashion: Going Green*, there was little discussion of the industry's environmental and social impact prior to the mid-twentieth century. Our exhibition provided a historical context for today's sustainable fashion movement by examining the past two centuries of fashion's bad (and occasionally good) environmental and ethical practices.

The first step was to organize the framework of the exhibition. In order to make such a complex subject as visitor-friendly as possible, we began by identifying contemporary methods of "going green," with which we hoped many visitors would be familiar. Six prominent themes within the current sustainable fashion industry informed the selection of objects for the exhibition: repurposed and recycled clothing and textiles; quality of craftsmanship; material origins; textile dyeing; labor practices; and treatment of animals.

The majority of curatorial choices were already part of the MFIT collections. In fact, it would be possible to explore the topic of sustainability using nearly any collection of historical clothing: many such collections contain garments that have been altered for continued wear, for example, or that were colored using chemical dyes. The materials, manufacture and/or construction of objects provide fascinating new avenues for research.

Another element crucial to the exhibition was the selection of contemporary sustainable fashion. These new acquisitions were not only featured in *Eco-Fashion: Going Green*, but they also became part of The Museum at FIT's permanent collection. In accordance with the Museum's mission to collect aesthetically and historically significant "directional" clothing, contemporary styles were selected for their designers' devotion to best fashion practices, as well as to high style. As many design theorists predict that sustainability will be integral to the future of fashion, we perceive these garments to be an important part of the Museum's collection not just today, but in years to come.

How is this book organized?

The six themes that formed the framework for the exhibition *Eco-Fashion: Going Green*— and many of the museum pieces that were used to exemplify them—were used to structure the six chapters of this book.

Chapter 1: Repurposed and Recycled Clothing and Textiles
"Repurposed and Recycled Clothing and Textiles" examines the wearing of secondhand clothing, the repurposing of existing fabrics into new garments, and the recycling of old fibers into new textiles. Techniques of repurposing and recycling are often viewed as especially sustainable, as they eliminate or minimize the need for new material production.

Chapter 2: Quality of Craftsmanship
"Quality of Craftsmanship" considers the creation of clothing with lasting value. Since the mechanization of textile and apparel production in the nineteenth century, the quality of many fashion goods has steadily declined, eventually resulting in the current "fast fashion" phenomenon. Inexpensive, poor quality clothing is all too often considered disposable. Many sustainable fashion designers, however, are working to bring conscientiousness and superior craftsmanship back into fashion production.

Chapter 3: Material Origins
"Material Origins" explores the processes surrounding the growth of natural fibers, as well as the manufacture of manmade and synthetic fibers. Plant- and animal-based fibers such as cotton and wool are often considered superior to synthetic fibers, but the chemicals used in their cultivation can be irreversibly damaging. On the other hand, while manmade and synthetic fibers are generally deemed harmful to the environment, there are some positive attributes to their production. In recent years, nature and technology have been combined to create more sustainable fibers that may inspire future innovations.

Chapter 4: Textile Dyeing
"Textile Dyeing" discusses one of the primary pollutants generated by the production of garments and textiles. Beginning with the development of various synthetic dyes during the nineteenth century, chemical dyes have largely displaced traditional plant or insect dyes, but their chemical components can generate toxic wastewater. In response, contemporary researchers and designers are exploring lower-impact and/or sustainable alternatives to harmful dyeing practices, including the preference of some for traditional methods of hand-dyeing and natural materials.

Chapter 5: Labor Practices
"Labor Practices" covers the health and ethical well-being of fashion industry workers, an issue on which the clothing and textile industry has been inconsistent. Unsafe or unfair working conditions characterized nineteenth- and early twentieth-century textile mills and garment factories. Unions formed to promote fair wages and healthy work environments in the United States. However, this has prompted an increase in the outsourcing of production overseas, where pay is likewise low and working conditions are often dangerous. To combat this, modern initiatives include cooperatives and Fair Trade agreements.

Chapter 6: Treatment of Animals
"Treatment of Animals" discusses the debate over the responsible and humane use of animal products, focusing on two categories of animal product: fur and feathers. Feathers were the controversial animal product during the nineteenth century, but have since been supplanted by outrage over the wearing of fur. Although prominent anti-fur campaigns of the early 1990s have sparked greater debate than ever before, numerous designers continue to use fur in their collections today. Some, however, are turning toward the use of ethically sourced products, faux furs or cruelty-free alternatives.

Conclusion
The book's conclusion focuses on the future of sustainable fashion, and features six interviews from designers, educators and entrepreneurs who bring awareness of environmental and ethical concerns into their work. Their responses provide insight into the viability and challenges of the sustainable fashion industry.

1

REPURPOSED AND RECYCLED CLOTHING AND TEXTILES

This chapter explores the wearing of secondhand clothing, the repurposing or remaking of garments, and the recycling of existing fabrics into new textiles. Each of these ideas is examined within the Western apparel market from the eighteenth century to the present. The objects outlined are organized chronologically within their respective concepts.

The term *secondhand* is used to refer to clothing that was re-distributed to new owners, either through being passed down (to family members or servants, for instance), or through resale at a secondhand shop or market. Many secondhand garments were modified to suit their new owners, but items of used clothing could also be entirely *repurposed,* meaning that they were substantially altered from their original forms—or, in some cases, fully refashioned from existing garments or textiles. While the terms repurposed and *recycled* are often used interchangeably, there are distinct differences between the two. In this text, the word recycled describes fabrics that have been reprocessed and converted into new materials.

Practices of repurposing and recycling clothing and textiles have existed for centuries. Yet although these methods have long been an integral part of the fashion industry, they were rarely documented (and were, in fact, frequently stigmatized) prior to the mid- to late-twentieth century. Within today's fashion industry—in which a trendy t-shirt may cost less than a cup of coffee—it is hardly necessary for consumers to purchase secondhand goods, or to mend or alter their clothing for longevity. For the eco-conscious shopper, buying used clothing is considered a particularly sustainable choice, as it reduces textile waste and minimizes the need for new production. In addition, numerous fashion designers are experimenting with ideas to craft unique fashions from the surfeit of discarded, seemingly valueless garments. The recycling of used clothing into new materials has also become vital to the preservation of valuable—and quickly diminishing—natural resources. In the past, however, secondhand or recycled cloth goods were typically utilized for markedly different reasons, such as thrift, economic necessity and appreciation for well-made materials. Prior to the industrialization of textile production in the nineteenth century, fabrics and clothing were costly, cherished commodities that were quite literally used to shreds.

Secondhand clothing: A brief history

Repurposed garments are often easily identified within museum collections, but it is not usually known if an item of clothing was part of the secondhand market. Few objects are acquired with an extensive knowledge of their provenance, and this is especially true of garments dating to the nineteenth century and earlier. Yet research on the "rag trade" has proven that the sale of secondhand clothing was widespread. Well into the nineteenth century, used garments made up a substantial portion of nearly every person's wardrobe in Europe and North America—with only the exception of the very wealthy.[1]

Tailors frequently sold used goods, and also allowed such objects to be exchanged in partial payment for the making of new clothes—meaning that secondhand clothing could act as an "alternate form of currency."[2] Many other specialized vendors, such as breech makers, milliners and shoemakers, sold used fashions alongside new offerings. In fact, some fashion historians consider such garments to be the first "ready-made" items, meaning that consumers were familiar with pre-made clothing long before it was mass produced.[3]

Even after ready-to-wear garments were made easily available, however, the market for cast-off clothing did not diminish. Records indicate that many consumers continued to enhance their wardrobes by purchasing secondhand goods—but to do so was increasingly stigmatized, and such transactions often remained as covert as possible. For example, in the essay "Smart Clothes at Low Prices: Alliances and Negotiations in the British Interwar Secondhand Clothing Trade," author Celia Marshik outlined the discretion necessary to the sale and purchase of secondhand garments among upper and middle class women. Such sales were often prudently managed by a middlewoman. Women of the upper classes were not necessarily wealthy, but it was important for them to remain well dressed. Many such women needed to make a profit from the sale of old clothing in order to purchase new garments—which in turn benefitted less affluent consumers. "Many women only came into contact with clothing designed by Chanel and Poiret—as well as with less august names—after other women had worn the garments and decided to sell them,"[4] Marshik wrote. Yet even clothing from the most fashionable labels had to be carefully considered and redistributed, as outdated styles would have immediately signaled a woman's inability to purchase the latest designs—and, more specifically, may have directly indicated that she was buying secondhand. While the stigmatization of wearing secondhand clothing dissipated substantially as the twentieth century progressed (see "At a glance: Vintage clothing"), there are undoubtedly sellers and consumers of used clothing who prefer to keep their transactions private even today.

Repurposed clothing

Repurposed clothing tells an even more complex tale than that of secondhand garments. Until recently, clothes that were extensively altered from their original form were frequently overlooked in museum collections, as it was believed that their alterations rendered them inauthentic. Today, however, analyses of such objects by scholars like Alexandra Palmer,[5] fashion curator at The Royal Ontario Museum, Toronto, as well as the embrace of repurposing techniques by high-end fashion labels such as Maison Martin Margiela, have imbued altered objects with newfound significance. Such clothing is now used to provide insight on the high value placed on textiles in the past, as well as to how that value has diminished over time. Examining remade garments also highlights a resourcefulness and skill that is all but lost in the contemporary fashion industry. In many ways, these garments acted as early models of sustainability.

Eighteenth-century materials

A woman's reticule[6] bag (c. 1800), provides a fascinating example of a repurposed object in the collection of The Museum at FIT (plate 1a). The bag is made from ivory silk that is artfully embellished with multicolor embroidery, silk fringe and tassels. When dress styles were too simple and lightweight to easily accommodate pockets during the early nineteenth century,[7] this type of bag was essential to a woman's wardrobe. Intriguingly, this object was constructed to highlight a different type of pocket: one that was originally part of the eighteenth-century waistcoat from which it was repurposed. The waistcoat pocket was purely decorative, however—a construction detail that indicates the waistcoat was made in the late eighteenth century, when functional pockets were thought to interrupt the lines of closely fitted clothing. Consequently, many waistcoats merely suggested the inclusion of pockets through the application of pocket flaps.[8] The bag's silhouette—a simple pouch that ends in three scalloped points at the bottom edge—is carefully contoured to correspond to the shape of the original embroidery of the waistcoat. Many reticules from this period were round or hexagonal, meaning that the design of this bag was not dissimilar to other fashionable examples. Nevertheless, the material from which the bag was fashioned must have been quite apparent, particularly as it was constructed not long after the embroidered waistcoat fell out of fashion.

Elaborately embroidered waistcoats were fashionable for men throughout the eighteenth century. Embroidery designs were carefully engineered, meaning that they were first selected by the customer, and then stitched onto panels of uncut fabric in a shape that contoured to the silhouette of the finished garment. The cloth was later cut and made into the waistcoat itself. Over the course of the mid- to late-eighteenth century, the fashionable silhouette of the waistcoat changed, becoming shorter and cutting away from the body.

Like the purchase of secondhand clothing, the practice of updating and altering existing garments was prevalent at nearly all class levels. As Elizabeth Sanderson wrote in her essay on the secondhand clothing trade in eighteenth-century Edinburgh, "people made their clothes last as long as possible; we find their clothes being turned, dyed, scoured, eked, cut down, let out, or simply 'helped'."[9] Yet it would have been difficult to alter waistcoats with such precisely placed embroidery and pockets.[10] As a result, men's embroidered waistcoats often remained intact, with few alterations made during their wearable life—but it is evident that they were repurposed in other ways.

By the time this reticule was made in the early nineteenth century, elaborately embroidered waistcoats had fallen out of fashion. Yet even unfashionable clothing and accessories held value in the secondhand market during the eighteenth and nineteenth centuries. Garments were priced according to how fashionable they were, but also by the quality of their materials. An item such as a stunningly embroidered, finely woven silk waistcoat would have retained significant worth. While the original waistcoat may have been given to the maker of the bag, it is also possible that it was purchased secondhand, and then remade into an entirely different object by its new owner.

A later example of a refashioned waistcoat provides further insight into the value of eighteenth-century embroidered silks (Figure 1.1). This object, dating to c. 1950, takes a more literal approach to the refashioning of a man's waistcoat, transforming the garment into a woman's vest. A good deal of the original waistcoat remains intact, particularly at the bottom edge, which preserves the integrity of the embroidery. The armholes and neckline, however, were entirely adjusted. The top of the waistcoat was cut off and re-fitted, becoming shorter to sit just above the hips. The original standing collar of the waistcoat was removed, cut into pieces, and reattached at the front of the armholes, creating decorative flaps that were not part of the original design. The shape of the waistcoat was also considerably altered through the addition of long darts over the waist, resulting in a more fitted silhouette. The original back fabric of the waistcoat was replaced with black silk.

This vest was part of a 1989 donation to The Museum at FIT from Sylvia Slifka. The donation also included haute couture clothing by Cristobal Balenciaga, Christian Dior, Yves Saint Laurent, Lucien Lelong and Emanuel Ungaro. The vest was, therefore, notably different from the other objects worn by Mrs Slifka. Although it is unknown how or when the donor wore this vest, its construction indicates that it was worn as a fashionable garment, rather than as a costume. The alterations were thoughtfully planned, particularly in the placement of the long darts over the waist. Not only did they better serve to highlight the wearer's figure, they also allowed the bottom edge of the vest to flare over the hips. A pronounced hourglass shape was the predominant silhouette of the 1950s, and the precise re-tailoring of this vest assured that it adhered to the fashionable norm, in spite of its unusual origins.

The years following World War II are often associated with increased consumerism. Particularly after adherence to fabric rationing and the "Make Do and Mend" ethos of the war years (see "At a glance: Make do and mend"), many women were eager to update their wardrobes with newly feminine and comparatively extravagant styles. Although there continued to be an active market for secondhand garments (including pre-worn couture) in the post-war economy,[11] wearing secondhand clothing remained somewhat stigmatized and covert. While the waistcoat used to make this vest would have been considered more "antique" than merely secondhand by the 1950s, it was nevertheless an atypical choice for a woman who was otherwise buying couture clothing. Once again, the appeal of the original waistcoat seems best explained by its exceptional quality and rarity. The hand-woven silk and intricate embroidery used to make the eighteenth-century garment would likely have surpassed even the finest 1950s couture garments in craftsmanship. Nevertheless, Mrs Slifka's appreciation of antique dress is noteworthy, as it

Figure 1.1 Woman's vest re-fashioned from a man's eighteenth-century waistcoat, ivory silk with multicolor embroidery, c. 1950, USA. Collection of The Museum at FIT, 89.54.2. Gift of Sylvia Slifka. Photograph © The Museum at FIT.

foreshadowed the embrace of secondhand clothing as a fashion statement by nearly 20 years.

Women's dresses from the eighteenth century offered even greater opportunity for repurposing, as they were frequently fashioned from long, uncut lengths of fabric. Textiles were significantly more costly than the labor it took to alter them, and as a result, most garments were modified numerous times to keep up with changes in fashion.[12] Many eighteenth-century dresses, particularly those from the first half of the century, were constructed with relatively crude stitches, indicating that the effortless deconstruction of the original gown was a consideration.[13] As the study of the aforementioned reticule underscored, fabrics retained value even when they were not in fashion. Hand-woven silks, cherished for their quality and beauty, were sometimes passed down through generations.

The heavy silks of the eighteenth century were not suited for the simple, slender dress silhouettes of the early nineteenth century, but such silks were again appropriate for women's garments from approximately 1835 to 1845. It is during this time period, in particular, that a number of dresses in museum collections prove to have been remade from eighteenth-century silks. Despite innovations in the production of textiles and clothing over the course of the nineteenth century (some of which will be discussed in Chapters Two and Three), high-quality clothing continued to be a significant expense for all but the wealthiest consumers. The successful transformation of an old fabric or gown into a new, fashionable garment would have attested to the cleverness of its wearer—or perhaps her dressmaker.

The collection of The Museum at FIT contains several dresses from c. 1840 which were remade from eighteenth-century fabric. One particularly interesting example was fashioned from silk brocade made in Spitalfields, a renowned silk weaving center located just outside of London in the eighteenth century (Figure 1.2). Anna Maria Garthwaite, a prominent English textile designer, may have created the fabric's floral pattern, which dates to c. 1760. While the silhouette and construction of the dress corresponded to the fashions of the early 1840s, closer inspection reveals its origins even beyond the earlier date of the fabric. It is clear that the original bodice of the dress was turned back-to-front, and a fashionably pointed waistline and ruched neckline were added. Although the original gown's sleeve ruffles were removed during its reconfiguration, they were preserved. Extant remnants from altered garments are rare and particularly valuable to the understanding of the original object.

Nineteenth-century materials

While expansive lengths of eighteenth-century silk provided more than ample material for nineteenth-century gowns, they were not the only fabrics to be repurposed into other garments. A dress and matching handbag dating to the late 1880s, for instance, were remade from a shawl (Figure 1.3). The style of shawl used to make this garment may be referred to in several ways: Kashmir (the geographical origin of the shawl's design), cashmere (the Western spelling of the word, which referred to both the design

Figure 1.2 Dress re-fashioned from eighteenth-century fabric, ivory silk brocade, c. 1840, England. Collection of The Museum at FIT, P87.20.7. Museum purchase. Photograph © The Museum at FIT.

Figure 1.3 Dress remade from paisley shawl, multicolor wool and burgundy velvet, c. 1889, USA. Collection of The Museum at FIT, 89.154.12. Gift of Maria Burgaleta-Larson. Photograph © The Museum at FIT.

of the shawl and its fabric), and Paisley (the region of Scotland that dominated Western production of imitation Kashmir shawls in the nineteenth century). Kashmir shawls had become fashionable luxury items for women by the 1790s, and were imported to both Europe and the United States. Made from goat hair, the shawls were soft and warm, and they became ideal accompaniments to the slender, lightweight dresses of the early nineteenth century. In addition to their inherent functionality, Kashmir shawls were considered exotic.[14] Prices of imported shawls ranged considerably, but by 1860, some of the longest and most luxurious examples cost over $2,000.[15] By the 1870s, however, shawls were falling out of fashion. This was due primarily to changes in dress silhouette—in particular, the introduction of the bustle. Shawls often added too much bulk when paired with voluminous bustle skirts, and more fitted styles of outer garments were devised to better suit the new silhouette. Although the shawls themselves were no longer worn, however, they did not necessarily lose their value.

Household and etiquette manuals from the late nineteenth century frequently encouraged women to be as resourceful as possible with their clothing and textiles. While advice for reconfiguring men's and women's garments into children's wear was prevalent,[16] large, uncut lengths of cloth would have offered even greater possibilities for repurposing. The dress in the MFIT collection was cut in the "princess" line, a one-piece style that created a lean, elegant silhouette.[17] The construction of the dress underscores the expanse of cloth that it required, as its back (including a short train) was cut and tailored from a single length of fabric. Likewise, the front panels of the dress were fashioned from lengths of cloth that were uncut from shoulder to hem. Although the shawl fabric is thick, the dress was fully lined in several different prints and colors of silk—indicating that the lining was perhaps made from repurposed or scrap fabrics as well. The velvet accents, as well as a patch pocket on the right front side of the dress, indicate that it was probably worn as a practical form of afternoon garment, sometimes referred to as a carriage dress. The corresponding handbag has a wide border that was made from the same material as the dress, but the body of the bag appears to have been fashioned from an entirely different shawl. It was somewhat more crudely made than the dress, and included a raw-edged handle braided from leftover strips of fabric.

Methods of repurposing paisley shawls into clothing continued well into the twentieth century, but more recent examples appear to have valued aesthetics over necessity or resourcefulness. A man's suit in the MFIT collection, for instance, was custom-made from a paisley shawl by the high-end Italian tailoring firm, Cifonelli (Figure 1.4). Mr. Valerian Stux-Rybar, a renowned interior designer, commissioned the suit in 1960. Rybar was referred to as "the world's most expensive decorator,"[18] and he designed rooms for an exceptionally high-profile clientele. He was known for his meticulous selection of fabrics[19]—a sensibility that must have also extended to his wardrobe choices. While it is clear that this suit was made from a paisley shawl, the fabric's appearance is quite different from that of the aforementioned nineteenth-century dress. This is because the fabric of the shawl was "turned," meaning the wrong side of the fabric faces outward. Historically, the method of turning fabric was meant to extend the life of a garment. Clothing made from fabrics that were reversible—including woolens, plain silks and damasks—could be taken apart, turned and re-stitched if the material became stained,

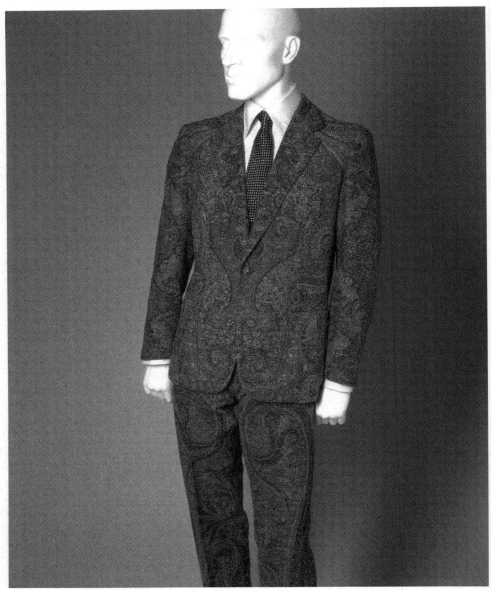

Figure 1.4 Suit remade from paisley shawl, multicolor wool, 1960, Italy. Collection of The Museum at FIT, 90.149.32. Gift of Mr. Jean François Daigre. Photograph © The Museum at FIT.

faded or otherwise dilapidated. Turning was not an uncommon practice, particularly in the eighteenth century. For example, historian Linda Baumgarten found documentation that George Washington had some of his garments turned.[20]

The antique paisley shawl from which this suit was made may have been damaged in some way, and thus the face of the fabric could not be shown. It is even more likely, however, that Rybar requested that the fabric be turned for aesthetic reasons. The shawl's colors are equally vibrant on its reverse, but the exposed threads offer more texture and visual interest. In either case, it is almost certain that the decision to reuse the shawl fabric was not made out of necessity, as the suit was commissioned by a successful entrepreneur and meticulously made-to-order by a premier Roman tailor. In addition to the jacket and trousers pictured, the suit has an additional pair of trousers—emphasizing once again that a single shawl could provide an enormous amount of fabric.

The slim cut of the suit was the hallmark of sophisticated Italian tailoring in the late 1950s and early 1960s. While the suit's silhouette was at the height of fashion, the fabric selection was decidedly ahead of its time. In 1971—in the midst of the new trend for wearing and remodeling vintage clothing—the *New York Times* specifically mentioned the remaking of shawls in an article entitled "For One-of-a-Kind Fashions." Its author profiled a New York City shop called Juicy Miss Lucy's, in which the proprietors, Carene Beatty and Lisa Price, sold "old embroidered shawls ... transformed into puff-sleeved jackets." The jackets sold for a costly US $100,[21] but Beatty would also "turn a customer's own shawl into a jacket or blouse for $50,"[22] proving that the antique shawls were worth as much as the labor required for a custom design.

A man's dressing gown from the 1930s exemplifies another creative reuse of existing materials (plate 2). It was made from a crazy quilt, an American handicraft that was at its peak in the late nineteenth century. Crazy quilts were assembled from fabric scraps of irregular shape and size, lending them a haphazard appearance. Many of the quilts also featured elaborate embroidery. They emerged in the 1870s, and it is typically thought that they were inspired by the Japanese decorative arts on view at the Centennial Exposition in Philadelphia—specifically Japanese silk screens, marquetry boxes and "crazed-glaze" pottery,[23] for which the quilt style was likely named. While the use of scrap fabrics into quilts is an established tradition in American needlecraft, it is perhaps less known that similar practices are also customary in Japan.[24]

The scraps of fabric that were used for crazy quilts were initially just that—scraps that were taken from unwearable or discarded articles of clothing. Pieces of material with sentimental value (a bit from grandmother's wedding dress, for example) further added to the appeal of the crazy quilt fad. An 1883 article in *The Decorator and Furnisher* magazine advised readers that scraps of fabric "need not be thrown away or sold to the ragman or sacrificed to the insatiable flames," but they could instead be transformed into a stylish quilt.[25] Also by the 1880s, crazy quilting had become so popular that kits were available for purchase, eliminating the need to hunt for scraps. This marketing strategy coincided with an increase in silk production in the United States.[26]

In spite of its name, the crazy quilt was not a traditional quilt. There was no batting inserted between the two layers, and scraps of fabric were simply attached to a backing material. Purely decorative embroidery was applied instead of typical quilting stitches. Crazy quilts were neither warm nor sturdily constructed, and were therefore used ornamentally, draped over furniture, for example, rather than as functional bed coverings. By the 1930s, many such quilts were dilapidated, but they continued to be passed on as family heirlooms.

While the origin of the crazy quilt used to construct this dressing gown is unknown, it seems to have been made with affection. New embroidery motifs were added to the left sleeve, including the name Phil (presumably the name of the wearer), and 1935 (the year the robe was made). Through careful examination, it is also evident that the quilt was substantially mended, probably by the maker of the robe. For example, patches cut from more contemporary fabrics were overlaid onto some of the original silk patches, in order to disguise material that was damaged. The robe was edged and lined in black moiré fabric. As the moiré is made from a manmade fiber (meaning that it was produced in the twentieth century), it is unlikely that it was also a repurposed material.

The dressing gown was made during the height of the Great Depression, indicating that the reuse of an existing expanse of material may have been as necessary as it was sentimental. Although *Vogue* and *Harper's Bazaar* continued to enthusiastically present the latest fashions throughout the 1930s, even they could not entirely ignore the effects of the Depression on the fashion industry. In 1933, for instance, *Vogue* referenced the need to economize by mentioning "the growing practice of making one costume do duty as several by changing accessories."[27] Yet even a cursory study of other sources from the Depression era indicates that maintaining a wardrobe was often a greater challenge than simply changing one's accessories. A guidebook entitled *Dyeing, Remodeling, Budgets,* published by The Woman's Institute of Domestic Arts and Sciences in 1931, outlined several ways in which women could maintain their families' wardrobes in a spendthrift manner. "Among the factors that aid her to increase the producing value of the dollar are the dye pot, the ability to remodel clothes, an intelligent treatment of clothing, and the observation of a clothes budget," it stated. The guide even went so far as to assert, "extravagance in dress conveys to thinking persons a feeling of doubt as to a woman's intelligence. Thrift, intelligent application of knowledge, and skill with the hands are worthwhile factors in life and are recognized by such persons qualified to judge."[28] Although this manual pre-dates the "Make Do and Mend" booklets released during World War II (see "At a glance: Make do and mend"), their ethos is quite similar.

For many people, however, extravagance in dress was not even an option in the 1930s. In Studs Terkel's seminal oral history of the Great Depression, *Hard Times,* a number of the interview subjects, particularly women, mention clothing in their recollections of the time period. Mary Owsley, who lived in Oklahoma from 1929 to 1936, spoke of dust storms that ruined the clothing that she had hung outside to dry: "They was never fit to use, actually. I had to use 'em, understand, but they wasn't very presentable."[29] Jane Yoder, who was a child living in Illinois at the time, recalled being laughed at for wearing an "Indian blanket coat" one winter. Nevertheless, it was the only warm outer garment she owned, and she wore it gratefully.[30] This dressing gown would have been strictly for at-home use, and its fashionableness (or lack thereof), was likely of little concern to its wearer.

Twentieth-century materials

In the mid- to late 1960s, the wearing of select secondhand, or "vintage," clothing began to develop into a veritable trend among the young and fashionable (see "At A glance: Vintage fashion"). By 1970, vintage clothes were such a fashion statement that they

Figure 1.5 Yesterday's News (Harriet Winter), dress made from vintage fabric, multicolor printed rayon, orange rayon, black rayon, 1970–1, USA. Collection of The Museum at FIT, 94.27.146. Gift of Harriet Winter. Photograph © The Museum at FIT.

were prominently featured in upscale department stores, such as New York's B. Altman. There, an in-store boutique aptly named "Yesterday's News" offered carefully chosen secondhand clothes. "One thing that's been missing in department stores is the thrift shop," wrote the New York Times. "That breach has been filled by Altman's with a cozy, lamp-lighted room on the sixth floor called Yesterday's News."[31] The article went on to discuss the vintage clothes that filled the shop, many of which had been collected by its owner, Lewis Winter, over a number of years. Prior to opening Yesterday's News, Winter had worked as a merchandiser in New York's Seventh Avenue fashion district, and would have been especially attuned to upcoming fads.

What the article does not mention is that Yesterday's News also sold clothing made from repurposed or deadstock[32] vintage fabrics. A two-piece dress from Yesterday's News in the collection of The Museum at FIT dates to 1970—the same year that the shop at Altman's was opened (Figure 1.5). The dress was made by its donor, Lewis Winter's wife Harriet (also called Mrs H. Winter), who later went on to have her own fashion line. In a 1977 interview for the New York Times, Mrs Winter recalled that her interest in designing clothes was inspired by the vintage styles she had collected for resale with her husband.[33]

The dress was made from vintage rayon fabric in a bold, geometric print, dating to circa 1930. The accent bands in rust-orange and black were made from new rayon fabrics. Although the ensemble itself was newly made, it was styled in a "retro" fashion, emulating the look of a 1920s sportswear ensemble. Thus the dress successfully combined two prevailing trends of its era—the wearing of vintage clothing, and the contemporary reinterpretations of past styles. It is not clear if this piece was one-of-a-kind, as the amount of vintage rayon that was available is unknown, but at most it would have been part of a limited run of such styles. Making new clothing from vintage fabrics was a technique that Mrs Winter continued to experiment with in her design career, even after the "thrift shop craze" had waned.[34] A line of her 1930s-style sundresses, for example, was crafted from old fabric that Lewis Winter found abandoned on a dock. In addition, many of Mrs Winter's coats were remade from wool blankets, which she selected for their sculptural and sometimes graphic qualities.[35]

The appearance of secondhand and repurposed clothing within the realm of high fashion resulted in its greater acceptance and de-stigmatization. By the 1970s, a number of publications focused on the wearing of used clothing as a stylish fashion statement. Diane Funaro's The Yestermorrow Clothes Book (1976), for example, featured detailed instructions on how to repair and update old clothes. In addition to ideas for adding patches or embroidery, she gave tips for altering hemlines, sleeves and necklines to make garments more fashionable or eliminate flaws. Ellen Weiss presented similar ideas in her 1981 book, Secondhand Super Shopper, avowing, "secondhand clothing has come out of the closet. Even the clothes: no more snobbery about somebody else's old rags, nothing shameful about hand-me-downs: it's all chic."[36]

By the end of the twentieth century, the acceptance of secondhand clothing as a part of the fashionable wardrobe had taken a new turn. "Since the 1990s, as a backlash to globalization, recycling clothing has been a way of intervening in the ongoing supply of new consumer products," wrote fashion theorist Jennifer Craik.[37] Indeed, growing awareness of the ecological benefits of recycling in all fields also fuelled interest in

Figure 1.6 XULY.Bët (Lamine Kouyaté), dress and jacket made from repurposed materials, multicolor sweaters, brown wool plaid, red nylon, Fall 1994, France. Collection of The Museum at FIT, 95.7.1. Gift of XULY.Bët. Photograph © The Museum at FIT.

"recycled" (or repurposed) clothing at the end of the twentieth century. Although numerous designers experimented with ideas of repurposing old garments into bold new high-fashion styles, Martin Margiela and Lamine Kouyaté—working under the labels Maison Martin Margiela and XULY.Bët, respectively—were two especially well-known designers within the genre. Both were featured in an exhibition held at The Museum at FIT in 1994–5, entitled *Hello Again: Recycling for the Real World,* which included clothes, home furnishings and other objects made from repurposed or recycled materials. At that time, Margiela and Kouyaté each donated several important pieces of their work for inclusion in the Museum's permanent collection. These objects exemplified a new type of avant-garde, one-of-a-kind clothing, and their design concepts remain integral to today's sustainable fashion industry.

Belgian-born, Paris-based designer Margiela—referred to as "fashion's founding father of recycling" by fashion journalist Suzy Menkes[38]—began showing work under his own label in 1989. From the label's inception, Margiela's unique, critical perspective on the traditional fashion industry was evident. T-shirts were crafted from cut-up plastic bags,[39] and his first runway show was held in a crumbling, abandoned warehouse in Paris. To showcase his fall 1992 collection, the designer staged a runway presentation within a Salvation Army store,[40] where guests sat atop pieces of used furniture and among racks of secondhand clothing. Although the setting was atypical, it was appropriate, as many of Margiela's designs were made from discarded items. "Maison Martin Margiela is partial to materials with a momentary character and to throwaways of little commercial value. Such materials do not hide the course of time, but carry along the traces of a garment's previous life and incorporate it in the new item,"[41] observed fashion curator Kaat Debo, who organized an exhibition to celebrate the Maison's 20th anniversary in 2008.

In a group of objects in the collection of The Museum at FIT, Margiela's process of assembling a woman's sweater from old army socks is demonstrated (plate 3). The designer made no attempt to disguise the raw material from which the sweater was formed—in fact, he emphasized the process by providing versions of the sweater in various stages of completion. Margiela began with a simple bundle of socks. The socks were then cut and pinned together to form an intricate patchwork, which slowly took the shape of the female torso. Finally, the patchwork was refined and stitched into a completed garment. Margiela masterfully utilized the shape of each sock to guide its placement in the pattern of the sweater: the contours of the sock heels, for example, formed the curves of the elbow, shoulder and bust. "Many of Margiela's 'raw materials' are fashion detritus when he starts with them: second-hand or army surplus clothing is the commodity form with the lowest exchange value in the fashion system,"[42] wrote fashion theorist Caroline Evans. Yet Margiela's completed garments exemplify how such "lowly" objects can be ingeniously (and even somewhat simply) transformed, leaving one to question the perceived value of any material.

Although it was officially announced that Margiela had left his namesake label in December 2009, the Maison continues to explore avant-garde design. The spring 2013 Artisanal Collection[43] featured 1920s beaded dresses remade into stunning new ensembles that, in some cases, scarcely hinted at their origins. As style.com reported, "The process involved restoring the beadwork, then bonding it to a trench, a 'cigarette line' coat, or a K-Way windbreaker jacket,"[44] to create pieces that resembled outerwear, while other vintage dresses were cut and reassembled with contemporary materials to create entirely new silhouettes. The last three of the 19 looks in the collection were made from thousands of metallic candy wrappers, painstakingly embroidered onto a silk backing to give the dresses an unusual, dimensional effect that took 70 hours to complete.[45]

The collection was generally well received, but the ethics surrounding the deconstruction of seemingly beautiful historic dresses became a subject of debate among fashion historians, as the origin and condition of the original dresses was unknown. There has been little such debate, of course, over Margiela's destruction of army socks. Regardless, the reuse of vintage garments adhered to the beliefs of Martin Margiela himself. When questioned about his use of secondhand clothes in 1993, the designer explained, "Often they are too small to wear today. I like to collect old clothes and give them another life. When they are lying here, they are dead."[46]

Lamine Kouyaté debuted his line of repurposed clothing in 1992, as part of the first major XULY.Bët collection.[47] A native of Mali (although he presents his collections in Paris), Kouyaté cites his background as the reason for his interest in repurposed fashion. "It's an African—and any Third World Nation's—philosophy to use things up. You don't waste anything, but create new from old,"[48] he explained in a 1994 interview. Kouyaté's clothes are assembled from a mix of garments he purchases at thrift stores, flea markets and discount stores. The designer does more than simply alter the clothes he acquires, however, often deconstructing and reassembling them to the extent that their original function is not apparent.

One of several XULY.Bët ensembles in the collection of The Museum at FIT includes a dress made from an irregular patchwork of mismatched, patterned sweaters (Figure 1.6). A heavy woolen winter coat, cropped at the waist, is worn over the dress. The final layer of the outfit is a wrap jacket in bright red nylon, assembled from old pantyhose— a signature of Kouyaté's work. The lightweight jacket is worn stretched over the coat, creating an intentionally bulky appearance that questioned conventional notions of beauty and the idealized body. Kouyaté's selection of unique materials ensured the exclusivity of this ensemble, thereby imbuing it with one of the fundamental characteristics of couture clothing. Yet the designer's work eschews the exacting craftsmanship that is another keystone of couture. He reassembles the existing garments in a manner that deliberately calls attention to their deconstruction—using coarse, bright red thread to highlight seams, for example, and leaving the original tags from the repurposed clothing intact and exposed.

In today's fashion lexicon, the practices employed by both Margiela and Kouyaté would be considered *upcycling*, a term popularized by William McDonough and Michael Braungart in their influential book *Cradle to Cradle: Remaking the Way we Make Things*.[49] Upcycling was defined by sustainable fashion expert Sandy Black as "design using reprocessed or waste materials to make a product of equal or higher, not lower quality."[50] It may seem from the aforementioned examples of repurposed clothing that upcycling has already existed for centuries—but it is important to remember that secondhand clothing prior to the late twentieth and early twenty-first centuries was purchased and remade

Figure 1.7 Rebecca Earley, *Ever and Again* shirt "upcycled" from used blouse, multicolor heat photogram-printed polyester, 2007, England. Collection of The Museum at FIT, 2010.42.1. Gift of Rebecca Earley. Photograph © The Museum at FIT.

Figure 1.8 Betsey Johnson, maxi dress with Woolmark label, multicolor space-dyed wool knit, 1971, USA. Collection of The Museum at FIT, 93.27.1. Gift of Betsey Johnson. Photograph © The Museum at FIT.

primarily for economic or aesthetic purposes—and sometimes both. Upcycling, however, is used to describe clothing that has been remade for ecological reasons.

Upcycling is often perceived as one of the most sustainable practices within the contemporary fashion industry, as it eliminates the need for newly manufactured goods—and functions as a distinctive alternative to mass-produced fashions. Similar to vintage clothing, the one-of-a-kind nature of upcycled garments is important to contemporary consumers who place particular emphasis on individuality through their dress. In today's fashion world, there is no one "correct" way to look, and a unique appearance is often perceived as an especially valuable attribute. Yet the use of secondhand clothing in any form—whether worn "off-the-rack" or upcycled—does have disadvantages. To find and/ or alter existing garments can be an unfeasible time commitment for many shoppers and designers, particularly as most consumers are accustomed to the instant gratification provided by fast fashion. The secondhand customer must be patient and flexible, since a garment that suits their exact needs may not be easily located.[51] Rebecca Earley—fashion designer, scholar, and professor of Sustainable Textile and Fashion Design at Chelsea College of Arts—also notes that used clothing typically needs to be dry-cleaned using harsh, environmentally harmful chemicals, a process which negates the otherwise eco-friendly nature of secondhand attire.[52]

Earley's interest in sustainable fashion inspired the organization of a 2007 exhibition entitled *Ever & Again: Rethinking Recycled Textiles*. The exhibition was the result of a three-year research project on the subject of upcycling, for which Earley and her colleagues collected 100 white polyester blouses from thrift shops around the United Kingdom. Each item purchased was flawed or undesirable in some way. "A single stain means that a number of these otherwise high quality garments are quickly discarded by a certain type of customer,"[53] Earley noted. She and her colleagues gave new life to each of these cast-off blouses by utilizing upcycling techniques, thereby imbuing them with newfound fashionableness. The 100 pieces were separated into ten groups of ten, and a different design method was explored for each grouping (laser-etching or digital printing, for example).

A blouse in the collection of The Museum at FIT is one of the hundred completed garments from the *Ever & Again* project (Figure 1.7). It was printed using a heat photogram technique, creating patterns of leaves and honeycombs. The blouse extended over the hips (fitting somewhat like a tunic), and its waistline was emphasized by the addition of multiple sash ties in varying widths and patterns. Not only did these techniques give the blouse a fashionable new look and silhouette, they also successfully disguised any flaws that may have caused it to be discarded by its previous owner.

Recycled textiles

While upcycling is an increasingly popular way to make something valuable from discarded clothing, recycling fabrics is another viable choice in the prevention of textile waste. As mentioned previously, the use of the term "recycled" in this text refers to fabrics made from reprocessed waste materials. Recycled textiles gained prominence in the 1990s, when innovations such as fleece derived from plastic bottles made headlines. Yet textile recycling is one of the oldest forms of material reprocessing in the world[54]—and, with the exception of a few recent advancements, the production processes and uses of recycled textiles have changed little over their long history.

Textile recycling is primarily a mechanical process: the cloth is first pulled apart by cylinders with projecting teeth (if garments are being recycled, all labels, tags and linings are removed prior to the pulling process). The fibers are then collected into funnels for storage until the next processing stage, called garnetting, which both pulls and combs the fibers to prepare them for spinning.[55] While this technique is effective, it breaks the fibers, resulting in lower-quality yarns. Synthetic fibers can be broken down chemically—a process that is more energy-intensive than mechanical recycling, but does result in higher-grade yarns.[56] The benefits to recycling textiles are numerous: in addition to reducing landfill waste, textile recycling is a relatively low-impact process. Many recycled fibers are not re-dyed (or use less dye than new fibers), and thus chemical and water waste is lessened. With the exception of chemically recycled fibers, the process also uses significantly less energy than what is necessary to produce new fabrics.[57]

Most textiles are entirely recyclable, yet the amount of fabric waste that ends up in landfills is considerable. In 2009, it was estimated that just 1.3 million tons of fabric was recovered for recycling in the United States[58]—a fraction of the 12 million tons of textiles that were thrown away.[59] The European Union initiated its Waste Framework Directive in 2008,[60] a program that will require at least 50 percent of household waste to be recycled by 2020. Yet despite this initiative, many European countries continue to be careless about the items they send to landfills—and textiles, in particular. In 2013, it was reported that 75 percent of the 5.8 million tons of textile waste in Europe was simply thrown away or incinerated.[61]

There is a growing market for recycled fabrics. However, as the cost of new clothing has plummeted in recent years, the cost of textile recycling can seem high in comparison.[62] Furthermore, the actual process of recycling remains little understood.[63] Without greater consumer awareness, it is unlikely that the amount of recycled textiles will increase substantially. First and foremost, there are two distinct types of textile waste: *pre-consumer* and *post-consumer*. Pre-consumer waste—that which comes from the processing of fiber, yarn, and fabric, as well as the manufacture of clothing itself—is less problematic to recycle than post-consumer waste, which involves the disposal of a completed product. The recycling of post-consumer waste has posed a particular challenge to the contemporary fashion system. Fiber blends, which are commonly used today, are more difficult to sort and recycle. In addition, the fast fashion system has also produced an influx of clothing, much of which has little or no resale value. Up to 50 percent of clothing donated to charitable organizations is not considered saleable, and is instead sent off to be recycled.[64] Furthermore, the fibers, dyes, and finishes used on post-consumer waste are often unknown, adding another layer of difficulty to the recycling process.[65]

Although the uses for recycled fabrics have expanded in recent years—becoming especially important to the contemporary sustainable fashion industry—recycled fabrics have been used for "low-grade" (non-fashion) purposes for centuries. When shredded, the material can be made into paper, used as insulation or stuffing, or quite literally used as rags (called wipers) for wiping or polishing. Leftover materials made from natural fibers can be composted.[66]

Historically, the first and primary fabric to be recycled was wool. Beginning around 1815, the demand for wool exceeded supply, prompting its reuse. The strength and quality of wool fiber was such that it was especially well suited to recycling.[67] When the recycling process was established and refined, however, it was extended to every fiber, excluding silk.[68] Such fabrics are known as "shoddy," meaning that the fiber was "cut, shredded, carded, or otherwise machined back to the fiber stage."[69] By the middle of the nineteenth century, shoddy cloths were purportedly "sold in all markets, consumed in all countries, and served to adorn the royalty and to clothe the crouching slave."[70] Most significantly, the use of shoddy cloth was integral to the burgeoning ready-made clothing industry,[71] fulfilling its purpose "to produce cheap, useful, tasteful, and economical cloths for wearing apparel, and other uses."[72] Beyond the worth of the cloth itself, the shoddy manufacturing process was a model of efficiency. Rag dust was used as crop fertilizer, for instance, while other refuse was utilized for bed stuffing or made into chemical agents for fabric dyeing.[73]

Despite the merits of shoddy wool, it was viewed with some prejudice even early in its history.[74] Although the quality of the fabric varied (depending on the strength of the original fiber), shoddy cloth became associated only with the cheapest of clothing. Today, shoddy is a general term that is used to describe products of inferior quality. While an aversion to shoddy wool had been developing for decades, the material nearly vanished from the market in the mid-1960s. This corresponded to the development of the Woolmark label in 1964, and the brand's promotion of high-quality wool over an influx of new, increasingly popular synthetic fabrics (many of which will be discussed in Chapter 3). The Woolmark company, which is still in existence today, described the motivation behind its establishment: "A new enemy emerged during World War II by the name of synthetic fibre and by the 1960s polyester and acrylic were fast becoming household names. To combat this rise of unnatural competition IWS Australian general manager William Vines penned the idea of a unique label which would guarantee the quality and authenticity of wool."[75] A maxi-length sweater dress by Betsey Johnson, from 1971, is made from wool yarn in shades of blue, green, red and yellow (Figure 1.8). Its fashionably casual appearance is underscored by a "natural" motif of birds. The dress included a Woolmark label, meaning that it was made from virgin, non-reprocessed wool—promoted for being of much greater quality than its recycled counterpart. Such labels were commonly seen in high-end, woolen clothing, particularly in the 1970s.

In recent years, recycled textiles have made a comeback, and a few manufacturers have shown remarkable innovation. One major development, mentioned briefly at the beginning of this section, was the ability to produce polyester fleece material from recycled plastic bottles, an idea pioneered in the early late 1970s[76] and refined in the following decade. In the simplest terms, the bottles are "melted down to a basic polymer, extruded into fiber, and knit into fleece."[77] Recycled fleece has rarely made its way into high fashion (although *Vogue* declared that "models can't live without Patagonia's

Figure 1.9 FIN (Per Åge Sivertsen), dress, grey/blue organic cotton and recycled polyester, summer 2010, Norway. Collection of The Museum at FIT, 2010.10.2. Gift of Per Sivertsen of FIN. Photograph © The Museum at FIT.

fleece vest" in its January 1998 issue[78]), but it has been a great success, especially for use on casual clothing. Patagonia is a leading sportswear company with a long-held commitment to environmental responsibility, and it recycles 25 plastic bottles to make a single coat. Over a ten-year period, Patagonia, in tandem with plastics recycling firm Wellman, Inc., used 86 million plastic soda bottles to produce their fleece—bottles that would have otherwise ended up in landfills.[79] The bottles are cleaned, shredded into chips and extruded into fibers that can be spun into yarn.[80] Today, Patagonia's fleece is made from a combination of "used soda bottles, unusable second quality fabrics and worn out garments."[81]

Patagonia's continued experimentations with recycled polyester fibers have also led to the development of fabrics better suited to high fashion. Although polyester production is ecologically damaging in many respects (see Chapter 3), it does have some positive attributes—especially its ability to be recycled innumerable times into a product of the same quality.[82] A chic mini dress by the Norwegian high-fashion label FIN was made from a luxurious, innovative fabric blended from recycled polyester and organic cotton (Figure 1.9). Like most fiber blends, the fabric was designed to capitalize on positive features of both fibers: the drape and longevity of polyester, for instance, with the porous qualities and softness of cotton. Without looking at the garment's label, consumers would be unable to tell that this dress was made from recycled fibers—an impression that is extremely important to the promotion and sale of such "eco-friendly" fabrics.

The use of recycled materials in recent high-fashion collections underscores that they have become more widely accepted than ever. High-profile campaigns aimed at educating and engaging consumers have also helped to further understanding of the importance of recycled fashions. In April 2012, for example, prominent British retailer Marks & Spencer launched its "Shwopping" campaign, an initiative that encouraged shoppers to trade items of used clothing when they purchased new garments in-store. As part of the campaign promotion, buildings on a street in London's Brick Lane were entirely covered and filled with used clothes (Figure 1.10)—the number of which was the equivalent of clothing that is thrown away every five minutes (approximately 10,000 garments).[83] The awe-inspiring display certainly made its point. The campaign was also launched and supported by British actress Joanna Lumley, who publicly stated her concerns over the amount of clothing that is simply thrown into landfills. "I think young people have been encouraged to buy something, wear it for months and throw it out, particularly if they're not very good at […] mending things. I donate a lot of my clothes to charity because I hate throwing things in the dustbin. It doesn't seem right to me. Hopefully, we will roll up to M&S with something we don't want anymore."[84] Not long after the Marks & Spencer recycling program was initiated, Swedish fashion retail giant H&M began a similar campaign.[85]

Conclusion

The practices of repurposing and recycling clothing and textiles have many important benefits, including the prolongation of the life of an item of clothing, the reduction of

Figure 1.10 Buildings covered in used clothing to promote Marks and Spencers "Schwopping" campaign, Brick Lane, London, April 2012. Photograph by the author.

environmentally harmful production processes, and the elimination of waste. In fact, this chapter is unique to this book, in that there is very little "bad" practice outlined. Recent initiatives in repurposing and recycling have proven how we can build a more sustainable future for the fashion industry—not just in theory, but also in actuality. Many designers and consumers are also looking to the past as a model for contemporary sustainable practices—in particular, to how clothing and fabrics used to be valued and altered over the course of many years. This idea is explored in further detail in the following chapter, Quality of Craftsmanship.

Suggestions for further reading

Baumgarten, L. (1998), "Altered historical clothing," *Dress*, 25: 42–57.
Ginsburg, M. (1980), "Rags to riches: the second-hand clothes trade 1700–1978," *Costume*, 14: 121–35.
Hawley, J. (2008), "Economic Impact of Textile and Clothing Recycling," in J. Hethorn and C. Ulasewicz (eds), *Sustainable Fashion: Why Now? A Conversation Exploring Issues, Practices, and Possibilities*, New York: Fairchild Books, 143–55.
Palmer, A. and H. Clark (eds) (2005), *Old Clothes, New Looks: Second-Hand Fashion*, Oxford: Berg Publishers.
Welters, L. (2008), "The Fashion of Sustainability," in J. Hethorn and C. Ulasewicz (eds), *Sustainable Fashion: Why Now? A Conversation Exploring Issues, Practices, and Possibilities*, New York: Fairchild Books, 7–29.

At a glance: Vintage clothing

In the latter half of the twentieth century, wearing secondhand clothing as a fashion statement (rather than as an economic necessity) developed as an important component of subcultural style. Hippies and punks, for example, were known to scour thrift stores and flea markets for inexpensive clothing, as a way to express their rejection of mainstream consumerist values. However, another market for secondhand clothing was developing simultaneously. By the end of the 1960s, the term "vintage" came to be used to distinguish a specific segment of the secondhand apparel market.

The choice of the word vintage—one that was traditionally used to describe wines— indicates the elite status of certain garments within the hierarchy of secondhand clothing. The term can be used to signify a garment that has a designer label, for example, or a style that fits within a trend in contemporary fashion. In other words, vintage clothing is imbued with a monetary or aesthetic value that sets it apart from an abundance of other used garments.

Buying vintage clothing often has little to do with thrift. Especially when compared to "fast fashion," a vintage garment often costs more than a new piece of clothing. Many consumers are willing to pay extra for vintage fashion, however, since it is perceived as more individual and exclusive than contemporary clothing.[86] Even by 1973, the *New York Times* had confirmed that "while antique dresses aren't necessarily inexpensive, they are elegant, one-of-a-kind fashion."[87]

Furthermore, vintage clothes are often considered to be of higher quality than more recent fashions. In the 1976 publication *The Yestermorrow Clothes Book*, for instance, author Diana Funaro wrote, "old period dresses come in a rich assortment of fabrics and styles that is hard to duplicate today."[88] The sentiment that old clothing was made from fabrics of superior quality—and that in general it was better constructed—is often echoed by vintage shoppers today. The wearing of vintage clothing by high-profile trend-setters such as Kate Moss furthered its appeal, and it became a mainstream fashion phenomenon in the 1990s. Couture garments were in particular demand at that time, and prices were skyrocketing. Fashion historian Richard Martin attributed rising sales in vintage couture to the decline of the couture industry itself. Meanwhile, while high-end, ready-to-wear fashion was becoming more expensive, quality of craftsmanship was declining.[89]

The market for vintage fashion continues to expand in the early twenty-first century. Wearing vintage is now linked to the sustainable fashion movement—yet as cultural theorist Angela McRobbie wrote in her study of secondhand apparel, "for every single piece rescued and restored, a thousand are consigned to oblivion."[90] Nevertheless, the widespread acceptance of vintage fashion has helped to elevate the status of secondhand clothing in general—or at least remove some of its residual stigma. While members of subcultural tribes continue to frequent thrift shops, one is just as likely to encounter an average shopper who is simply looking for something unique to add to his or her wardrobe. The trend for wearing secondhand clothing has also sparked debate about the use of the term vintage—what if the clothing was homemade, or it was not of high quality? Should vintage be used to describe garments that are less than 20 years old? The quickening pace of fashion cycles can suddenly transform the dated into the desirable. In a market saturated with secondhand clothing dealers, it seems that it is up to the buyer to decide if an article of vintage clothing is worth its price tag.

Suggestions for further reading

Hansen, K. (2005), "Secondhand Clothes, Anthropology of," in V. Steele (ed.), *Encyclopedia of Clothing and Fashion,* Detroit, MI: Charles Scribner's Sons.
McRobbie, A. (1988), "Second-Hand Dresses and the Role of the Ragmarket," in A. McRobbie (ed.), *Zoot Suits and Secondhand Dresses, an Anthology of Fashion and Music*, Boston: Unwin Hyman, 23–49.

At a glance: Make do and mend

World War II had an enormous effect on the fashion industries in England, France and the United States. Clothing and fabrics were rationed in order to conserve material necessary for wartime supplies, such as parachutes made from silk or nylon. With new clothing in limited supply, it was essential that existing garments be cared for or repurposed as thoughtfully as possible—and the "Make Do and Mend" ethos was born.

Apparel-making supplies were certainly not the only items to be rationed. Food, for example, was also carefully apportioned. Yet the campaign to make do with existing clothing was met with impressive innovation—and even with enthusiasm in the United States, where many women seemed to view the conservation of fabric as their patriotic duty.[91] In addition to fastidiously maintaining clothes that were already in their closets,

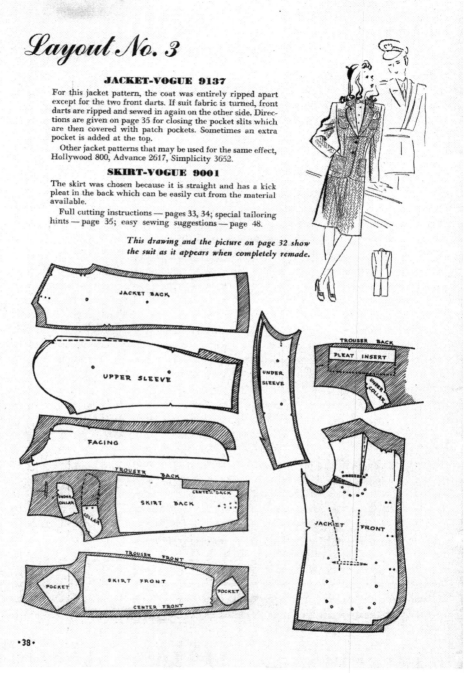

Layout No. 3

JACKET-VOGUE 9137

For this jacket pattern, the coat was entirely ripped apart except for the two front darts. If suit fabric is turned, front darts are ripped and sewed in again on the other side. Directions are given on page 35 for closing the pocket slits which are then covered with patch pockets. Sometimes an extra pocket is added at the top.

Other jacket patterns that may be used for the same effect, Hollywood 800, Advance 2617, Simplicity 3652.

SKIRT-VOGUE 9001

The skirt was chosen because it is straight and has a kick pleat in the back which can be easily cut from the material available.

Full cutting instructions — pages 33, 34; special tailoring hints — page 35; easy sewing suggestions — page 48.

This drawing and the picture on page 32 show the suit as it appears when completely remade.

• 38 •

Figure 1.11 "Layout No. 3," instructions for converting a man's suit to a woman's suit. From the book *Make and Mend for Victory,* The Spool Company, 1942. Collection of the author.

some women relied on the purchase of secondhand goods that could be altered or remade into new fashions.[92]

Numerous publications and articles were written on the topic of making do, all of which provided clever ideas for maintaining, mending or repurposing existing clothing and textiles. In a 1943 booklet released by the Board of Trade in the United Kingdom (where "Make Do and Mend" was a governmental campaign), women were given tips on how to help clothing last longer, make repairs to material, wash and iron garments, renovate existing clothes, and unpick knit garments so that the yarn could be re-used. "No material must lie idle," readers were instructed, "so be a magician and turn old clothes into new."[93]

In the United States, The Spool Cotton Company released a similar booklet, entitled *Make and Mend for Victory*, in 1942. This publication focused on alterations and mending, and also included a special layout devoted to crafting unique accessories from existing materials. A section called "You Have the Goods on Him" detailed four different ways to refashion a woman's suit from a man's (Figure 1.11). Another page with the heading "There's Life in the Old Girl Yet" showed that companies such as Butterick and Simplicity sold special sewing patterns that demonstrated how women could convert their old clothes into a variety of new styles.

Other sources show the Make Do and Mend philosophy in practice. In 1943, the *New York Times* reported on a runway show that featured garments inspired by the "rag bag." Designed by students at the Traphagen School of Fashion, the materials used for the clothing included "new versions of dad's cast-off shirts, the upholstery that was meant for the family automobile, the bedspread that brother burned a hole in and the checkered tablecloth that was 'too shabby to use'," in addition to a bathing suit made from a shower curtain. Although the show also featured clothing that had simply been altered from past styles, the fully repurposed goods purportedly received the most attention.[94]

A video by Britain's Board of Trade, entitled *How to Make-Do-and-Mend,* features footage from a special exhibition held at upscale London department store Harrod's. The exhibition was devoted to "showing the housewife how to turn old things into something quite different and as good as new," and also included a fashion show featuring repurposed garments. One of the highlighted ensembles featured a woman's dressing gown made from an old quilt (similar to the man's dressing gown in the MFIT collection), worn with pajamas made with "material found in the attic—presumably grandmama's bed valance."[95]

Today, many items of contemporary clothing can be purchased at an extremely low cost, and there is little need to care for or remodel garments. Yet the ingenuity and resourcefulness of the Make Do and Mend ethos often serves as an inspiration to those working within the sustainable fashion movement. In fact, many of the techniques used by designers who "upcycle" are directly related to practices outlined in Make Do and Mend publications. In addition, experts on sustainability frequently suggest that consumers purchase fewer garments of higher quality, and then care for and alter those clothes over a number of years. In short, the philosophy of Make Do and Mend has taken on a new, ecologically minded significance in the twenty-first century.

Suggestions for further reading

Board of Trade by the Minister of Information (1943), *Make Do and Mend*, repr., Sevenoaks: Sabrestorm Publishing, 2007.
Spool Thread Company (1943), *Make and Mend for Victory*, New York: Spool Thread Company.

2
QUALITY OF CRAFTSMANSHIP

This chapter examines changes in the ways that textiles and clothing were made and valued from the eighteenth century to the present. Many of the garments featured were selected for the meticulous or thoughtful ways in which they were crafted. Others highlight how the mechanization of textile and clothing production has made an indelible impact on the environment. All of them relate to an important ethos in the sustainable fashion industry: that an understanding of how our clothing is made is essential to changing production methods for the better.

The fashion industry has undergone a metamorphosis over the past 300 years—and it continues to evolve rapidly. Fuelled by technological advancements, changes in the way clothing is manufactured and consumed have likewise transformed our perceptions of how contemporary fashion should be valued. Today, many consumers can afford to buy hundreds of garments per year, should they choose to shop in the countless trend-driven stores specializing in low-priced, "disposable" clothes. In the frenzy to buy into the latest look, however, few shoppers stop to consider the full life cycle of the clothes they purchase—and not just where and how the clothes were made, but what will become of them after they are worn a few times and discarded.

The advent of true "fast fashion" (further outlined in At a Glance: Fast Fashion) only occurred about 20 years ago, but it has nearly eradicated all memory of how our clothing was manufactured, sold and cared for prior to the 1990s. While the fast fashion production cycle is often blamed for today's overabundance of cheap, seemingly valueless clothing, however, faster and less expensive production of fabric and clothing was a vital part of the Industrial Revolution in the nineteenth century. Many historians believe that the Industrial Revolution was, in fact, principally generated by the demand for more textiles. The framework for today's methods of clothing manufacture can be traced back to the establishment of the ready-to-wear industry during the mid-nineteenth century, yet such clothing was typically of better quality than it is today. It also made up only a small part of most women's wardrobes until the twentieth century. Ready-made clothing was usually worn to supplement more complex garments that were made by a couturier, a dressmaker, or at home. When garments were custom-made for their wearers, only the "right amount" of clothing was produced—eliminating the potential for excess supply of mass-produced fashion.[1]

Historically, the cost of clothing was high, especially prior to industrialization. In most eighteenth-century households, for instance, expenditure on clothing was second only to food.[2] As a result, the average person owned far fewer clothes than do most of us today. The high cost of clothing also ensured that it was meticulously cared for and often altered to maintain its value over a long period of time. In addition, many sustainable design experts believe that consumers of the past developed an emotional attachment to their clothing—both because it was a highly valued commodity, and because it was commonly made especially for them. This sense of connection to our clothing is all but lost today.

The eighteenth century

Three centuries may seem like a long time, and advancements in fashion production—like those in any field—are only natural. When we consider how fabrics and clothing were produced prior to mechanization, however, it becomes apparent that drastic changes in the fashion industry have actually occurred quite rapidly. Prior to the nineteenth century, every process necessary to the manufacture of clothing—from spinning yarn, to weaving fabric, to sewing elaborate gowns—was done by hand. Many processes involved the skills of multiple, specialized workers. The tremendous amount of time and labor required to produce clothing accounted for its lasting value, meaning that clothing and textiles were reused and used up, rather than simply discarded.

A few period sources provide intriguing glimpses into the workings of the eighteenth-century fashion and textile industries. For instance, a set of plates that was originally part of *L'Encyclopédie, ou Dictionnaire Raisonné des Sciences, des Arts et des Métiers,*[3] written from approximately 1750 to 1771, illustrates several day-to-day operations related to weaving, dyeing and the sale of clothing during the eighteenth century. The story of the *Encyclopédie* is itself an interesting one: in short, the project was designed to give readers a summary of world knowledge. It focused especially on the operations necessary to all types of manufacturing processes in eighteenth-century France, from the construction of bridges to silk weaving. According to historian Philipp Blom, "Nothing of this magnitude had ever been attempted … a survey of manual work undertaken for the general reader was unheard of."[4] Although the encyclopedia had multiple contributors, philosopher Denis Diderot led the project, acting as its general editor and also becoming one of its primary authors. Diderot visited tradesmen and craftsmen in their workshops, taking notes and making sketches of what he observed. His encyclopedia became a bold assertion of the importance of manual labor to the everyday lives of the people of France.[5]

Some of the most illustrative plates from the series are those that show weaving in progress. Although the 1769 plate entitled "*Tapisserie de Haute-Lisse des Gobelins*"[6] features a loom used in the Gobelins tapestry manufactory, the process for weaving dress silks was similar (Figure 2.1). All looms were operated manually, and they required great skill to master. At least two people were needed to work at each loom and, as the plate shows, several more people were often employed. The spinners, weavers and "draw boys" (the persons needed to manually operate the looms) in this plate show just a few of the numerous tasks involved in the creation of a length of fabric. Draw looms could not really be considered machines, therefore, but rather served as devices for weaving.[7]

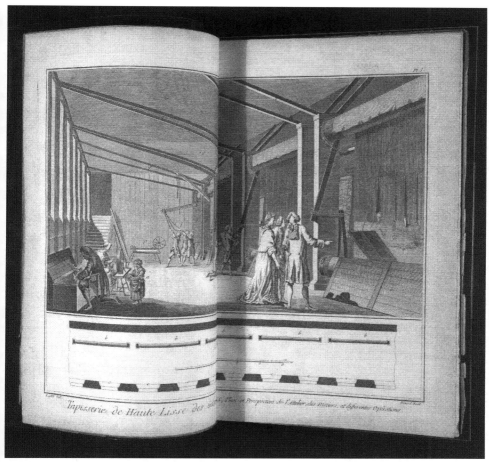

Figure 2.1 Denis Diderot, "Tapisserie de Basse-Lisse des Gobelins," from *L'Encyclopédie, ou Dictionnaire Raisonné des Sciences, des Arts et des Métiers*, 1769. Collection of The Museum at FIT, P84.15.2c. Museum purchase. Photograph © The Museum at FIT.

Silk brocades were particularly difficult and expensive to produce, ranking as luxury materials alongside lace, velvet, embroidered fabrics and gilded textiles.[8] A robe à la française[9] c. 1760 was made from violet and pink silk brocade with a meandering floral pattern (Figure 2.2). The gown survives intact and is in excellent condition, yet close examination reveals that it was carefully altered, probably to update its silhouette. This is not surprising, as the pattern of the silk dates to approximately 15 years earlier than the style of the gown. As Chapter 1 underscored, fabrics and garments were frequently remade or repurposed simply because their wearers could not afford new cloth. "Even the wealthy saved fabrics, remodeled clothes, and sold unwanted items in the secondhand market," observed fashion scholar Linda Welters. "Sustainability was a way of life."[10] Indeed, although change is inherent to fashion, the remodeling of existing clothing, rather than buying new, was a widespread practice. It is rare, in fact, to find an eighteenth-century dress that does not show some sign of alteration. The cost of having a gown made, or remade, was only

Figure 2.2 *Robe à la Française*, lavender and pink silk brocade, c. 1760, Denmark. Collection of The Museum at FIT, P84.8.1. Museum purchase. Photograph © The Museum at FIT.

about half the cost of the textile itself,[11] and could be significantly less, depending on the type of fabric. In addition to updated dress silhouettes, accessories and trimmings played an important role in refreshing old clothing styles. For example, the addition of a row of lace on a bodice was an economical alternative to the full replacement of a gown.[12]

It is believed that the styles of many mid- to late-eighteenth-century gowns derived from a dress style that was prevalent early in the century, usually referred to as a mantua. Essentially a loose gown with large pleats at the shoulders to fit it slightly to the body, the mantua's simple shape showcased intricate silk patterns to their full advantage.[13] Wide pleats also meant that significant widths of the gown's fabric remained uncut. As dress silhouettes evolved over the course of the century, many mantuas were picked apart, and their material was reused to fashion more up-to-date gowns. Heavy, patterned silks such as that used for the robe à la française in the Museum's collection were fashionable until the 1760s. Like the mantua, the silhouette of this dress style (which was also referred to as a sack gown) was considered ideal for displaying elaborately patterned silks.[14]

Technological advancements

Many eighteenth-century textiles are still admired for their beauty and longevity. Yet research has shown that in England, at least, fabrics became lighter and less durable over the course of the century, requiring them to be replaced more often.[15] At any quality level or price point, however, the manufacture of textiles remained a manual process. Draw looms had reached their technical capacity by the late eighteenth century,[16] and the sheer difficulty of producing fabric impeded the growth of the textile industry. With fabrics in high demand and short supply, change was imminent.

Although the nineteenth century is usually considered to be the most critical era to the development of the modern fashion system, the groundwork for technological advancement was laid in the previous century. In 1770, for example, English inventor James Hargreaves patented the spinning jenny—a machine that mechanized the spinning of yarns for weaving. In mid-eighteenth century England, it was purported that:

> Weavers were unemployed a great part of every day, the time being spent in wandering over the country seeking weft amongst the spinners; whilst the latter, though there was a considerable increase in their numbers, owing to the comparatively large sums they were enabled to earn, scarcely cared to work more than half their time. It was in this state of the trade that Hargreaves' invention appeared, promising relief from the most pressing difficulty of the trade.[17]

The spinning jenny required just one person to operate, and its actions mimicked those that were performed by hand.[18] When those actions were mechanized, they allowed for much faster production of weft yarn, but the spinning jenny was not ideally suited to making warp yarns.[19] This created a need for further technological development, such as the spinning mule of the later 1770s. An improvement on the spinning jenny, the spinning mule was itself improved upon in subsequent years, becoming automated and producing stronger yarns. In other words, the wheels of textile invention were fully in motion.

The nineteenth century

The Jacquard loom

As mechanization was clearly vital to the expansion of fabric manufacturing, the textile industry was the first to make the complete transition from hand labor to machine operation. The introduction of the Jacquard loom, which mechanized silk production, was one of the most significant (and controversial) technological developments of the nineteenth century. Joseph Marie Jacquard patented the loom in 1804, and it was widely regarded as the most complicated machine in the world at that time.[20] In fact, some historians regard the Jacquard loom as the first "computer." The operation of the loom is somewhat complex, but its basic operation can be briefly summarized. An automated punched card system continuously feeds information about the next line of weaving to the loom. The resulting patterns range from basic to complex, depending on the number of cards used. A greater number of cards gives more information to the loom, resulting in more intricate weave structures. The patterns woven on Jacquard looms were often as visually compelling as their hand-woven counterparts—and sometimes even more so. A dress, c. 1830, in the collection of MFIT was made in the fashionable silhouette of its era (with voluminous "leg-o-mutton" sleeves) from a Jacquard woven silk in a shade of aubergine (see plate 9). Up close, the woven pattern is strikingly sharp and geometric— so much so, in fact, that it seems to have been purposely designed to highlight its manufacture on a Jacquard loom.

Intricately woven fabrics could be produced over 24 times faster on the Jacquard loom than on handlooms. A single weaver could operate an entire loom, eliminating the need for assistants. Whereas manual looms could only make up to one inch of fabric per day, Jacquard looms could produce an astonishing two feet of fabric in the same amount of time.[21] In addition to the efficiency of time and labor offered by the Jacquard weaving process, the looms themselves were economical. They were built in such a way that the patterns woven on them could be easily changed, without necessitating that the entire loom be rebuilt.[22] In spite of its efficiency, however, the Jacquard loom was not an immediate success. It was, in fact, met with "violent opposition" by weavers who did not understand its workings, and some machines were publicly disassembled by the *Conseil des Prudhommes* (the Labor Court).[23] Eventually, the loom was accepted—and even lauded—as an important French invention. Although the French government attempted to keep all Jacquard looms within France, the looms were gaining popularity in England by the early 1830s, where they were further enhanced by steam power.[24] The quickening speed of fabric production was well underway.

Dressmaking techniques

In spite of such important technological advancements, however, attitudes toward the value and maintenance of clothing and textiles did not change overnight. Many women's clothes in the nineteenth century continued to be thoughtfully and efficiently made. Fabric

Figure 2.3 Dress with added pelerine and long sleeves, pale green silk, c. 1840, USA. Collection of The Museum at FIT, P87.20.48. Museum purchase. Photograph © The Museum at FIT.

Figure 2.4 Dress with evening bodice, pale green silk, c. 1840, USA. Collection of The Museum at FIT, P87.20.48. Museum purchase. Photograph © The Museum at FIT.

remained a significant expenditure, even after the mechanization of its production, and many dresses were designed for maximum wear. Since skirts necessitated the greatest quantity of fabric in a dress, the same skirt would often be worn with different bodices—usually one for day and another for evening. A dress in pale green silk, c. 1840, took an even more economical approach to fabric conservation (Figures 2.3 and 2.4). It had just one bodice, with a low-cut neckline and short sleeves that were appropriate for eveningwear. A matching *pelerine* could also be worn over the bodice, disguising the low neckline and transforming the dress into a style appropriate for daywear. A pair of long sleeves could also be added to the dress, further allowing the wearer to convert its appearance.

In today's fashion lexicon, this dress would be described as transformable or multi-functional—meaning it was designed "with more than one use or configuration."[25] The concept of multi-functionality was integral to dressmaking in the nineteenth century, but it is nearly obsolete today. The ready availability of clothing in the contemporary market-place means that many consumers wear a garment only a handful of times before simply buying something new. Outside of the sustainable fashion market, a multifunctional garment would likely be viewed as a short-lived novelty item.

Other nineteenth-century dressmaking techniques underscored the value of fabric in different ways. For instance, a handbook from 1874 entitled *How to Dress on £15 a Year* offered tips on how to save fabric when cutting and making a dress at home. "By careful attention to all these little things a reduction of two or three yards can frequently be gained. An inch or two here or there soon mounts up to yards in cutting out a costume,"[26] it advised. As dresses of the period frequently required 13 or 14 yards of fabric,[27] such tips could have spared a dressmaker nearly 20 percent of the total amount of cloth needed. Such an idea is akin to the current concept of *zero waste*, to be discussed later in this chapter.

The contemporary sustainable fashion movement focuses not only on how clothing is made, however, but also on how it is cared for after it is purchased and worn. Washing our clothing is a simple, automated process today, and we rarely consider the environmental impact of laundering (such as the amount of energy and fresh water used, which can be four times as harmful as the manufacture of the garment itself[28]). In the nineteenth century, however, laundering clothing was an enormously labor-intensive task. A study of nineteenth-century laundry practices in the United States found that some clothing was likely constructed so that it could be taken apart and cleaned with greater ease.[29]

The sewing machine

While the mechanization of fabric production was well underway, another vital innovation to the manufacture of clothing was forthcoming. The introduction of the sewing machine forever changed the way most clothing was made. Designed by an American named Elias Howe, the first sewing machine was patented in 1846. Early examples were prohibitively expensive, costing nearly US $3,000[30]—and large factories required up to 40 machines to operate.[31] Nevertheless, the benefits of the sewing machine were too great to ignore, and sales increased slowly. The rate of machine stitching was approximately seven times faster than that done by hand, and it was also neater and stronger.[32] Prices dropped considerably over the next 20 years, as the sewing machine gained prominence. By 1866, the average cost of a machine was US $60, and there were purportedly 750,000 sewing machines in the United States alone.[33]

The introduction of the sewing machine (and its subsequent variations by other entrepreneurs, such as Isaac Singer) offered a substantial boost to the American economy. The sewing machine also helped to cement the role of the United States as an industrial nation.[34] Ideas to improve upon the original invention were enacted almost immediately after its introduction. A booklet published in 1867, entitled *History of the Sewing Machine,* mentioned that "by means of the various improvements and attachments, the sewing machine now performs nearly all the needle ever did. It seams, hems, tucks, binds, stitches, quilts, gathers, fells, braids, embroiders, and makes buttonholes. It is used in the manufacture of every garment worn by man, woman, or child."[35] While "every garment" was surely an overstatement, the sewing machine did enable enormous change to take place in the ready-made garment industry. In 1860, for instance, a shirt manufacturer based in New Haven, Connecticut reported that his factory made 800 shirts per week, using 400 sewing machines and operators. The work produced was the equivalent of that done by 2,000 hand sewers. As a result, labor costs were reduced from US $6,000 per week to $1,600 per week.[36] This data clearly shows that the large-scale production of clothing at a drastically reduced price point was becoming increasingly feasible.

In relation to sustainability, the rise of ready-made fashion is considered a key progenitor of problems within the industry—including excessive waste, pollution and poor labor conditions. Numerous scholarly studies have outlined the history of ready-to-wear, and it is largely discussed as a mid-nineteenth century phenomenon. While it is true that ready-to-wear became more prevalent at that time, the advent of ready-made clothing in parts of Europe actually took place much earlier. London's East India Company, for example, offered mass-produced garments by the late seventeenth century, and tailoring and dressmaking shops also sold a selection of ready-made clothes (although these were typically of a simple nature).[37] In the United States, ready-made clothing was first available for men. While its growth was generated at least in part by the need for Civil War uniforms, it appears that a demand for standardized work wear instigated the production of men's ready-to-wear prior to the 1860s.[38]

Ready-made clothing for women became more widespread as the nineteenth century progressed, but the selection of garments was generally more limited than that which was available for men. This was due in part to the precise fit necessary for many items of women's clothing, in addition to the fact that dressmakers were both prevalent and relatively inexpensive. If a woman could not afford a dressmaker, she typically sewed her own clothing at home—perhaps only purchasing ready-made garments for the men in her family.[39] Furthermore, as a general rule, factory-made clothing was believed to be poorly constructed and quick to deteriorate.[40] But the convenience of ready-made clothing could not be ignored. Its "democratic" nature allowed many people of lesser means to more easily keep up with fashion for the first time, even if their garments were not especially well made. The sewing machine also played a role in boosting the popularity of certain ready-made items for women, such as wraps, cloaks and crinolines. For example, the cage crinoline—an essential undergarment during the 1860s—was much easier to sew by machine than by hand, and machine production also helped to substantially lower its price.[41]

At the end of the nineteenth century, the shirtwaist blouse became the first widely mass-produced garment for women. The shirtwaist was considered a "separate," meaning it could be easily mixed and match with other items in a woman's wardrobe. The simplest styles were worn with tailored suits, or paired with skirts for at-home wear or sportswear. Dressier options—those made from better fabrics and trimmed with lace, for example—were acceptable for more formal afternoon occasions and eveningwear.[42] The relative simplicity and ease of fit of shirtwaists meant that they were simple, and therefore inexpensive, to manufacture. An example by the New York-based company Stanley, dated to c. 1894, typifies the informal style of shirtwaist (Figure 2.5). Made of simple cotton, the blouse buttons down the center front, and is tightly pleated under the collar and at the waist to create fullness over the bust. The sleeves are very full, and gathered into plain, wide cuffs at the wrist.

An advertisement for Macy's department store in New York included an extensive listing of available shirtwaist styles in "all the 1899 styles in the fabrics that wear and wash best … Don't let the little prices scare you. Every garment looks and launders beautifully."[43] Stanley shirtwaists were specifically mentioned, and ranged in price from US $0.59 (for a shirtwaist in striped percale) to $1.89 (for a style made from dressier crepe fabric).[44]

While many ready-made clothes in Europe still carried an aura of cheapness,

Figure 2.5 Stanley, shirtwaist blouse, white cotton, c. 1894, USA. Collection of The Museum at FIT, P91.33.1. Museum purchase. Photograph © The Museum at FIT.

American factory production was coming into its own, providing increasingly fashionable, low-priced alternatives to custom-made clothing.[45] This allowed Americans to become "the best dressed average people in the world"[46] by the turn of the twentieth century. For certain consumers, such as young, unmarried women, there was a certain gratification in purchasing something brand-new and fashionable for themselves.[47] It could be argued that this attitude still exists to some extent, particularly as many fast-fashion chains target a youthful clientele. Yet also like today, inexpensive clothing prices were primarily made possible by two main factors: mechanization and poorly paid employees (more on the history of fashion industry workers is outlined in Chapter 5).

The end of the nineteenth century also saw the development of several other machines that aided in the production of ready-made clothing. These included the button sewer (1875), a steam-powered cutting machine (developed in the 1870s), and the electric-powered rotary knife (invented in the 1890s). The latter two innovations allowed more than 20 layers of fabric to be cut at a single time.[48] It must be noted, however, that most machines used in fashion production—both past and present—still require some degree of human operation. While technology has increased the speed and efficiency of production, therefore, it has not eliminated the need for labor.

The twentieth century

The ready-to-wear clothing industry prospered during the early twentieth century. By 1910, every item in a woman's wardrobe was available ready-made.[49] New and inexpensive manmade fibers, such as rayon, also came to be a logical choice for mass-produced fashion. This helped to decrease clothing prices, while simultaneously increasing the speed of the fashion cycle. By the 1920s ready-to-wear styles were sold in greater quantity than ever before, in part because the simple, tubular silhouette that dominated the era allowed garments to be easily manufactured.[50] As a 1924 handbook entitled *Principles of Clothing Selection* observed, "at present our standard of dress is based upon fashion. Quality and beauty are not important, because fashion changes so rapidly that garments are discarded long before they are worn out."[51] It is therefore evident that concerns over the "disposability" of fashion have existed for decades. Moreover, especially in reaction to a decline in clothing sales during the Great Depression, the concept of separates became more important. Items such as individual skirts, sweaters, or blouses were much less expensive to replace than entire suits or dresses, and could be worn in multiple ways to different effect. It was through the purchase of ready-made separates that the average consumer's wardrobe began to expand.[52]

World War II and the golden age of couture

While the Depression had a lasting impact on fashion production, World War II brought even greater change to the industry. Consumers were encouraged to "Make Do and Mend" (see "At a glance: Make do and mend"), but there remained both a need and a desire for new clothing as well. While Paris—long the leader of the fashion industry—was under German occupation, it became especially critical for designers and apparel manufacturers in the United States to assert themselves as an integral part of their nation's industry. Although popularly priced ready-to-wear had become standard attire for many Americans by the 1940s,[53] there was also a market for higher-end fashion, provided by a number of prominent American designers.

Hollywood costumier-turned-fashion designer Gilbert Adrian was one of the most famous tastemakers of the World War II era. In his work for Metro-Goldwyn-Mayer (MGM) studios in the 1930s, Adrian successfully costumed hundreds of films, becoming well known for his theatrical creations (providing the costumes for *The Wizard of Oz,* for example), as well as his forays into high style (dressing Joan Crawford in chic clothing that accentuated her slim, broad-shouldered physique). Adrian's fashion label, founded in 1941, was an immediate success. Offering both custom-made and high-end ready-to-wear clothing, he became especially known for his elegant, ingeniously designed suits. The "clothes hanger" shape that Adrian had devised for Crawford, with its padded shoulders, narrow waistline and slim skirt, had been fashionable for women's suits in the 1930s—but the style's austere silhouette and ease of wear also proved ideal for women's practical wartime fashions.

One example of an Adrian suit, from c. 1942, exemplifies the designer's clever methods of construction (plate 4). The label designates that the suit is an Adrian Original, meaning that it was ready-to-wear. Nevertheless, it was impeccably crafted. The suit jacket was made from an engineered wool fabric that, at first glance, appears to be several different textiles pieced together. Wide bands of dark grey pinstripes were interspersed with bands of tan and grey houndstooth, as well as thinner stripes in bright blue and red. The blue and red portion of the fabric was also used to create one of Adrian's most recognizable design elements: the addition of decorative flaps. In this instance, the flaps were placed vertically at the left front waist and on the right sleeve. These small scraps of fabric may have held greater significance than mere visual interest, however. It is possible that they also related to the measures the designer took to follow L-85 restrictions (described in "At a glance: Make do and mend), instated just after he started his clothing label. Although following the restrictions was mandatory, Adrian embraced them with particular enthusiasm. His use of fabric scraps, which would have otherwise been swept from the cutting room floor and discarded, may have been a clever way to maximize fabric in a time of scarcity. Although this is only speculated, Adrian's feelings on fabric rationing were documented. Upon presenting his fall/winter 1942 collection, he stated: "We feel privileged at this vital time in world history to present a collection of clothes carefully attuned to Government Order L-85."[54] Adrian's streamlined silhouettes were already attuned to rationing ideals, but some of his newer ideas, such as collarless necklines or self-tie fastenings, proved that he was constantly refining his designs.

Adrian's clothing was in great demand and frequently sold out at New York department stores, but his designs were not inexpensive. The lowest priced Adrian Original suit cost about US $50—just slightly above the average price of a wool suit in the 1940s[55]—but most sold for nearer to $125.[56] This underscores that, even in wartime America, some consumers were willing to pay a premium for clothing—and especially for garments lauded for their quality and longevity. As fashion historian Claudia Kidwell stated in a 1978 article on Adrian, "[The suits] were special, which is why so many women bought them to get married in. They were practical yet beautiful."[57] In the same article, a woman recalled that she had purchased an Adrian suit in 1944—and she continued to wear the style 34 years later.

Other sources reinforce that the appreciation for well-designed, beautifully made garments spared them from disposal. A 1970 article in the *New York Times,* entitled "Those Vintage Dresses That Defy All the Whimsies of Fashion," profiled a number of society women who refused to replace some of their most cherished articles of clothing. The article underscored that the women usually chose to wear their old dresses "for reasons unrelated to economy ... there is often nostalgia and sentiment involved in the decision to keep a dress, but there are also far more tangible reasons. Construction, quality of fabric and the timelessness of the design are the three most frequently mentioned."[58] Styles described ranged from a 12-year-old coat by Pauline Trigère to more authentically vintage pieces, such as two Christian Dior couture dresses from 1950. Those dresses were initially made for the wedding trousseau of Mrs William Buckley, Jr., who began to wear the dresses again in the mid-1960s. "They are as chic as they ever were," Buckley stated. "Even more chic."[59]

In spite of the growing market for mass-produced fashion in the mid-twentieth century (or more likely in reaction to it), the years 1947 to 1957 are often viewed as "The Golden Age of Couture." In order to re-assert its influence following World War II, the Parisian couture industry promoted the elegance and luxuriousness of its clothing more than ever before. Although there were numerous prominent couturiers, including Cristobal Balenciaga and Pierre Balmain, it was Christian Dior who dominated. A 1951 Dior dress provides insight into the perfection of couture technique (Figure 2.6). The heavy ivory silk was densely embellished with polychrome ribbon, silk flowers and bright blue rhinestones. The ornamentation was applied entirely by hand, and the dress itself was almost entirely hand-stitched (a hallmark of couture craftsmanship). The interior of the dress was also immaculately constructed, featuring a fully boned bodice and a separate crinoline petticoat made from layers of stiff netting.

While it is easy to imagine that women cherished their beautiful couture dresses over a long period of time, the 1950s, in particular, was a decade rife with consumerism and change. A meticulously crafted couture dress was made to last, but not all couture clients were content to wear the same dress for years. Dior himself continued to introduce new ideas season after season, and his latest designs were quickly distilled into simpler versions for the ready-to-wear market. It could also be said that Dior created a "need" for women to replace or drastically update their wardrobes immediately following World War II. In 1947, he presented what became known as the "New Look"—characterized by an hourglass silhouette, long, full skirts, and an overall sense of luxurious femininity that is exemplified by this evening dress. In other words, the New Look was a direct reaction to the austere styles that women had worn during the war years.

A 1948 survey by the *Women's Home Companion* questioned its readers on their wardrobes after "the change" (referring to the introduction of Dior's New Look). Just

Figure 2.6 Christian Dior, evening dress, ivory silk satin with multicolor embroidery and rhinestones, 1951, France. Collection of The Museum at FIT, 75.86.5. Gift of Despina Messinesi. Photograph © The Museum at FIT.

ten months after the new silhouette was presented, the women surveyed had already purchased an average of three dresses in the latest style, and half had also bought a new suit and coat. Yet the same survey showed that women continued to be resourceful with their clothing as well: nine out of ten readers had altered existing garments in an attempt to make them conform to the fashionable New Look, and most of the alterations were performed by the wearer herself, rather than a dressmaker.[60] The average amount of money that readers spent on dressing themselves was US $186[61]—but that sum was likely underestimated, being that most women could not remember all of their fashion expenditures. Approximately half of the total money spent was on ready-made clothing, followed by shoes, hats and other accessories.[62]

The 1960s and "disposable" fashion

Concerns over the abundance of ready-to-wear fashion, particularly in America, were outlined in Vance Packard's 1960 book *The Waste Makers*. Packard, a journalist, frequently questioned practices aimed at increasing consumerism, and *The Waste Makers* focused primarily on planned obsolescence in American manufacturing and marketing. The book covered a range of products, from telephones to automobiles, and specifically mentioned the fashion system. Packard wrote:

> For centuries women have craved a new dress, and so have become co-conspirators with the dress marketers. When a woman already has a closetful of good-as-new dresses, the best excuse she can offer her husband (who usually considers himself financially hard-pressed) for further splurging is that every dress she owns is out of style. In recent years the dressmakers have stepped up to the pace of style obsolescence, so that by 1960 fashion ran through a full cycle every seven to ten years.[63]

Although Packard's writing may seem somewhat sensationalized, his observations on the fashion industry summarized the desire for "disposable" fashion that further developed over the course of the 1960s. Often considered the decade that revolutionized the fashion industry, the 1960s fostered a seemingly endless array of new ideas, from teenaged design entrepreneurs to battery-powered, light-up dresses. Rapid change also meant that inexpensive, ready-made clothing became even more important. Whereas 1950s couture garments were defined by their elegance, 1960s clothing had a different focus. "Clothes are just not that important," asserted Rudi Gernreich in a 1967 interview for *Time* magazine. "They're not status symbols any longer. They're for fun."[64] Gernreich was a top ready-to-wear designer of the era, whose bold styles—including a topless bathing suit—placed him at the forefront of experimental fashion.

The most obvious example of the movement toward "fun," disposable clothing in the 1960s was the trend for so-called paper clothes—items typically made from a variety of nonwoven fibers (rather than actual paper) that were, quite literally, intended to be thrown away after being worn one or two times. The fad began somewhat inadvertently. In 1966, Scott Paper Company offered paper dresses in two different prints—promotional items that were designed to match a new line of disposable tableware. The dresses could be ordered with a mail-in coupon for just US $1.25. Over a period of just a few months, Scott had sold 500,000 copies of the dresses.[65]

Paper clothing in a variety of styles was a wildly popular—albeit short-lived—phenomenon in the late 1960s, but paper garments were not a new idea. They were, in fact, quite prevalent during the eighteenth and nineteenth centuries. As few of these items exist today, however, it seems that they have been largely forgotten in the history of fashion. In a master's thesis on the early history of paper clothing, Jennifer Feingold Kibel found that such items were in production as early as 1718, and that paper was used not because it was inexpensive, but because it was novel.[66] It was not until the nineteenth century that items such as bonnets, collars, cuffs, and shirtfronts were made from paper for reasons of economy. Although paper had not dropped in price at that time, traditional cloth goods had become more expensive, making paper a comparatively affordable alternative.[67]

Kibel also pointed out that "the waste and disposal of materials is a significant by-product of twentieth-century society. In contrast, nineteenth-century disposability was viewed as a novelty."[68] However, paper clothes of the 1960s were little but novelty items as well. While most examples were simply designed, a dress from the Museum at FIT collection proves that, in some cases, ideas of what was considered disposable were quite extraordinary (plate 5). The dress was made from paper in a swirling "psychedelic" design in shades of yellow, orange, green and pink. Its very construction marks it as unusual: while most paper dresses were made in a simple shift style, with perhaps some darts over the bust, the full skirt of this example was carefully gathered at the bust and stitched onto a separate bodice. The bodice fastens with a center back zipper. Likewise, while the hems of most paper dresses were cut straight across, this dress has a "fishtail" hem, beginning at the knee in front and extending almost to the ankle in back. Most notable, however, is the large collar of bright pink ostrich plumes. Once considered as valuable as diamonds, ostrich feathers had come to be used as decoration on a garment intended for quick disposal.

In a 1967 article on the paper dress fad, William Guggenheim III, the proprietor of a New York City boutique called Dispensable Disposables, proclaimed, "I believe implicitly that disposables are here to stay."[69] While Guggenheim surely meant that he felt that the fad for paper clothing would last (it did not), traditional clothing was, indeed, increasingly viewed as something of little value. In 1975, the style handbook *Cheap Chic* lamented:

> We've become spoiled in America. Surrounded by mass manufacturing and mass marketing, we stuff our closets with masses of mistakes. Fashion seduces us from Sears to Sak's in a dizzying array of styles, prices, fabrics, and colors. We end up with far too many clothes, without stopping to consciously work out our own personal style and gather together the basic elements we need to get it going.[70]

This sounds eerily similar to some of the concerns expressed in twenty-first century publications that examine the overconsumption of fashion, such as *To Die For: Is Fashion Wearing Out the World?* by Lucy Siegle (2011), and Elizabeth L. Cline's *Overdressed: The Shockingly High Cost of Cheap Fashion* (2012).

Contemporary fashion

The major changes to the fashion system in the 1960s resulted in the decline of the couture industry, which had long been the driving force in fashion. Perhaps not surprisingly, the introduction of revered couturiers in the mid-nineteenth century—most notably Charles Frederick Worth—corresponded to the rise of mass-produced clothing. Garments that were made to order from a fashion authority had a cachet of stylishness and quality, setting them apart from clothing made by the average dressmaker—and most certainly ranking them above ready-to-wear garments. "The signature of a designer served the same purpose as the signature of an artist on a painting,"[71] wrote Karl Aspelund in his study of haute couture. Today, however, most fashion trends revolve around clothing styles produced by high-end, ready-to-wear labels, rather than couturiers. The allure of the brand name is sometimes all that is needed to attract customers, and high prices do not necessarily translate to quality of craftsmanship or fine materials. "Luxury used to have a shelf life,"[72] recalled Ilse Metchek, executive director of the California Fashion Association, but today's so-called "luxury" goods often hold little more lasting value than their fast-fashion counterparts.

A potential antidote to the questionable quality and inherent sameness of mass-produced goods may lie in the fusion of ready-made production principles and artisanal techniques. A 1994 dress by Karl Lagerfeld for the French label, Chloé, demonstrates this idea (Figure 2.7). It was embellished with multicolor floral motifs that were carefully hand-painted, cut out, and appliquéd onto the floor-length skirt of the dress. The handcrafted elements of the dress make it one-of-a-kind, despite the fact that it was produced by a ready-to-wear brand. Founded in 1962, the Chloé label was, incidentally, the first to introduce the idea of luxury ready-to-wear to the French fashion market. Prior to that time, French women relied on either dressmakers or couturiers for their clothing.

Similarly, designers working in the sustainable fashion industry have begun to perceive elements of high craftsmanship and individuality as key to creating garments with lasting value. John Patrick, who founded his label, Organic, in 2007, takes multiple approaches to the concept of sustainability (more on Patrick's fabric selection is included in Chapter 3)—but his focus on artisanship is prime among them. In a 2008 ensemble, Patrick hand-painted a blouse and skirt in shades of purple (plate 6). The skirt's colorful border was hand-embroidered in Peru. Patrick has consistently worked with Peruvian artisans and organic farmers since launching his label.

Patrick ensures that his production practices are transparent, and he maintains strong personal and business relationships with craftspeople around the globe. Such business models are, unfortunately, a rarity within the fashion world. Many workers in countries such as India and Malaysia are taxed with the production of hand-embroidered garments, but few of them are paid fairly for their skills. Many work from their homes in abysmal conditions. As Lucy Siegle concluded in *To Die For,* "in luxury [goods], the handworker is celebrated; in Big Fashion she is an inconvenient truth."[73] It becomes apparent, therefore, that simply purchasing clothing with unique, handcrafted elements is not enough—conscientious consumers must also research the conditions under which such embellishments were produced.

Figure 2.7 Installation shot from *Eco-Fashion: Going Green* (The Museum at FIT, 2010). Chloé (Karl Lagerfeld), evening dress, off-white silk net, multicolor painted silk appliqués, spring 1994, France. Collection of The Museum at FIT, 95.131.1. Photograph © The Museum at FIT.

John Patrick's one-of-a-kind ensemble holds even greater significance than the beauty and ethics of its craftsmanship, however. It was made for the 2008 Council of the Fashion Designers of America/Vogue Fashion Fund Award,[74] for which Patrick was nominated. The selection of John Patrick's label for such a prestigious award was a major coup for the sustainable fashion industry—which, in the past, was often critiqued for its focus on "earthy" designs that were decidedly out of the realm of high fashion. The origins of the sustainable fashion movement are often traced back to the 1970s—the time period in which hippies used handmade and secondhand clothing to express their anti-fashion ideals, as well as their concern for the environment. As the sustainable fashion movement has evolved, it has been somewhat of a struggle for designers to shed the associations with hippie culture in favor of a more high-fashion appearance. The designers are keenly aware, however, that the ability to produce fashion that is ethically, emotionally and aesthetically pleasing is essential to the future of their businesses—as well as the sustainable fashion industry as a whole.

Alabama Chanin, a label founded in 2006 by designer Natalie Chanin, has become especially recognized for the integrity of its designs, in addition to its business practices. Chanin's company epitomizes what has become known as the *slow fashion* movement (a direct contrast to the fast-fashion industry). Modeled after Carol Petrini's concept of slow food, the slow fashion model focuses on transparent production models with "less intermediation between producer and consumer," the use of local resources and economies, and the production of goods with greater value and longer lives.[75]

Alabama Chanin's clothing is made from "organic, custom-dyed cotton jersey that is cut, painted, sewn, and embellished by hand in America by skilled artisans."[76] The label was started after the brand with which Chanin was previously involved, Project Alabama, moved its manufacturing to India.[77] The designer works from her small hometown of Florence, Alabama, where she focuses on entirely local production—from the growth of the organic cotton used in her garments to the skilled craftspeople she employs to make them.

A three-piece Alabama Chanin ensemble from spring 2010 consists of a wrap-style top, a skirt, and a jacket (Figures 2.8 and 2.9). It was entirely hand stitched from the label's signature knit cotton fabric, dyed a shade of light blue. While the silhouette of the ensemble is basic, the embellished fabric is decidedly elaborate. Each garment was constructed from two layers of fabric. In some areas, leaf shapes were cut out from the top layer of fabric, the edges of which were painted and topstitched. The leaves were then filled in with small silver beads. On other parts of the cloth, smaller organic shapes were sketched, painted, and outlined with the same white topstitching. The final result took months to complete—a far cry from the minutes it takes to produce most fast-fashion garments.

Alabama Chanin's clothing is never trend-driven, and it is designed to be versatile, comfortable, and flattering to many different body types.[78] These qualities are essential, as the impeccable craftsmanship of the clothing comes at a high price. For those who can purchase the garments, they are intended to be "investment" pieces that can be worn for many years. In an industry dominated by US $5 T-shirts, however, the label has been criticized as "elitist" and "inaccessible." It is for that very reason that Chanin has published two lavishly illustrated books on her work, giving step-by-step instructions

Figure 2.8 Alabama Chanin (Natalie Chanin), ensemble: coat and two-piece wrap dress, light blue organic cotton jersey, Spring 2010, USA. Collection of The Museum at FIT, 2010.19.1. Museum purchase. Photograph © The Museum at FIT.

Figure 2.9 Alabama Chanin (Natalie Chanin), detail of organic cotton jersey fabric, Spring 2010, USA. Collection of The Museum at FIT, 2010.19.1. Museum purchase. Photograph © The Museum at FIT.

on how to make Alabama Chanin clothing at home. In freely revealing her company's production practices, Chanin hoped to "shed light on not only how we can preserve and protect precious natural resources but also how we can preserve and protect techniques that were once understood as essential survival skills."[79]

Since the fashion industry is structured around the very idea of obsolescence, however, many people have questioned if slow fashion is a legitimate strategy for the future of clothing manufacture. In theory, the development of slow fashion on a larger scale is feasible, but it would necessitate that consumers focus on making the aforementioned investment purchases—items of higher value that they would plan to wear for a longer period of time. This would allow a greater number of designers and manufacturers to shift their focus to making items of much better quality—and, most importantly, of higher cost. This change cannot happen overnight, of course—especially since many consumers rely on the so-called "bargains" and instant gratification they can obtain through fast fashion—but public awareness of harmful fashion production practices has increased dramatically over the past decade.

New York-based designer Mary Ping began her conceptual clothing label, Slow and Steady Wins the Race, in 2002. The name of the brand underscores its ideology: to create a line of clothing and accessories in a slowed-down production cycle, specifically through its dedication to non-seasonal designs that are "timely and timeless."[80] Clothing and accessories from the label's earliest collections are still available over a decade later—creating what Ping refers to as a "living archive,"[81] and underscoring the lasting relevance of the designs.

Just shortly after launching her label, Ping introduced a line of handbags. The collection was produced at the height of the "It bag" craze—a time in which demand for the latest designer bags resulted in exorbitant prices, even if the bags were quickly replaced by the next trendy style. "People sort of hit the saturation point with the status handbags ... Increasingly, I couldn't see where the design lay within the status it-bag,"[82] remembered the designer. Ping's bag designs were modeled after recognizable styles from several prominent fashion houses, exemplified by her version of the ubiquitous "Postal" bag by Balenciaga (Figure 2.10). Rather than using traditional handbag materials, however, Ping's versions were crafted from inexpensive cotton canvas, relying solely on their silhouettes and minimal hardware to convey their design origins. The designer explained her concept as a "logical dissection of fashion, an investigation into the basic elements of what we wear, and a considered response to the hyper-consumerist pace of fashion."[83] Stripped of their luxury skins and extraneous design elements, the bags took on an unassuming appearance. The line was inspired by forgeries of designer bags available on New York City's Canal Street for next-to-nothing prices, meaning that Ping's bags were like "knock-offs of knock-offs."[84] The designer's work was thought-provoking: while the owner of a real Balenciaga may not have carried it more than a few seasons (for fear it would look outdated), Ping's unique version transcended trends. She continues to produce pared-down versions of iconic designer handbags, which are made to order.

Zero waste has also gained exposure as part of the sustainable fashion movement, but its concept has deep historical roots. In her book Cut My Cote, textile and dress historian Dorothy Burnham explored ancient practices of making clothing, observing

Figure 2.10 Slow and Steady Wins the Race (Mary Ping), "Postal" bag, unbleached cotton canvas, Fall 2002, USA. Collection of The Museum at FIT, 2005.63.1. Gift of Mary Ping. Photograph © The Museum at FIT.

that "weaving far outstripped the techniques of cutting and sewing, with the result that garments were made with the cut edges as straight as possible and with selvages cleverly utilized to save the sewing of hems and to give strength where needed."[85] Economy of material continued to be an important component for hundreds of years. In eighteenth-century France, for instance, a garment was considered to be successfully designed when it produced no more scrap fabric than could fit in one hand.[86] Even in the late twentieth century—when cloth was easily available and frequently wasted—traditional notions of dressmaking and appreciation for fabrics were not entirely lost. Designer Yeohlee Teng (known professionally as Yeohlee) began crafting garments that centered on minimal fabric wastage in the 1980s, including a one-piece coat crafted from three yards of material. In some of her other designs, any leftover fabric was used to create elements such as ties and pockets.[87]

Figure 2.11 YEOHLEE Fall 2009 runway presentation, model wearing a *ballerina* bodysuit and *Zero Waste* sarong. Photograph by Dan Lecca, courtesy of YEOHLEE.

More recently, Yeohlee created her entire fall 2009 collection "on the principle of economy in design, fabric and execution,"[88] and many of the garments presented utilized every inch of fabric. One example from that collection featured a floor-length sarong, made from four layers of uncut black organza that were simply folded and stitched (Figure 2.11). When tied on the body, the sarong's elegant silhouette belied its zero waste construction. For the runway presentation, however, Yeohlee chose to highlight how her garments were designed. Over the course of the show, several models removed their zero waste outer garments (they wore basic black body suits underneath), and arranged the clothing over outlines of the pattern pieces used to construct them, which had been taped out on the runway floor (Figure 2.12). It was astounding to observe how such seemingly simple, geometric patterns could result in fashions that looked so complex when worn.

Such thoughtfulness in regard to fabric usage is a rarity in today's fashion industry. On average, about 15 percent of the cloth used to make an adult-sized garment is wasted—and that scrap fabric is usually sent straight to landfills.[89] Although Yeohlee does not consider herself a sustainable fashion designer, she incorporates numerous principles of sustainability into her practices. In addition to her consideration for economy of cloth, Yeohlee concentrates on functionality and adaptability in her work, offering clothing that

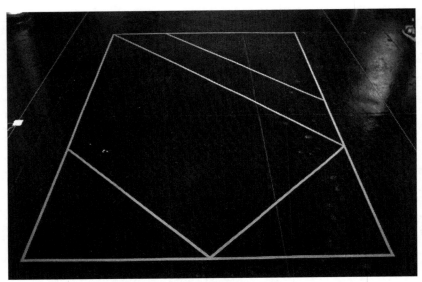

Figure 2.12 YEOHLEE Fall 2009 runway presentation, featuring a *Zero Waste* pattern by Yeohlee Teng. Photograph by Dan Lecca, courtesy of YEOHLEE.

can be layered or mixed-and-matched for maximum wear. The aforementioned body suits, for example, are wardrobe staples that can be paired with a variety of different garments. Yeohlee's work is at once contemporary and timeless: it can be worn for decades without looking dated. It could even be said that it exemplifies a new type of luxury dressing, which emphasizes high-quality materials and immaculate, long-lasting construction over ostentation or "branding."

The manufacture of Yeohlee's clothing is also of great importance to her work. She has become a prime supporter of Save the Garment Center, an organization that strives to "promote, preserve, and save New York City as fashion capital of the world."[90] In recent decades, New York's Seventh Avenue—long the garment-manufacturing center of the United States—has nearly been obliterated due to the demand for cheaper, faster clothing production. In 1963, Bernard Roschco, author of the book *The Rag Race: How New York and Paris Run the Breakneck Business of Dressing American Women,* wrote that "no other major manufacturing industry in this country has so much of its design, production, sale, and distribution facilities concentrated in so small an area."[91] Yet even at that time, manufacturers of low-end clothing were looking for ways to minimize production costs by moving their factories to New York City's outer boroughs, to nearby states such as Pennsylvania, and to the American South.[92] This was merely a precursor to the drastic rise in overseas production, which can provide rock-bottom production prices—usually at the expense of quality craftsmanship, by a poorly-treated, drastically underpaid workforce (more on labor conditions in the fashion industry is discussed in Chapter 5).

Today, only 5 percent of clothing sold in the United States was made in America—a number that has dropped an astounding 90 percent since 1960.[93] Local production is considered to be an integral part of the sustainable fashion industry, as it usually provides step-by-step transparency within the manufacturing process. In addition to a list of designers who produce their clothing in New York (including Yeohlee), the Save the Garment Center website offers a list of resources, helping to locate New York City-based factories, suppliers, and business development agencies.

Conclusion

It is clear that changes in fashion production practices over the past 250 years—and the resulting overconsumption of clothing—have led to severe problems such as waste, pollution and appalling labor conditions. Although these problems are not new, they have compounded in recent years, and many of us have more clothing in our closets than ever before. While a dedicated group of contemporary designers is attempting to counteract long-standing concerns over production and consumption, much of the best-made clothing is out of the reach of the average consumer—and fast fashion remains a temptation. So what can we do to make a difference?

Making more thoughtful clothing purchases is an essential (and relatively simple) way to change current patterns of consumption. Buying fewer items, while simultaneously considering which clothes will have some degree of longevity in our wardrobes, is a step in the right direction—even if what we consume is not "sustainable" in the true definition of the word. Properly caring for our garments, rather than treating them as disposable commodities, is also essential. "There is a saying that of the three desirable qualities [in fashion]—fast, cheap, and good—only two of the three are possible in any one project,"[94] wrote Sandy Black in *Eco-Chic: The Fashion Paradox*. Basic knowledge of the contemporary fashion system allows consumers to make the best possible choice—and smart decisions by individuals can add up to make a substantial difference.

Suggestions for Further Reading:

Clark, H. (2008), "SLOW + FASHION—an oxymoron—or a promise for the future...?" *Fashion Theory: The Journal of Dress, Body & Culture* 12 (4): 247–446.
Essinger, J. (2007), *Jacquard's Web: How a Hand-loom Led to the Birth of the Information Age*, Oxford: Oxford University Press.
Kidwell, C. (1974), *Suiting Everyone: The Democratization of Clothing in America*, Washington, DC: Smithsonian Institution Press.
Lemire, B. (2009), "Developing Consumerism and the Ready-made Clothing Trade in Britain, 1750–1800," in P. McNeil (ed.), *Fashion: Critical and Primary Sources*, Oxford: Berg, 2: 241–65.

At a glance: Fast fashion

The term *fast fashion* refers to garments that are made as cheaply and quickly as possible. Driven by the latest, fleeting trends, fast fashion is intended to be worn just a handful of times before it is disposed of. Its quality of craftsmanship, therefore, is of little concern to both manufacturers and consumers. Stores specializing in fast fashion introduce new styles on a monthly basis, and almost never restock items once they have sold out. The sense of urgency created by the short shelf life of such clothing encourages frequent and impulsive purchases, which quickly leads to overconsumption and waste.

The fast-fashion phenomenon truly took off in the late twentieth century, but its roots go back much further. "In its journey downward and outward, fashion becomes not only less expensive, but less diversified,"[95] observed journalist Bernard Roshco in 1963. Since that time, the dissemination of fashion trends has sped up considerably, allowing low-priced clothing chains to copy and sell high-fashion looks just weeks after they are presented on the runway. Since the number of ideas is limited, however, fast-fashion chains often continuously introduce "new" styles by making small changes to existing models. Some fashion theorists believe that this method will destroy "true style" entirely, foregoing ingenuity in favor of mediocrity.[96]

Devotees of fast fashion often laud such clothing for its "democratic" nature, as it allows nearly anyone to look fashionable. Because clothing has become so readily available, many consumers seem to think that the garments simply "appear" in shops. They give little thought to how such clothing was made or how it reached the store—not to mention what will become of it once it has become unfashionable. Consideration of the full life cycle of a garment is referred to as the "cradle to grave" metaphor. If fast-fashion consumers do stop to think about the life of their purchases from cradle to grave, however, the result is bleak.

As the fast-fashion industry continues to grow, competitors search for ways to manufacture clothing at ever-lower prices. This has resulted in a huge shift to overseas manufacturing, where employees often work for very little pay in unsafe conditions—literally risking their lives to provide the cheap clothing demanded by the Western market. The fabrics from which the clothing is made must also be taken into account: rarely is an inexpensive material also one that is environmentally friendly, and the labor conditions surrounding the production of such materials are often shockingly poor.

Once the clothes are made, they must be shipped to their far-off destinations—another tax on natural resources. After they are purchased, fast fashions will not last very long—but that is of little concern, since most consumers will discard such clothes before they even begin to wear them out. In addition to their poor quality, however, the mass quantity in which the clothes were produced means that they have little value in the resale market. In their final stage, many fast-fashion items end up in landfills.

Changing the way we consume means we must first come to terms with the harsh realities of the ethical and environmental effects of fast fashion. This will not be an easy task, as many shoppers seem to be "addicted" to fast fashion—even if they are aware of its harmful nature. Perhaps another method, then, is to underscore the short-term satisfaction and limited value that such clothing provides. As designer Geoffrey B. Small pointed out, "The math is very simple. Fast fashion is not cheap. If you buy something for ten Euros that lasts only a month, you have to buy another one every month."[97] Although a little money spent on clothes here or there may seem inconsequential, many consumers find that, if pressed, the total amount they spend on fast fashion in a year is vast—and all for goods that provide little long-term satisfaction. In the end, selecting high-quality pieces over trend-driven items is the greatest bargain, but a change in consumption habits will require an enormous shift of focus within the fashion industry.

Suggestions for Further Reading

Cline, E. (2012), *Overdressed: The Shockingly High Cost of Cheap Fashion,* New York: Portfolio.
Siegle, L. (2011), *To Die For: Is Fashion Wearing Out the World?*, London: Fourth Estate.

3
MATERIAL ORIGINS

Fabric selection is essential to clothing manufacture. It is only logical, therefore, that many fashion innovations—past and present—have centered on new or improved fibers. This chapter provides a brief history of the cultivation and production of a selection of fibers, focusing on those that are especially pertinent to the discussion of sustainable fashion. It begins with several important *natural fibers*, including cotton and wool, and proceeds to discuss the invention of *manmade* and *synthetic fibers*, such as rayon and polyester. The positive and negative attributes of each fiber in relation to its environmental impact are highlighted.

Fabric selection is one of the most important and frequently discussed components of sustainable fashion. The impact of fiber production on the environment is profound, ranging from excessive water waste, to polluting pesticides, to climate changes—just to name a few. As the world's population has more than tripled over the past 60 years (from US 2.1 billion to US 7 billion[1]), the resulting depletion of natural resources has become a prime source of concern. Coupled with consumers' ever-expanding desire for new clothing, the creation of more sustainable fabrics is crucial to the longevity of the fashion industry—as well as to the environment as a whole.

Some companies perceive the use of sustainable materials as a "quick fix"[2]—a relatively simple way to appear more eco-friendly, without necessarily incorporating more sustainable or ethical practices into their business operations as a whole. This concept can be traced back to at least the 1980s, when a number of fashion labels adopted what was referred to as the "ecology look," a style that expressed its concern for the environment through eco-centric graphics and prints, as well as through fabrics that had the appearance of being "natural" or "unprocessed." While such clothing made a statement—particularly as a reaction against heightened consumerism—it did little to solve the long-term environmental problems brought on by the fashion industry.[3] Additionally, in spite of the push for natural materials, manmade fibers have become more popular than ever, now comprising almost 60 percent of all textiles—a 20 percent increase from 1990.[4]

Without knowledge of how different fabrics are produced—or how they will decompose—it is easy to conclude that fabrics made from natural fibers are "good," while those made from synthetic materials are "bad." In reality, the distinction between good and bad fibers is much more complex. As sustainable fashion expert Kate Fletcher notes, "we have to be aware of the impacts of our fibre choices on whole interrelated product life-cycles, which include cultivation, production, manufacturing, distribution, consumer laundering, reuse, and final disposal."[5]

Natural fibers

Cotton

Cotton is one of the most widely used and oldest known fibers. It has been cultivated continuously for at least 5,000 years,[6] and its importance to the apparel industry has been a source of inspiration, innovation and political conflict. Since raw cotton was not a natural resource in Europe—meaning its importation was necessary—it took hundreds of years for the fiber to become an integral part of European fashion.[7] Once cotton took hold in Europe in the late seventeenth century, however, it was used extensively. Cotton was especially revered for its "chameleon-like" quality, meaning that it could be used in some ways like linen, and in other ways like lightweight wools or silks.[8] Imports of fine Indian cotton, in particular, were easily cleaned and cared for, could be beautifully printed or painted, and were fine enough to be pleated and draped.[9] Cotton was also a relatively inexpensive fiber, furthering its popularity. Throughout most of the eighteenth century, much of the raw cotton used in Europe was shipped from the West Indies and the eastern Mediterranean, until the United States also began to export cotton at the century's end.[10]

In addition to providing raw fiber for the national and international market, the United States made another vital contribution to cotton production at the end of the eighteenth century: the invention of the cotton gin. Patented in 1793 by Eli Whitney, the cotton gin was said to have unlocked "the imprisoned resources of the South"[11] through the mechanical separation of the sticky cotton fiber from its seeds—a task that was previously completed by hand (and in the American South, typically performed by slaves). Whereas a skilled picker could get through one pound of cotton per day, an average of fifty pounds could be completed in the same amount of time using the cotton gin. As Whitney himself wrote of his invention, "this machine may be turned by water or with a horse, with the greatest ease, and one man and a horse will do more than fifty men with the old machines. It makes the labor fifty times less, without throwing any class of People out of business."[12] The impact of Whitney's invention was profound: in 1791, a reported two million pounds of cotton was produced in the United States. By 1860, that number had leapt up to 1,650 million pounds.[13] Not surprisingly, the use of cotton was greater than that of any other fiber in the mid-nineteenth century, and comprised almost 70 percent of all textiles produced.[14]

The seemingly insatiable desire for cotton only continued to expand. In 1900, consumers purchased around 3.4 million tons of fabric, which consisted of approximately 25 percent wool and 75 percent cotton.[15] Yet cotton is a natural fiber, meaning its growth is easily hindered by conditions such as pests, drought, or an overly rainy season. In an 1854 article in *Harper's New Monthly Magazine,* the author mentioned just a few of the challenges faced by cotton farmers: the "rust" and "rot" of cotton plants in the wet season, which was often followed by an infestation of worms, and the devastating invasion of army-worms, which could eat an entire crop in a matter of hours. "They seem to spring out of the ground, and fall from the clouds,"[16] he wrote despairingly. It was clear that ways to counteract pests were crucial to meeting (or exceeding) the high demand for cotton—and thus began the use of chemical pesticides in the twentieth century.

Pesticides—a term that encompasses fungicides, herbicides and insecticides—are used to deter pests and weeds. They are also utilized to control soil quality, as traditional cotton crops quickly deplete their soil of nutrients. Heavy usage of pesticides enabled the amount of cotton grown to triple in the past 80 years, yet the percentage of land dedicated to cotton farming has scarcely expanded. This has resulted in a variety of serious environmental crises, such as reduced soil fertility, loss of biodiversity, and life-threatening health problems to those who have been exposed repeatedly to the toxic chemicals used in pesticides.[17] Awareness of the hazards surrounding the use of pesticides is not new—Rachel Carson specifically mentioned them in her seminal 1962 book *Silent Spring,* the publication that is widely believed to have initiated today's environmental movement—yet cotton crops continue to use nearly 25 percent of the total amount of pesticides used worldwide.[18] Pesticides allow farmers to produce as much cotton for as little cost as possible—a model that corresponds to the ever-growing demand for cheap clothing.

In addition to the pesticides often deemed necessary for cotton production, its crops require enormous amounts of water. One kilogram of cotton fiber—which is the amount necessary to make a single pair of jeans—requires between 7,000 and 29,000 liters of water,[19] and much more water is wasted if irrigation systems do not function properly. In addition, the diversion of water away from its original source, in order to provide for cotton farming, is increasingly devastating to the ecosystem. As scholar Marie O'Mahoney pointed out, Uzbekistan is currently one of the largest exporters of raw cotton, in spite of the fact that the country's climate is unsuited to cotton growth.[20] The Aral Sea is rapidly diminishing as a result, having shrunken from the world's fourth largest lake to the eighth largest.[21]

These grave concerns led to the development of one of sustainable fashion's most recognized fibers: organic cotton. The fiber was first grown in the United States and Turkey in the late 1980s, followed by Egypt, Uganda, India and Peru.[22] It began to be marketed in the following decade, in correspondence to other "eco-friendly" fashion trends, such as recycled clothing. Organic cotton was not an immediate success—due in large part to its relatively high cost—but it has now become a popular choice of material for nearly any clothing brand that is looking to market itself as sustainable. For some companies, offering clothing with an organic label is a relatively easy way to assert themselves as "eco-friendly" (a concept that is sometimes referred to as *greenwashing*). For others, the selection of sustainable fabric is just one step in a number of conscientious design and business practices.

Organic cotton has a great number of benefits that have placed it at the forefront of sustainable fabrics. First and foremost, organic cotton is highly saleable: physical differences between organically grown and traditionally grown cotton are scarcely perceived, meaning that organic cotton has found easy acceptance among designers and consumers. Furthermore, its impact on the environment is much less than that of traditional cotton, as organic cotton farming prohibits the use of chemical pesticides and fertilizers. Natural enemies are introduced to crops to rid them of unwanted pests instead. To counteract the depletion of soil nutrients, organic famers rely on crop rotation, which helps to enrich soil. By extension, the nutrient-dense soil requires less water. Farmers who grow organic cotton also receive higher incomes—as much as 50 percent more than that of their peers who farm non-organically.[23]

In spite of the many positive attributes of organic cotton, it is not a "perfect" fiber choice. Although the production of cotton requires relatively little energy, all cotton—whether conventionally grown or organic—requires cleaning. The cleaning process involves desizing, scouring and bleaching, using chemicals that are usually toxic. In addition, organic cotton still made up only about 0.02 percent of the overall amount of cotton grown in 2009,[24] even though demand for the fiber had increased by an average of over 40 percent per year since 2001[25] (and sales of organic cotton continue to rise). The fiber is also limited in quantity, due in part to the way in which it is grown—yields of organic cotton tend to be 20 to 50 percent lower than those of their pesticide-enhanced counterparts.[26] In addition, organic cotton farming is best suited for growth on small farms, where crop rotation is often already in practice.[27] While organic cotton is often lauded as an ideal sustainable choice, its current output simply cannot meet demand. In addition, the fiber's designation as organic often ends at harvest, without accounting for further stages of its life cycle—many of which are not sustainable.[28] Nevertheless, organic cotton production is in many ways being viewed as a model—or perhaps more aptly, an experiment—for how to cultivate sustainable fibers in greater quantity in the future.

Organic cotton has been a well-known commodity in the apparel market for a number of years: huge companies such as Nike, Wal-Mart and Woolworths have all become known for their usage of the fiber. In addition, a number of high-fashion designers are further popularizing the use of organic cotton by including it in their collections. John Patrick, for instance, clearly emphasizes his interest in sustainable fibers in the name of his label: Organic. Patrick—who had years of experience working in the conventional fashion industry—began making his name as a sustainable fashion designer in 2003, when a friend writing for *Organic Style Magazine* asked him to make something to feature in one of her articles. The resulting design was an apron made from organic cotton canvas, and it received an outpouring of interest. It was at that point that the designer realized he could "incorporate a lot of things that didn't fit into fashion and design, make them, tell a story, and do the right thing."[29] Although Patrick takes an ethical approach to design overall (also working with collectives, for example), the selection of sustainable materials is especially crucial to his work. His interest in organic cotton, in particular, led him to Peru, where he learned firsthand how the fiber was planted and grown.[30]

An Organic by John Patrick dress from The Museum at FIT dates from the spring 2009 *American Gothic* collection (Figure 3.1). Patrick's designs were inspired by the 1930

Figure 3.1 Installation shot from *Eco-Fashion: Going Green* (The Museum at FIT, 2010). Organic by John Patrick, shirt and jumper, white Japanese organic cotton mesh, light blue and white organic cotton shirting, Spring 2009, USA. Collection of The Museum at FIT, 2010.43.1. Gift of John Patrick. Photograph © The Museum at FIT.

Grant Wood painting of the same name, and were conceived as modern interpretations of what the designer referred to as "dust bowl creativity"—pieces that "paid homage to prairie life"[31] and could be mixed-and-matched in different ways. In this example, a pinafore dress was fashioned from organic cotton shirting fabric in pale blue and white stripes. Patrick worked with the Peruvian textiles company Creditex for a year to have the fabric manufactured to his specifications. Creditex is known for its use of Pima cotton— an especially soft, silky fiber that is manually harvested by local farmers. The company is also dedicated to ethical practices, receiving certification annually for its compliance to issues of plant security, staff training, infrastructure, production process, distribution of merchandise and more.[32] The jumper was paired with a white blouse made from organic cotton by Avanti, a Japanese company that began working with organic cotton in 1990. Avanti is dedicated to transparency in all aspects of its production processes.

The Danish luxury label Noir, founded in 2005, has likewise centered many of its designs on the use of organic cotton. The company works in tandem with Illuminati, a Fair Trade and organic cotton brand based in Uganda. Noir's founder, Peter Ingwersen, conceived of Illuminati after finding it difficult to source the high-quality organic fabrics he desired for his label.[33] Illuminati cotton was first used in Noir's fall 2009 collection.[34] By spring 2013, the selection of Illuminati cotton fabric had expanded to include seven different styles, including basic cotton, voile and jersey.[35] In addition to its goal to expand organic cotton production, Illuminati seeks to aid the local community and the 4,000 farmers that work for the brand, providing tools for farming, health care and education. In addition, Illuminati seek to continuously improve and broaden the selection of their fabrics.

The relationship between Noir and Illuminati provides an interesting model for the successful marriage of high fashion and sustainability. An evening dress from Noir's fall 2010 collection exemplifies the label's goal to fuse sexy, cutting-edge design with sustainable materials and corporate social responsibility (Figure 3.2). Made from ruffled tiers of black organic cotton, the floor-length halter dress has a plunging neckline, and it is nearly backless. The resulting design is a far cry from the "ecology look" of the 1980s. Noir understands that the production of sophisticated, contemporary clothing is essential to its survival, as studies done by the company proved that clients consistently value aesthetics over ethics.

In conclusion, it is important to note that there are other types of cotton to be considered as well. Naturally colored cottons, for example, are cultivated to eliminate the need for bleaching and dyeing the fiber, and can be grown in shades of brown, green and red. Over the past two decades, genetically modified cotton has been developed to significantly reduce the need for pesticides, and has been in use in large cotton-producing countries including Australia, China and the United States. Although Fair Trade cotton is not necessarily grown differently from conventional cotton, it assures that workers at the very bottom of the production chain are paid fairly for their labor. Like conventional and organic cotton, however, each of these alternative fiber choices has both positive and negative attributes.

Figure 3.2 Noir (Peter Ingwersen), evening dress, black Illuminati II cotton, silver studded leather, Fall 2010, Denmark. Collection of The Museum at FIT, 2010.11.1. Gift of NOIR. Photograph © The Museum at FIT.

Wool

Like cotton, wool has a long history: its cultivation can be traced to over 6,000 years ago.[36] Wool acts as a natural insulator, and it can keep the body warm or cool as necessary. It repels dirt, stains and water. It has also proven to be an extremely versatile and durable fiber. Historically, wool was cotton's greatest rival, and both fibers were suited to a variety of apparel types. While cotton reigned as the most common plant-derived fiber, wool was the predominant animal-derived fiber. In eighteenth-century England, especially, wool production was a crucial component of the nation's economy. People of all classes in England wore domestically produced wool garments in the early part of the century,[37] and woolen fabrics were available in varying qualities and blends, such as wool and silk or wool and linen.[38] Although imports of cotton fabric gradually challenged wool's importance to English fashion, wool production continued to rise. From 1721 to 1774, the amount of wool cloth shipped to the United States from England increased over 500 percent, a number that exceeded the rise of the US population.[39] Over 800 new mills opened in England between 1835 and 1874, and employment in woolen mills rose from just under 53,000 to nearly 139,000 persons.[40] Likewise, business in the export of woolen fabrics increased steadily over the course of the century. By the nineteenth and early twentieth centuries, New England had itself become established as an important hub for wool production. Although cotton was increasingly used for blankets, summer suitings and other items that had previously relied on wool,[41] American production of wool fiber continued to expand into the 1920s.

It was also in the early twentieth century, however, that wool began to face another serious competitor: manmade fibers. By the 1950s, a US study showed that Orlon, an acrylic fiber, was used more often for winter sweaters than wool.[42] Synthetic fibers were especially popular among young people, and were liked for being easier to wash and care for than natural materials.[43] In an attempt to counteract the encroaching dominance of synthetics, The Woolmark campaign[44] was launched in 1964, touting natural virgin wool as a superior fiber. Woolmark ads featured the tagline "People who have everything wear wool," and promoted the quality of woolen clothing. The campaign must have been somewhat effective, as wool production did increase over the course of the 1970s and into the 1980s, particularly in developing nations and the United States. Yet synthetic fiber production remained, on average, over twenty times that of wool.[45]

More recently, the Prince of Wales launched The Campaign for Wool in January 2010, "as an initiative to expand the market for British and Commonwealth wool and promote awareness of its environmental benefits."[46] It has since expanded its focus to support small business and local farmers across the globe. In spite of such efforts, the wool industry still represents only about 1.5 percent of fiber production worldwide.[47] In correspondence to the rise of the sustainable fashion movement, however, wool is being reevaluated for its potential viability as an eco-friendly fiber. Wool is naturally occurring and renewable, and taken from an animal that can thrive on land unsuited to farming— thus leaving arable soil elsewhere for vegetable, fruit and grain crops. In addition, sheep help to fertilize the soil they graze upon.[48] More specifically, studies by the Australian-based Wool Carbon Alliance have found that "wool fiber production systems, based on renewable grass and natural vegetation, complement current demands to reduce carbon emissions."[49] Wool is also fully biodegradable.

Much like cotton production, however, pesticides came to be used for wool over the course of the twentieth century—albeit in significantly smaller quantities. The sheep themselves can be dipped in pesticide baths, or they may be injected with pesticides to deter parasites. These pesticides can also be hazardous to farmers' health, and they are polluting to water supplies.[50] In addition, raw wool requires scouring, a task that removes dirt and the natural grease that the sheep deposit in their wool. While the grease byproduct is often refined and used as lanolin for cosmetics and soaps, it frequently contains residual pesticides. Finally, the total life cycle of wool must be considered—it is typically a material that cannot be laundered, and must therefore undergo dry-cleaning, a process with its own environmental repercussions.[51]

The introduction of organic wool has become a more sustainable fiber option in recent years. While not necessarily "organic" in any standardized sense, the use of the term implies that the fiber was obtained from sheep that were not subjected to pesticide baths or inhumane treatment.[52] Stella McCartney used a blend of alpaca and organic wool to make her *Cocoon* sweater dress in 2009 (see figure 6.8). More recently, McCartney designed one of her signature chain-edged bag styles using wool that was taken from sheep raised at her own farm in the Cotswolds, England.[53] The use of organic wool by a high-profile fashion designer has helped the fiber to gain recognition, but production of organic wool is still extremely limited. In 2009, less than 0.1 percent of the UK 1.1 million tons of wool produced globally was organic.[54]

Hemp

The use of hemp fiber also dates back at least 6,000 years. Alongside flax, hemp prevailed over fiber production in Asia, Europe and North America during the eighteenth century.[55] As cotton eventually proved cheaper and easier to harvest, however, hemp slowly began to lose its dominance. The fiber's decline was aggravated by its prohibition in the United States and Western Europe (excluding France) around World War II, for its association with marijuana.[56] Hemp's lack of popularity has been due in large part to that association, despite the fact that the industrial hemp plant is grown solely for its fiber. It contains only a trace amount of the psychoactive constituent tetrahydrocannabinol (THC), and therefore has no narcotic properties. Even today, the differences between the types of hemp plant are often unclear to consumers—a problem that many sustainability advocates are hoping to change.

Hemp offers a multitude of ecological advantages. It grows extremely quickly, and requires only about one fifth of the water necessary to grow cotton.[57] Hemp is naturally resistant to harmful insects and weeds, thus eliminating the need for pesticides. The hemp crop is also an ideal choice for land that is in transition to certified organic status[58] (a process that requires three years of plant growth without pesticides). Hemp plants improve the structure of the soil in which they are grown, and can thrive on land that has been polluted with heavy metals.[59] They are also carbon-negative, removing five times more carbon dioxide from the atmosphere than trees.[60]

Throughout much of its history, the typically coarse hemp fiber was best suited for use in industrial textile products, such as ropes and sail fabric. In the 1980s, however, the development of a new processing technique allowed for finer yarns,[61] and hemp became better suited for use in apparel fabric. The cloth has a silky texture that is more porous than cotton, takes well to dyes, and is durable. These attributes provide hemp fabric with the potential to displace both cotton and petrochemical-based materials. However, the hemp plant is somewhat difficult to harvest, often requiring costly and time-consuming hand labor. While mechanical techniques for fiber extraction have been developed, those processes tend to weaken the fibers.[62] The cultivation of hemp is likely to remain limited until a better harvesting process is discovered.

For many years, the use of the hemp fiber for clothing was also hindered by its associations with an "alternative lifestyle" that had little in common with the world of high fashion.[63] More recently, however, a number of sustainable designers have begun to utilize hemp fabrics for their stylish, fashion-forward creations. Nina Valenti, founder of the Brooklyn, New York-based clothing brand naturevsfuture®, selected a hemp and Tencel blend fabric for a dress from her spring 2009 collection (Tencel is the trademark name of lyocell, discussed in the following section). As the name of the label suggests, naturevsfuture® explores the dichotomy between technology and the natural world—a key concept to the future developments in the sustainable fashion industry. Valenti incorporates a variety of sustainable materials, including organic and recycled fabrics, into her garments. Her clothing is also designed to minimize waste, and can be worn for years without looking dated. This dress took a contemporary twist on the classic shirtwaist style, and was cinched at the waist with Valenti's signature "obi" belt (Figure 3.3). The fabric was dyed a dark purple, exemplifying how well the hemp fiber takes to color. Valenti's clothing is also locally produced and retails at a fairly low price point (ranging from about US $200 to $400), proving that although hemp fabric retails for about twice the cost of cotton, it is still not prohibitively expensive.

Manmade fibers

Rayon

A multitude of fiber innovations occurred in the twentieth century—the various benefits and problems of which still affect the apparel industry today. Viscose rayon, the first commercially produced manmade fiber, was patented in 1892 by a British chemist named Charles Cross and his associates.[64] In 1904, the first manufacturing plant devoted to rayon production was built.[65] Rayon was conceived and initially marketed as a substitute for silk, which was notoriously difficult and costly to produce. Several of the positive attributes of silk—including its luster, handle and drape—can be mimicked with the rayon fiber, which also takes well to various dyes and finishes. In addition, rayon was stronger than silk and—most importantly—inexpensive. In the early 1920s, raw silk cost US $8.65 a pound, whereas rayon cost just US $2.80 per pound.[66]

Figure 3.3 naturevsfuture® (Nina Valenti), dress with obi belt, purple hemp/Tencel blend, Spring 2009, USA. Collection of The Museum at FIT, 2010.39.1. Gift of naturevsfuture® Photograph © The Museum at FIT.

As a result, many inexpensive, mass-produced clothes began to be made using rayon fabrics. The Viscose Company, a New York-based manufacturer, reported that fiber production rose from 350,000 pounds in 1911 to 28,000,000 pounds in 1924.[67] That was an increase of 80 percent in just over a decade—and yet the company still struggled to keep up with demand. "There is hardly an end to the myriad ways in which rayon serves you," claimed an ad for Drecoll rayon in 1928. "It is made into apparel of every kind, from dainty lingerie to formal evening gowns."[68] A day dress, from c. 1928, provides an example of the basic yet stylish clothing that was most often associated with rayon in the 1920s (plate 7). Although the dress does not have a label, it was likely American-made, and purchased at a mid-priced department store or via mail order. Sears, for example, featured similar rayon dresses in its 1928 catalog, which ranged in price from US $0.98 to $3.89.[69] This dress was knit in the simple, tubular silhouette of the era, from a blend of rayon and cotton yarns dyed a vibrant shade of orange. Fibers are often blended in order to benefit from the positive qualities of both: in this case, for example, the rayon prevented shrinking and wrinkling, while the cotton fiber allowed the dress to be more breathable and comfortable on the skin. The ruffles applied to the front of the dress, as well as the piping at the neckline and pockets, were made from printed cotton.

By the late 1920s, the production and use of rayon had expanded beyond inexpensive clothing styles, and a number of couturiers began to work with the fiber for their designs. Elsa Schiaparelli, in particular, was known for her close associations with several textile manufacturers. As curator Dilys Blum wrote in her extensive monograph on Schiaparelli's work:

A number of times she found inspiration in a mill's discards and experimental pieces, which gave her the reputation of making successes out of other people's mistakes. In Schiaparelli's hands synthetic fabrics became chic, and she was credited with making rayon fashionable by using unique weaves that took on the appearance of wools, linens or silks but still retained the distinctive draping quality that was one of the fabric's greatest assets. She made a success of rayon crepes in bold, rough textures and relief patterns.[70]

Rayon's ever-increasing importance to the textile industry resulted in the production of nearly US two billion pounds of the fiber by 1938.[71]

Rayon is an especially interesting fiber in relation to its environmental impact. It is classified as a manmade fiber, rather than a synthetic, meaning that it is chemically produced from cellulose (a substance derived from the cell walls of plants). Easily grown trees, such as beech, allow cellulose to be regenerated with relatively little ecological impact. In addition, because rayon is derived from a natural material, it is biodegradable. Nevertheless, rayon production is highly energy intensive, and far from eco friendly. It requires that wood be ground into pulp and spun—a process that requires multiple trips around the rayon factory. The energy needed to simply run such large factories is also vast. In addition, the production of rayon is exceptionally polluting to both air and water. Nevertheless, sales of rayon have increased substantially, in reaction to the rising cost of cotton fabric.[72]

Bamboo

In recent years, textiles made from a "new" natural fiber, bamboo, have entered the marketplace. Upon its introduction, bamboo was touted as a valuable fiber within the sustainable fashion market, and it does, indeed, have many positive attributes. The bamboo plant grows quickly—much more quickly that cotton—and reaches its full height in just three months.[73] It is also less expensive to cultivate than cotton, and requires very little irrigation, pesticides or fertilizers. Mold and bacteria do not easily affect bamboo, and its plants actually improve—rather than deplete—the soil in which they are grown. In addition, bamboo fibers are more easily extracted than those of some other natural fibers, such as linen and hemp.[74] A printed mini dress from Fall 2010 by FIN, made from bamboo satin, demonstrates the aesthetic qualities that have rendered the bamboo fiber a fashionable choice (Figure 3.4). Bamboo's capacity for drape is highlighted in the fitted, knee-length skirt, constructed from soft, irregular folds of fabric. The smoothness and sheen of the bamboo fiber are also appealing to designers and consumers.

In spite of these many benefits, however, the use of bamboo fabric has become a point of contention within the sustainable fashion community. As Todd Copeland, strategic environmental materials developer at Patagonia, has pointed out, "Most bamboo fabric has a smooth hand that feels like rayon—because that's essentially what it is."[75] Although the fiber itself is a natural, quickly regenerated material, its method of production is, indeed, commonly adapted from that used for rayon. This process has allowed for bamboo fabric to be manufactured on a larger scale[76] (prior to this method of manufacture, the fiber was used for apparel in much smaller amounts). The problem is, of course, that the process of producing rayon is especially polluting, chemical laden and energy intensive.

Furthermore, although bamboo grows well and quickly on its own, there is evidence that some farmers still choose to use chemical pesticides to further enhance its growth. This is especially true in China, where bamboo is grown on a commercial scale—and where there is a lack of environmental regulation overall. Increased demand for bamboo has also led to deforestation in China, in order to provide more land for bamboo plants.[77] In spite of these issues, however, bamboo remains a highly regenerative fiber with many ecological benefits, and eco-conscious manufacturers are working to develop less energy intensive and more sustainable methods of production.

Lyocell

Lyocell (also known by its brand name, Tencel) has made a significant impact on the traditional rayon fibers market in recent years.[78] Courtaulds Fibres, the creator of Tencel, began developing the fiber as part of its "Genesis" research project in 1987, an initiative aimed at creating a product that could compete with both the cost and physical characteristics of viscose rayon, but that was also ecologically sustainable.[79] Lyocell was first made commercially available in the late 1980s; by 1993, it was already being used for clothing by Calvin Klein, Girbaud and Esprit, among other labels.[80] Like rayon

Figure 3.4 FIN (Per Åge Sivertsen), dress, blue organic bamboo satin, Fall 2010, Norway. Collection of The Museum at FIT, 2010.3.2. Gift of Per Sivertsen of FIN. Photograph © The Museum at FIT.

and bamboo, lyocell is a cellulosic fiber that is derived from easily grown woods such as beech, eucalyptus and pine. Unlike other cellulose-based fibers, however, lyocell utilizes a closed-loop manufacturing process, meaning that all but 0.05 percent of the non-toxic chemical solvent and water used for the fiber's production are reclaimed and used again. Although waste is almost entirely eliminated, however, the process remains energy intensive.

In addition to the closed-loop manufacturing process, lyocell has many characteristics that have established it as an important sustainable fiber. It is as comfortable and absorbent as cotton, and it is fully biodegradable. Lyocell has the strength of a synthetic fiber, and it can be easily blended with other materials for even higher performance characteristics. Since lyocell was specifically designed to reduce environmental impact, the forests from which its cellulose is obtained are also carefully managed and harvested. Lyocell yarn can be woven on conventional looms and, as sustainable fiber expert Richard Blackburn wrote, "current lyocell factories are designed and operated to achieve world-class low levels of emissions and minimize energy consumption."[81] Perhaps most importantly, the highly successful lyocell manufacturing process has provided a template for the potential improvement of production methods for other fibers.

The contemporary sustainable fashion industry is embracing lyocell enthusiastically. Sarah Ratty's elegant *Grecian Drape Nymph* dress from 2010, created for the designer's UK-based sustainable fashion label, Ciel, was made from lyocell jersey in dove grey and metallic silver (Figure 3.5). The fabric drapes beautifully, and it is cool and silky to the touch. As lyocell is also easily laundered and requires little ironing, the garment's environmental impact during its wearable life is minimized. Ratty was a pioneer of the sustainable fashion industry (she started her first label, Conscious Earthwear, in the early 1990s), and she has based much of her work on the selection of high-quality, sustainable fabrics. Her clothing is simultaneously simple and luxurious. "We're not trying to reinvent the wheel, we're just trying to make dresses for women to feel good in, but using interesting fabrics," Ratty stated in a 2007 interview. "We're still challenged with fabrics and we have to develop a lot more, but every step of the way more is becoming available."[82]

Synthetic fibers

Nylon

The success of rayon led to the development of other artificial fibers in the first half of the twentieth century. "The rapid increase in materials with new and strange names appearing from season to season sometimes makes choice bewildering. New fibers, new weaves, new finishes are constantly changing the appearance and feel of fabrics,"[83] lamented the author of a 1940 clothing handbook for women. Just two years before, Du Pont had introduced the first fully synthetic, "miracle" fiber, nylon. Dr. Charles Stine, one of the chemists involved with nylon's invention, spoke of the merits of his new fiber for the *New York Herald Tribune* Forum in 1938: "Nylon can be fashioned into filaments as

Figure 3.5 Installation shot from *Eco-Fashion: Going Green* (The Museum at FIT, 2010). Ciel (Sarah Ratty), dress, grey and silver metallic printed lyocell, 2010, England. Collection of the Museum at FIT, 2010.47.1. Gift of Ciel. Photograph © The Museum at FIT.

strong as steel, as fine as the spider's web, yet more elastic than any of the common natural fibers and possessing a beautiful chemical luster."[84]

The fiber's qualities were especially well suited to women's hosiery, which was made commercially available in 1939. Nylon hosiery was worn in place of delicate, more costly silk stockings, and it was an immediate success. Foundation garments made from nylon soon followed. With the advent of World War II, however, nylon became an essential material for products such as parachutes and tents.[85] Therefore, the manufacture of nylon hosiery was ceased during the war years, but began again immediately following the war. Between 1947 and 1952, shipments of nylon fabric increased from 25.4 million to 134.1 million pounds.[86] As the nylon fiber proved to be remarkably versatile—it could be made to resemble anything from silk satin to wool[87]—its use for clothing also expanded during that time.

Claire McCardell, a premier American sportswear designer, was known for using materials that were inexpensive, washable and generally easy to care for. One of her most famous designs, the "pop-over" dress, was made from cotton denim, and retailed for just US $6.95 when it was introduced in 1943.[88] While McCardell frequently used humble cotton or wool fabrics for her designs—even for eveningwear—she was also known for her selection of new or unusual materials. In 1950, for instance, she introduced a Grecian-style evening dress made from white nylon tricot, printed with a pattern of red roses (Figure 3.6). Such fabric was typically relegated to the lingerie market (and McCardell's dress did, in fact, resemble night gowns from the era), but in her hands, its use resulted in "subtly sexy evening wear designs" that could "hold their own against dresses costing ten times as much."[89] McCardell continued to use nylon for various designs, as evidenced by a 1954 Du Pont advertisement that featured two more of her dresses. "Hand-washable, they dry effortlessly, need only the merest pressing, and never lose their just-starched appearance," the ad proclaimed. "Du Pont nylon is the fashion fiber that makes possible fashions that are fragile in looks only—that measure up to all the demands of today's busier living."[90] Indeed, a survey conducted by the United States Department of Agriculture that same year indicated that nylon was the most widely known synthetic fiber at the time, and that it was praised for its laundering qualities and durability.[91]

The idea of "wash and wear" clothing was developed in the 1950s. Such garments were made from a variety of synthetic fibers, including acrylic, polyester and nylon. A man's suit in the collection of The Museum at FIT, manufactured by a company that was actually called "Wash 'N' Wear," dates to c. 1958 (Figure 3.7). Although the suit's appearance is typical for its era, it was constructed from grey seersucker fabric made from nylon, rather than the traditional wool, cotton, or linen. In 1958, the *New York Times* observed that "For the past three summers the big news in men's clothing has been the improvement—and acceptance—of the hot-weather suit known as wash-and-wear."[92] Sales of wash and wear suits had risen from 1,200 in 1952 to 2,000,000 in 1958, meaning that they came to account for approximately one third of suit sales overall.[93] Such suits were easy to launder (whereas suits from traditional materials required dry-cleaning), and they dried easily. Many wash and wear fabrics were promoted for their resistance to wrinkles—although that claim was not always entirely accurate, as evidenced by the appearance of this suit. Wash and wear clothing remained popular through the 1960s; according to a study in

Figure 3.6 Claire McCardell, evening dress, white printed nylon, 1950, USA. Collection of The Museum at FIT, 72.61.182. Photograph © The Museum at FIT.

Figure 3.7 Wash N' Wear, man's suit, grey nylon seersucker, c. 1959, USA. Collection of The Museum at FIT, P88.80.1. Photograph © The Museum at FIT.

1968, 73 percent of American women surveyed owned at least one garment made from wash and wear fabric.[94]

Nylon's wrinkle-resistant qualities reduce the need for routine ironing, which saves a great deal of energy over a garment's wearable life. The production of the nylon fiber, however, is especially harmful to the environment. Nylon relies on petroleum oil, a limited resource, and its manufacture is a highly energy-intensive process. In addition, nylon production generates nitrous oxide, a potent greenhouse gas. Even in small amounts, nitrous oxide is a dangerous contributor to global climate change. Although nylon can be recycled, much of the fiber ends up in landfills, where it will take hundreds of years to decompose. Nylon production has been in decline since the late 1960s, however, when polyester came to dominate the synthetic fiber market. Today, its primary usage is for carpeting and many home fabrics, as well as some hosiery, sportswear and sporting equipment.[95]

Polyester

Nylon paved the way for the development of a host of other synthetic fibers, including polyester, which was patented in 1941. Polyester was used for clothing by the 1950s, but it was not immediately popular. In addition to having to compete with more established synthetic fibers—especially nylon and acrylic—there were notable issues with early versions of polyester fabric. Excessive static during processing, difficulty dyeing and oily soiling were just a few of the numerous problems reported.[96] As the quality of polyester increased over time, however, it came to be used more frequently, and it began to displace cotton. By 1968, the production of synthetics had surpassed that of natural fibers,[97] and polyester was in the greatest demand. "Polyester Emerges from the Shadow of Nylon," proclaimed a New York Times headline that same year.[98] Similar to rayon and nylon, polyester was an inexpensive fiber, yet it ultimately came to be ubiquitous for both low- and high-end fashions.

A maxi-length halter dress by Giorgio di Sant'Angelo, dated to c. 1971, is an example of a high-end garment made from polyester dyed in three bright shades (plate 8). "Placement of color relating to construction is my important message," the designer said of his work in a 1968 interview, in which he also stated that he detested "anything that is a status symbol, that is chic or proper."[99] The low cut neckline and slinky fit of this dress were typical of Sant'Angelo's work, which often relied on stretchy, knitted materials intended to show off the figure. While many of the designer's clothes were costly (an article from 1970 stated that his garments typically ranged from US $200–250[100]), his knitwear was much less expensive, costing US $12–70.[101] Sant'Angelo's knit clothing was some of his simplest and most streamlined. Items such as this maxi dress, as well as a selection of bodysuits and other basics, counterbalanced the imaginative, "haute hippie" creations that characterized much of the designer's work. Yet the low price of his knitwear was undoubtedly due also to the use of inexpensive synthetic materials.

Like nylon, polyester is made from petroleum. In addition to being a non-renewable resource, the location and extraction of petroleum oil is incredibly taxing on the environment. It must also be transported to nations that are heavily oil-reliant.[102] Its production is energy-intensive, with dyeing, in particular, requiring high temperatures. The processing of petrochemicals also results in large quantities of hazardous waste, the emissions of which can be irreversibly damaging to air, soil and water. More environmentally responsible processing procedures would, however, be incredibly expensive, driving material costs upward by a considerable amount.[103]

In recent years, polyester has been a topic of frequent discussion in the fashion industry, due in large part to the volume at which it is currently produced. While polyester has long dominated the market for manmade textiles, it accounted for more than 50 percent of total fiber production in 2011.[104] As demand for the fiber continues to grow rapidly, it has become abundantly clear that current production practices are not sustainable. Yet there are some positive qualities to polyester production. It uses significantly less water than the manufacture of cotton, and sometimes does not require water at all. Polyester is also strong, easy to care for, and wrinkle resistant. Furthermore, it does not absorb moisture, reducing the need for machine drying after laundering. The polyester fiber can also be recycled numerous times into a material of equal quality—and is, in fact, one of the most commonly recycled fibers (see Chapter 1 for more information).

Conclusion

In a 2007 editorial, *Textile Outlook International* reported that "Between 1900 and 1950 total fibre production grew almost three times as fast as the world population. And between 1950 and 2006 it grew almost four times as fast."[105] This knowledge, coupled with even a fraction of an idea of the toxic chemicals, water and energy that go into producing most fibers and fabrics, paints a clear picture of the need for major change within the fashion industry. While the increased demand for materials such as organic cotton and lyocell indicates that there is greater awareness of the environmental impact of fiber production, finding sustainable solutions is still no easy task. Even within the organic textiles market, a lack of global standards and labeling makes it difficult for both designers and consumers to select fabrics that possess the sustainable qualities they desire. In addition, although there may be a multitude of companies hoping to make more sustainable choices, it is a costly endeavor that is just not feasible for some. Rather than simply ignoring the need for change, however, experts recommend that companies make short-term goals toward sustainability that are "realistic, achievable and beneficial,"[106] rather than focusing on larger, seemingly impossible tasks.

There is certainly hope for the future of sustainable materials. In March 2013, four leading home textile manufacturers organized an association called the Sustainable Textiles Coalition. The organization acts as the counterpart to the Sustainable Apparel Coalition, which formed three years earlier, and already boasts more than eighty members. These groups focus on transparency in fabric production. Of course, the selection of material from which to make a garment is still only a small part of the overall picture of sustainability, but it is an important task—and should, in the eyes of some, be a simple one. As Andreas Dorner, global marketing director of the progressive, sustainably minded textiles firm Lenzing AG pointed out in a 2012 interview, "You can have price and sustainability. Goods should be offered at an affordable price level, and to use sustainable fibers like Tencel or Lenzing Modal[107] is not much more expensive due to the fact that the fibre price accounts for less than 1% of the finished product. If the garment companies would start with real sustainability at the fibre stage … the world would become much better environmentally."[108]

Suggestions for further reading:

Baugh, G. (2008), "Fibers: Clean and Green Fiber Options," in J. Hethorn and C. Ulasewicz (eds), *Sustainable Fashion: Why Now? A Conversation Exploring Issues, Practices, and Possibilities,* New York: Fairchild Books: 326–57.

Bide, M. (2011), "Fiber Sustainability: Green is not Black + White," in Linda Welters and Abby Lillethun (eds), *The Fashion Reader: Second Edition,* Oxford: Berg: 577–85.

Blackburn, R. S. (ed.) (2009), *Sustainable Textiles: Life Cycle and Environmental Impact*, New York: CRC Press.

Fletcher, K. (2008), *Sustainable Fashion and Textiles: Design Journeys*, London: Earthscan.

Fletcher, K. and L. Grose (2012), *Fashion & Sustainability: Design for Change,* London: Laurence King.

At a glance: "Futuristic" materials of the past

Many manmade or synthetic fibers were developed to mimic or improve upon natural materials. Others were not initially intended for use in fashion, and have appealed primarily for their novelty. Cellophane, for example, was developed in the early twentieth century as a packaging product, but its light weight and shimmer proved intriguing to fashion designers and consumers alike. Especially in the 1920s and 1930s, cellophane was utilized for a variety of clothing and accessories, in addition to its intended function. The material was named for the primary component from which it was made: cellulose. Not surprisingly, the cellophane production process was similar to that of viscose rayon, meaning that it was both energy intensive and polluting.[109]

Woven strips of cellophane could be used in place of straw—making the material an especially popular choice for millinery—but it was also woven into other fabrics and used for clothing. A 1934 *Harper's Bazaar* editorial entitled "The Dawn of Synthetic Splendor: On with the Passion for Cellophane" included a description of a rubber coat embroidered with cellophane straw butterflies, designed by Alix. The magazine assured its readers that the garment "… was not madness but fact. The designers are plunging their shears into fantastic materials that might have come over the counters of Broadway's Dazians,[110] woven richly with a new kind of splendor."[111] That same year, Lucien Lelong, a leading French couturier renowned for his exquisite taste and sense of modernity, used cellophane in some of his designs. Lelong's elegant evening cape, in the collection of The Museum at FIT, was made from strips of dark blue cellophane that were attached to a

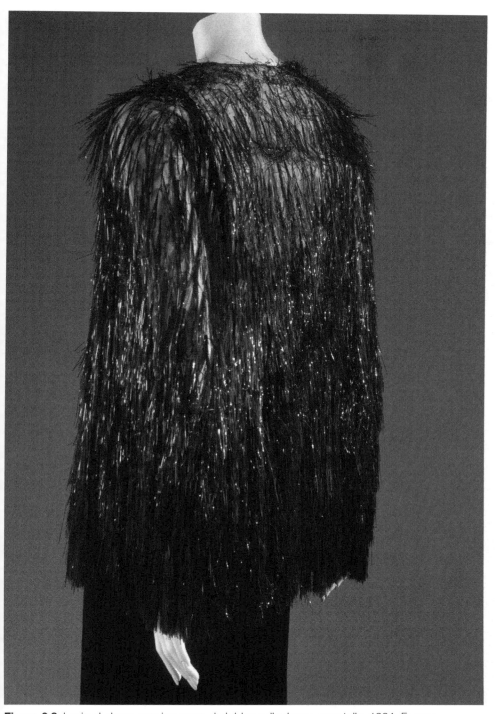

Figure 3.8 Lucien Lelong, evening cape, dark blue cellophane, navy tulle, 1934, France. Collection of The Museum at FIT, 76.196.30. Gift of Fernanda Munn Kellogg. Photograph © The Museum at FIT.

Figure 3.9 Installation shot from *Eco-Fashion: Going Green* (The Museum at FIT, 2010). André Courrèges, dress, black vinyl, black chiffon, tan silk, c. 1967, France. Collection of The Museum at FIT, 86.49.8. Gift of Sylvia Slifka. Photograph © The Museum at FIT.

silk tulle backing fabric (Figure 3.8). The design of the cape itself was simple, allowing all focus to be on the shimmery effect of the cellophane.

Polyvinyl Chloride (PVC) was discovered by accident in 1926, when a scientist working for B. F. Goodrich was attempting to develop synthetic rubber. The material was soon applied to outerwear, such as raincoats and umbrellas.[112] In the 1960s, shiny vinyl materials had a desirably "Space Age" appearance that furthered their appeal. British designer Mary Quant was among the first to experiment with PVC in her 1963 "Wet Collection," but technical problems surrounding the application of the material for fashion took her nearly two years to resolve. As the designer recalled in her autobiography, *Quant by Quant,* "by that time other designers on both side of the Channel were as bewitched as I still am with this super-shiny man-made stuff and its shrieking colors."[113]

Indeed, vinyl was an inexpensive, "futuristic" material that was utilized by a multitude of designers, and embraced for its overtly synthetic appearance. While the trend began with young, hip boutique designers such as Quant and Betsey Johnson, it was also used in high-end fashion. For example, a couture dress c. 1967, by André Courrèges, features an interesting mix of immaculate construction techniques and materials (an "openwork" effect created from hand-stitched pieces of nude silk and black chiffon), with cutout trim in black vinyl (Figure 3.9). While the vinyl clothing of the 1960s was soon displaced by the more "natural" look of the hippies, the material did not disappear from fashion. PVC and other plastics remain in common use, especially for inexpensive handbags and shoes. In spite of their sleek look, however, it is now known that plastics are highly carcinogenic, and their production relies on petrochemicals. Furthermore, plastics can off-gas toxic chemicals that leak into the ecosystem while they biodegrade—a process that will take hundreds of years.

Suggestion for further reading

Ferro, M. (2005),"Vinyl as Fashion Fabric," in Valerie Steele (ed.), *Encyclopedia of Clothing and Fashion,* Detroit, MI: Charles Scribner's Sons, 400.

4
TEXTILE DYEING

Introduction

This chapter explores the historical practices and problems associated with the dyeing of Western fashion and textiles, which were magnified by the advent of industrial production and the transition from primarily organic dyes to *aniline dyes*, or synthetic chemical dyes, during the nineteenth century. By addressing the historical evolution of fabric dyeing and its impact on the environment, namely through harmful chemicals and wastewater pollution, we can make connections to the corresponding problems faced by the contemporary fashion and textile industries—as well as the sustainable solutions proposed in response.

Fashion writer M. D. C. Crawford marveled, in retrospect, that "within a period of no less than a century a small group of mechanics … had changed methods of spinning and weaving, dyeing, and fabric decoration which had a previous history of perhaps ten thousand years."[1] The changes to the textile industry propagated by the Industrial Revolution of the late eighteenth and early nineteenth centuries were indeed astounding. Through mechanization and science, fabric production became more efficient than it had ever been. Dyeing, as Crawford pointed out, was no exception in the tide of progress. Prior to the mid-nineteenth century, that is, for most of history, dyeing was done using organic materials gathered from plants, insects, or minerals. The plant madder, for instance, or the insect cochineal were common sources of the color red; indigo or woad, both plant-based, provided blue; and the safflower plant was culled to provide yellow coloring. Dyestuffs were mostly determined by local availability, and generally speaking, waste was localized and produced on a far smaller scale than will be discussed later in the chapter.

Plate 9, which shows a dress produced around 1821, provides an example of the beautiful, but comparatively subdued, color palette available from natural dye sources. The dress is uniquely positioned in history, representing both old and new practices. Its multicolor zigzag pattern was achieved through a new industrial process, roller printing, which began to replace hand block and engraved copper plate printing early in the nineteenth century. With roller printing, a series of engraved cylinders could create intricate, multicolored patterns much less expensively than either previous method.[2] Although the dress's production process was modern, its dyes certainly were not. It would be another three decades before the dye industry would be subject to the same wholesale changes as the rest of fashion and textile production. Those changes, however, would leave an environmental legacy that we have yet to reconcile.

Synthetic dyes

During the mid-nineteenth and early twentieth centuries, dyes began to be synthesized from chemical sources, a revolutionary change to the clothing and textile dyeing industry. Interestingly, the first commercially successful synthetic, or aniline fabric dye, mauveine, was an accidental innovation. In 1856, chemist William Henry Perkin derived the dye from coal tar during an experiment, in which he had sought to create a synthetic version of the natural compound quinine. Perkin instead found himself with an entirely different product, which through additional testing produced his soon-to-be famous mauve dye.[3]

Mauveine was unlike anything the public had seen, its brilliance unmatched by any natural dye. Perkin himself marveled at the fastness (ability to withstand fading) of his purple dye. "The affinity of aniline purple for silk or wool is very remarkable," he wrote, "the mauve is the most permanent coal-tar purple known."[4] The brightness of these synthetic dyes is illustrated by the purple and black silk taffeta dress in plate 10. Some 150 years after it was produced, the dress's fabric still retains a marked intensity of color.

Perkin's mauveine transformed dyeing, paving the way for an influx of synthetic dyes that produced bold, vivid colors. Perkin solved the logistics of commercial development of synthetic dye, and as he said in 1868, "to introduce a new coal-tar colour after the mauve was a comparatively simple matter."[5] As the century progressed, new dyes were developed and marketed, one after another; magentas, reds, greens, and finally blues—the possibilities seemed endless. (See "At a glance: Indigo" for a brief discussion of the development of synthetic indigo.) Chemical "coal tar colours" dominated fashion for much of the late nineteenth century, displacing many traditional plant or insect dyes. "The use of natural colors in dyeing is disappearing year by year and artificial products from coal tar are steadily and surely taking their place. Nearly every color has been found to lurk in that black and uninviting substance called pitch or tar," reported the New York Times in 1893.[6] What made the new dyes so attractive, apart from the brilliance of the colors they produced, was that they were cost-effective. "One pound" of the red dye synthetic alizarin, cited the New York Times in 1915, equaled "the coloring power of ninety pounds of madder,"[7] the plant from which red had historically been procured.

Although it adored the bright synthetic colors, the public likely had little real understanding of the scientific process of synthesizing color from coal tar. "Frightful as it may seem, our wives and sweethearts are gradually becoming carboniferous," wrote the New York Times correspondent to the International Exhibition held in London in 1862, as their dresses were "in fact dipped and steeped in the essence of vile, smoky, stinky, crackly English coal."[8] Although its author tried to explain something of the reactions and components involved with synthetic dyeing, the statement emphasized most of all its great novelty.

Perkin, in a lecture delivered in 1868, explained that the term "coal tar colours" was easily misinterpreted. Coal tar is a material with many different chemical components, including the chemical liquid aniline, the base of and the term by which we now refer to these dyes. "It is not meant to imply that colouring matter actually exists in coal tar ... but that coal tar is the source of certain products which, when changed by various chemical processes, are capable of yielding coloured derivatives," Perkin said.[9]

Viewed as exciting and evocative of scientific progress, aniline dyes nonetheless presented something of an ecological conundrum. From a contemporary perspective, they have created a legacy of chemical pollution. They largely displaced the use of natural dyes, which in many parts of the world had an age-old history, and in doing so, also disrupted the industries and livelihoods of the people who grew dye-producing plants. Yet, at the time of their development, aniline dyes were praised not just for their modernity and beautiful hues, but also because the coal tar they utilized was waste material, and by all accounts one that was nasty, foul smelling, and difficult to dispose of. "From this singularly repulsive refuse, springs one of the most important of modern English manufactures," cried the *New York Times*,[10] lauding the new use for the by-product generated when coal was processed to form gas.[11] Although repurposing of waste products can be a good thing ecologically, aniline dyes still had significant drawbacks. Even as their popularity grew, the dyes received criticism for the impact their chemicals had on the health of textiles workers and wearers, as well as their chemical pollution of waterways.

Poisoning people

It is the direct impact on humans that we discuss first. Although the march of aniline dyes, with their inexpensive and radiant colors, continued undeterred through the latter half of the nineteenth century, their potentially toxic chemical makeup became a point of concern. It is now well known that many fashionable green dyes of the mid-nineteenth century contained the poison arsenic, including those widely used in the production of wallpapers, fabrics and clothing, such as the day dress in plate 11. Shades of green pigment, referred to by names such as Paris green, emerald green, or Scheele's green, were immensely popular. Scholar P. W. J. Bartrip, who studied arsenic in the Victorian environment, has written that during that era, "Any manufactured item coloured green was as likely as not to have been dyed with arsenic."[12] One source indicated that in 1862 English production of the dyes was as much as 500 to 700 tons.[13] Dr Alfred Swaine Taylor discussed these "arsenite of copper" pigments in an 1875 publication, confirming the widespread use of the dyes in fashion, particularly for artificial flowers and a thin cotton fabric called tarlatan, and warned of the dangers of arsenic poisoning.[14] Health risks to the textile worker as well as the wearer ranged from skin irritation to poisoning from inhalation of dust or fumes, although some experts felt that the most common method of transmission for the poison from fabric was through the skin.[15] "Girls employed in this manufacture, as well as dressmakers, suffer seriously from this form of poisoning," wrote Taylor, which harmed their eyes and respiratory systems.[16]

Although green was the most notorious, it should be noted that a great many other aniline dyes also contained arsenic. In 1878, a reporter from *Fraser's Magazine* observed the vast quantities of arsenic at a mine that supplied the chemical to the dye industry. He wrote, "More than 2,000 tons a year are sent out from this one mine, to be used mainly in those brilliant modern dyes by which our women can dazzle the sunshine at cheap expense." He was discomfited by the toxin's presence, and also unable to answer the basic question: "Is it safe to wear?" Experts had reached no consensus. However, the author noted one of the reasons that arsenic was so potentially dangerous: it could pass undetected.[17] Poisoning could happen slowly, without the awareness of its victim, which surely should have been a red flag in its use in products so intimately connected to the body.

As time went on, evidence mounted against the safety of working with or wearing clothing dyed with arsenic compounds. In 1891, Boston physicians lambasted the use of arsenic in wallpapers and textiles, hoping to persuade the state legislature of the dangers they presented. To illustrate the point, one doctor showed the blue cloth of a dress, which he claimed, "poisoned the physician's wife who wore it, the dressmaker who made it, and the seamstress who sewed it."[18] Around this time, the Bureau of Chemistry within the US Department of Agriculture undertook a study, "Arsenic in Papers and Fabrics," the results of which were published in 1904. The report, which summarized previous research and added its own findings, tried to quantify the arsenic problem. Red, black and green dyes seemed to be the biggest offenders, however: "the presence of large amounts of arsenic does not seem to be confined to any particular class of goods, since those containing the largest amounts include calicos, cashmeres, outing flannels, ducks, mohairs, and flannelets."[19] In all, 11 percent of the fabrics they tested contained a significant amount of the poison.[20]

Yet, arsenic was not alone in the dangerous chemicals employed in dyeing, and the danger was especially great for the workers in dye factories. As early as 1895 there was speculation, based on illnesses of workers in aniline dye factories, that components of chemical dyes could be carcinogenic[21]—a concern that has not abated in the contemporary industry. In 1868, when Perkin delivered lectures for the Society for the Encouragement of Arts, Manufactures, and Commerce, he made mention of one of the contemporary methods of manufacturing magenta dye, which included the use of mercury. Although "with care this process works very well, and the colouring matter produced is of good quality ...," he admitted, "the use of mercury salts is most undesirable on account of their fearfully deleterious influence upon the workmen."[22] Many years later, a 1921 Labor Department publication examined the potential effects of aniline dyes on workers, determining both fumes and skin contact could be problematic.[23] As they explained, coal-tar dyes contained a number of chemical compounds, not just arsenic, which could affect the health of employees:

The making of dyes has necessitated the production and use not only of benzene, nitrobenzene, and anilin, but also of an enormous number of derivatives, many of which have a toxic action on the skin, on the central nervous system, on the blood, or on all three.[24]

The dyeing of fabric is a complicated process involving dye preparation, numerous methods of application, and sometimes *mordants*, since some dyes, especially natural ones, require the addition of another substance to affix dye to fabric. Thus, the dye is not the only potentially troublesome factor in human and environmental impact. If the dye mixture is natural or nontoxic, with minimal environmental impact, but the mordant is not, then the process can still have an adverse effect. The aforementioned presence of arsenic in some dyes, for instance, was sometimes because it was an ingredient in the dye mix, and sometimes because it was present in the mordanting material.[25] As S. R. Cockett and others have observed, the resultant color on a dyed textile or garment can be greatly affected by the mordant chosen. Depending on the desired hue, a dyer might be inclined to choose one or the other, regardless of the toxicity. As an example, Cockett contrasted the varying colors generated by the mordants chromium, iron, copper, and aluminum when combined with the plant dye logwood.[26] Of the mordants listed above, chromium is a highly toxic material, one that was also heavily utilized historically in leather tanning. Chromium was a favored mordant, one writer explained, because as compared to other choices, it produced longer lasting color.[27] J. W. Slater, in his 1870 manual on dye colors, mentioned bichromate—a compound which, like chromium trioxide, also contained chromic acid—as particularly dangerous to work with. It was, he wrote, in common use, paired with logwood to produce black dyes. Yet, the danger to the workers was great: "The hands of dyers who work much with this salt, become swollen and ulcerated, and in time the mischief extends to the toes, palate, jaw-bones, etc."[28]

The harmfulness of particular dyes is, however, sometimes recognized only in hindsight. Another type of chemical dye, azo, first hit the market about a decade after Perkin discovered mauveine.[29] In 1921, Dr Alice Hamilton, writing under the auspices of the US Department of Labor, declared, "the making of azo dyes … the safest branch of the color industry."[30] Yet, azo dyes are a serious worry for many contemporary scientists and conservationists, as under certain conditions some may have carcinogenic properties as they chemically decompose.[31] As a result, their use is regulated and/or prohibited in many places,[32] but they continue to appeal to producers now, as they did then, because of their efficiency and color fastness.[33]

Poisoning the environment

Although it can be argued that many chemicals involved in the dyeing process, once stabilized in the fabric, are of no, or at least negligible, harm to the wearer, the same cannot be said of their effect on the environment if they are allowed to contaminate waterways through unregulated disposal. The sheer variety of dyes used by the textiles and clothing industry is immense, which means *dye effluent*, or the liquid waste generated during the dyeing process, fluctuates from factory to factory and season to season. The type of dye, as well as the process used, can yield vastly different mixtures and quantities, at various degrees of toxicity. As reported in a 1930s publication on textile pollution: "Textile waste liquors range from almost harmless to very toxic and putrescible mixtures."[34] It is also important to remember that by the time dyeing occurs, a yarn or a fabric may have been through various stages of pre-treatment and processing, such as cleaning or bleaching, which have their own chemical impacts on the environment. The complex technical and chemical processes associated with dyeing are beyond the scope of this chapter, but suggested reading provides references to further resources on the variables and their environmental consequences.

Although dye waste can be a highly visible effluent in lakes, oceans, and rivers, what is unseen can be equally, if not more, harmful. As scholar Anthony S. Travis noted in his study of dye pollution in Basel, Switzerland during the 1860s: "Compared with eyesores such as stagnant or dye-coloured streams and clouds of choking gas in industrial districts, subsurface water was certainly out of sight if not completely out of mind."[35] Drawing from Swiss archival documents, Travis explored the link between a dye plant, J. J. Müller-Pack and Company, and soil and groundwater contamination with toxins, including arsenic, from the dye-making process.[36] Poisoned well water extended the risks of aniline dye production from the workers in the plant to the surrounding environment and those who called it home.[37] In the seminal publication *Silent Spring*, Rachel Carson explained why groundwater pollution was so worrisome: virtually "all the running water of the earth's surface was at one time groundwater... so, in a very real and frightening sense, pollution of the groundwater is pollution of water everywhere."[38] The events described in Basel played out shortly after the first aniline dyes were discovered and had begun to be industrially manufactured, providing evidence that the danger of dumping dye effluent into water sources was evident early on.

In fairness, wastewater from dyes is a troublesome predicament to address, and always has been. A 1930s study conducted by the Textile Foundation, Inc. in Washington, DC, noted: "The textile waste treatment problem is more complex than many other industrial waste purification problems because of the fact that no two textile wastes are alike in character, nor can any two wastes be purified by exactly the same treatment."[39] Not only that, "the waste ... continually changes with the introduction of new processes or the change in market demands,"[40] hinting at the historical precedent of a problem that has since only grown with the increased speed of the fashion cycle.

In a 1969 publication on the modern factory, George M. Price reasoned as to why dye and other industrial wastes so frequently ended up in the earth's waterways: it was the practice that caused the manufacturer the least expense.[41] Shortly thereafter, during the environmentalist boom of the 1970s,[42] the United States Environmental Protection Agency recognized the severity of the problem, and in the proceeding decades collaborated with the textiles and clothing industry to establish standards for waste disposal.[43] Many other countries have also enacted regulatory measures and built filtration systems that limit chemicals and other materials in the effluent they release. Yet much of our clothing is now sewn, processed, and dyed in countries where regulations may be insufficient and enforcement lax. Ensuring proper filtration and disposal can be an added expense for textile producers, meaning the cheap and easy solution is still prevalent in many developing countries, where as environmental group Greenpeace points out, waterways become "a convenient dumping ground for all types of wastes."[44] As with transferring production to new locations for lower labor costs, there is the temptation for unethical manufacturers to target those areas where "environmental control is less stringent."[45] Likewise, Maria C. Thiry, in an article for *AATCC Review*, cited cost-prohibitiveness as the reason why some producers do not bother with "sustainable production practices"; the experts she interviewed indicated that up front this is perhaps true. However, the real benefit, ecological *and* financial, is in the long run.[46]

Past meets present in the search for solutions

Unfortunately, there is no one-size-fits-all solution to the problems presented by the dyeing of textiles and clothing. Any given choice may present a trade-off environmentally, as illustrated by the comparison of two dyeing methods, discharge printing and heat-transfer printing, in "At a glance: Lowering the impact of dyeing processes." Nonetheless, the quest for lower impact, more sustainable dyeing processes has generated enormous creativity and experimentation.

Furthermore, certain best practices have emerged within the industry. Better oversight and management of the dyeing process is one method of limiting dye waste materials. J. R. Easton, of DyStar, believes that mistakes in production can be costly not just for the environment, but also for a company's bottom line.[47] The single "most effective pollution prevention practice for textile wet processing is 'right-first-time' dyeing," Easton wrote.[48] As opposed to dealing with the end stage waste, it is far better to prevent it outright.[49] Filtering after the fact is "complicated, uneconomical, and time consuming," agreed J. N. Chakraborty.[50] Pollution "is a sign of inefficiency in industrial production."[51]

Recovery and reuse of waste (sending it back into the production cycle, as opposed to out of an effluent pipe) is prized and promoted, and most agree that it should be done whenever possible. "Closing the loop," as modern terminology would dub it, was the advice of scientists in the late 1930s, who concluded that, "in many instances waste liquors from one operation might be used to make up the bath in another."[52] The same recommendations are found in scholarly texts and practical guidelines today.[53] Designer and eco-fashion scholar, Dr Kate Fletcher has observed that certain circumstances make this more probable: "The likelihood of dye liquor reuse is increased especially when dyeing is limited to a few shades … where given the right conditions a dye liquor could be used up to ten times before the level of impurities limits further use."[54]

Despite our contemporary wealth of scientific knowledge and modern materials, some within the design community have proposed that solving the problems of the present requires us to reconsider the practices of the past and return to the use of naturally derived dyes. Cheryl Kolander, a master dyer based out of Portland, Oregon, has decades' worth of experience in the art of dyeing naturally. Explaining her motivation, in *Future Fashion White Papers*, she stated that contemporary dye factories, with their colored and chemical effluents, "are not the kind of industry that I want coloring my life."[55] Kolander has tried to overcome, and disprove through practice, prejudices held against natural dyes, which she noted include a supposed lack of fastness and limited range.[56] One thing she vehemently rebuts is the notion that the mordants required by plant and insect dyes render them as toxic as chemical ones.[57] Fellow author and dyer India Flint acknowledged that not all mordants used for natural dyes, past or present, are safe.[58] However, recognizing that a mordant is sometimes necessary, Flint's writing provides suggestions for viable substitutes for hazardous materials, such as chromium; many of her recommendations are things you might find in your kitchen.[59]

Natural dyeing has gained adherents, such as young designer Kate Brierley, to whom Kolander served as a mentor. Brierley was attracted to the rich palette of natural dyes, which she often uses in the production of her clothing line, Isoude, based out of her Newport, Rhode Island atelier. Her *Eirene* gown (plate 12) is the product of her experimentations with the natural dyeing process. The creation of the dress, she has said, "represented real beauty ... an artisanal process from A to Z." It was hand-colored by Cheryl Kolander using a natural madder root dye. The madder, Brierley explained, was cultivated in Afghanistan, but due to the military conflicts in the region, "it hadn't been culled in a very long time," causing its color to take on singular qualities. Brierley has said, "Natural dyeing is definitely an art form," likening its intricacies to the baking of bread as well as to winemaking. Each time she prepares a batch of dye, the end result varies slightly: "Because it's so tactile, there's an interaction with your subconscious and what's coming out." Yet, she is quick to stress that natural dyeing is, for her, solely an artisanal process, not something that can be translated to a large output.[60] Of course, that fits with Brierley's overall design philosophies—she does not design for mass production, preferring to focus on quality craftsmanship at each stage of the process. Her focus on quality and sustainable practices extends to other choices made in the design process, such as the use of tussah silk, the harvesting of which does not harm the silkworm, in the *Eirene* dress. The gown's subtle chevron embellishments are derived from a repurposed material, made by the Zanzibar Women's Pearl Shellcraft Cooperative and jeweler William Elliot Drake, utilizing portions of the Mabe pearl shell that are usually discarded.

While it can be argued, as Brierley does, that natural dyeing best serves artisanal production, some larger companies are attempting to incorporate it at the industrial level. The brand Eileen Fisher has given serious consideration to the ways in which dyeing fits into their supply chain, and the result has been a prestigious eco certification, bluesign®, for production in their Chinese factory. As reported in *Women's Wear Daily* in October 2012, Eileen Fisher has begun working to "create 'colors without compromise' using vegetable dyes and other nontoxic materials."[61] The company website, which provides transparency on its sustainable initiatives, further explains the goal of minimizing waste: "Rather than treating wastewater to remove harmful chemicals after the fabric is dyed, our dyehouse reduces toxins before they enter the manufacturing stream."[62]

Advocates of natural dyes, who support the embracing of tradition and the resurgence of dyes and methods that pre-date the Industrial Revolution, make an argument that is, in fact, anything but new. Anti-industrialist and leader of the Arts & Crafts movement, William Morris, asserted the same view, and put the idea into practice not long after synthetic dyes first rose to prominence in the late nineteenth century.[63] Morris, who eschewed synthetic colors in favor of natural ones, used natural indigo to dye the textile, *Bird and Anemone* (plate 13). Similarly, clothing and textile designer Mariano Fortuny was disinclined to follow trends of mass production. To create the beautiful hues of his clothing

Figure 4.1 Rafael, man's denim suit, cotton, c. 1973, Italy. Collection of The Museum at FIT, 85.161.8. Gift of Chip Tolbert. Photograph © The Museum at FIT.

and textiles, he preferred to source his own natural dyestuffs, rather than use aniline dyes.[64] Less well-known figures of the period also gave thought to natural dyes. In 1917 the *New York Times* praised New York woman Edith O'Neil MacDonald for her ingenuity in developing a natural dye using the leaves fallen from hardwood trees around her home in the Adirondacks, an idea inspired by the imprints of leaves left on sidewalks. Wartime had affected the supply of German-made synthetic dyes, making her discovery timely, but MacDonald thought about the bigger picture.[65] Her patent for the dye emphasized its ecological benefits—as a resource it was renewable and the non-toxic by-products could be recycled into fertilizer.[66]

Although these examples provide important historical context for modern solutions, we should be wary of viewing natural dyes as a panacea. Traditional dyeing, like that practiced by Morris and many others before him, has the capacity to pollute, and to adversely affect our planet, just like any other dyeing process, natural or otherwise, especially when done industrially. India Flint commented that Morris, despite his good intentions with natural dyes, "did not consider the environmental consequences of large-scale dyeing and the effects on local waterways."[67]

Likewise, contemporary designers and scholars have concurred that there are real obstacles in the broad implementation of natural dyeing. "Nowhere in the world do industrial natural dye-works, which could handle a department store-sized order, still exist," Kolander has pointed out.[68] Furthermore, Anne de la Sayette, horticultural engineer, in a May 2012 presentation at the *Coloring Fashion* symposium at New York's Parsons The New School for Design, observed that the knowledge of natural dye culti-vating, although its history is ancient, can be lost surprisingly quickly.[69] Textile chemist, Martin Bide of the University of Rhode Island, speaking at the same symposium, brought an interesting perspective to the debate. Natural dyes are not perfect, Bide indicated; they can be wasteful and water and energy intensive. Furthermore, in his observations, natural dyes could not possibly fulfill our demand for colorful fast fashion.[70] Kolander, too, has mentioned the lack of the plant resources for commercial applica-tions.[71] Additionally, Bide made the valid point that an incredible amount of land would have to be converted for the harvesting of natural dyes.[72] How can we justify this, concurred McDonough and Braungart, in *Cradle to Cradle*, when we still need to feed an ever-growing world population?[73] And is it sustainable, India Flint questioned, to use "plants harvested from fragile environments and shipped over great distances?"[74] All of their arguments warrant consideration in evaluating the adoption of natural dyeing practices. What's more, they point to the need for a shift not just in production, but also consumption patterns.

Conclusion

Very little in the way of greige (undyed or unbleached) goods ever appears in our stores or decorates our bodies, and this is unlikely to change. An entire industry exists to forecast color trends for each upcoming season. Unfortunately, as environmental organization Greenpeace notes, information can often be gleaned from "looking at the colour of the rivers in Mexico and China."[75] (For more on Greenpeace's efforts to publicize and combat wastewater pollution associated with the fashion and textile industry, see "At a glance: Greenpeace.") As this chapter has argued, the problems associated with contemporary fabric dyeing and pollution have an historical precedent in the development and "modernization" of chemical dye processes in the nineteenth century. The detrimental effects of effluent on our environment and chemicals on our bodies are not necessarily new concerns, but have taken on a new imperative in light of the increasingly large scale of industrial production to meet the demands of rapidly changing fast fashion.

Sustainable production in the context of textile dyeing means striving to minimize pollution, waste, and water use over the course of the dye production, application, and finishing processes. It can mean critiquing how we produce, diligently monitoring effluent, and finding better alternatives—an idea which has attracted scientists, designers, and environmentalists alike. Greenpeace, for example, advocates what they call the "the principle of substitution" where "hazardous chemicals are progressively replaced with safer alternatives."[76] Rather than simply blaming history for our present problems, some feel we ought to draw from the heritage of the past, using natural dyeing traditions as a way to move forward. Certainly, it would be foolish to discount the appeal of color, and no one is really suggesting that we cease to dye our clothing. As Jacky Watson has observed, this merely sidesteps the problem, and is not viable within the scheme of contemporary fashion.[77] The question then becomes, how do we mediate our desire for beautiful color with its potentially detrimental effect on the environment?

The initiatives of designers and researchers discussed here, as well as the countless unmentioned ones, offer exciting possibilities for improvement on what has been a formidable and enduring environmental problem—the dyeing of clothing and textiles. Perhaps like William Henry Perkin's serendipitous mistake, one of today's scientists will unlock a better way to dye—one that counteracts the chemical legacy with which, fair or not, Perkin will always be associated. A. Sherburne wrote that we have a responsibility to heed the "revolutionary call to grow up, and to reinvent the industrial revolution, by mimicking nature in a way that maintains a benign balance and not mixing it up in a way that disturbs global ecosystems and poisons us."[78] Combining philosophy and action, the present and future generations of designers and manufacturers have the potential to enact real and positive change for the environment.

Suggestions for further reading

Bartrip, P. W. J. (1994), "How green was my valance?: Environmental arsenic poisoning and the Victorian domestic ideal," *The English Historical Review* 109 (433): 891–913.

Blackburn, R. S. (ed.) (2009), *Sustainable Textiles: Life Cycle and Environmental Impact*, New York: CRC Press.

Kolander, C. (2007), "In Defense of Truth and Beauty," in L. Hoffman (ed.), *FutureFashion: White Papers,* New York: Earth Pledge.

Perkin, W. H. (1869), "The aniline or coal tar colours," *Cantor Lectures*, London: W. Trounce.

Slater, K. (2000), *The Environmental Impact of Textiles: Production, Processes, and Protection*, Cambridge: Woodhead Publishing.

Tobler-Rohr, M. I. (2011), *Handbook of Sustainable Textile Production*, Oxford, Philadelphia: Woodhead and Cambridge: In association with the Textile Institute.

Travis, A. S. (1997), "Poisoned groundwater and contaminated soil: The tribulations and trial of the first major manufacturer of aniline dyes in Basel," *Environmental History* 2 (3): 343–65.

Watson, J. (1991), *Textiles and the Environment: Special Report no. 2150*, London: The Economist Intelligence Unit.

At a glance: Lowering the impact of dyeing processes

The patterning on the day dress by designer Sophie, in plate 14, was achieved through discharge printing: the dress was first dyed and then selectively treated with a bleaching agent to create the floral design. This process, with the dye baths and chemicals it requires, is especially environmentally harmful. As textiles scholar Keith Slater has noted, discharge printing "combines the worst aspects of printing and dyeing."[79] Of late, however, scientists have worked to find safer alternatives to certain chemicals used in the discharge printing process. As noted in a recent report, the horseradish peroxidase enzyme is a viable, and non-toxic, substitute for harsh chemicals—the potentially dangerous formaldehyde sulphoxylate being the main example[80]—used in discharge printing. This research is a positive step, resulting in what could be a promising, less environmentally harmful process. However, the method of testing in this study reveals that the scientists have used bleached fabric as their base, and dyed it with a commercially available chemical dye.[81] Their proposed process, while it investigates part of the problem, discounts the issues of pollution still associated with bleaching and dyeing.

Heat-transfer printing, a technique that has existed since the end of the 1920s, presents an interesting alternative for creating attractive patterns on garments.[82] It does not require the preparation of dye baths, and instead, as the name explains, transfers dye via heat to fabric. Plate 15 shows a detail shot of a dress designed by Japanese designer and textile innovator, Yoshiki Hishinuma, who has used the technique to create the colorful decoration on the dress's appliqués. This method, using disperse dyes, removes one of the primary effluent concerns, water. Yet, the technique's ecological benefits and impact are debated. While it requires little water, heat-transfer can generate waste in the form of a transfer medium, paper. In 1986, researchers indicated that although "transfer printing is ecologically favorable" for some reasons, for "the enormous amounts of waste paper… no economical reuse has yet been indentified."[83] Additionally, many garments that are dyed or printed in this manner are made of polyester, which is the fiber most receptive to heat-transfer printing,[84] and one that has historically been, due to its natural resistance to water, difficult to dye.[85] Yet, polyester, as discussed in Chapter 3 is surrounded by its own ecological debate. Regardless, heat transfer is becoming an increasingly popular method, with prominent examples of contemporary applications, such as the partnership between the design label Costello Tagliapietra and the dyeing firm AirDye®.

The Brooklyn-based design team of Jeffrey Costello and Robert Tagliapietra, has for a number of seasons used AirDye® to color their collections. The dress in plate 16, the finale garment in their Fall 2010 ready-to-wear collection, described in the collection notes as "lava," was dyed with AirDye®'s signature heat-transfer method that eliminates water and significantly minimizes energy usage and greenhouse gas emissions. The company markets their technology as "today's sustainable alternative to traditional dyeing and decorating processes."[86] An informational hangtag, which accompanied Costello Tagliapietra's Spring 2010 runway show program, stated that with the use of this method, the amount of water saved is 45 gallons per dress. AirDye® has solved the problem of paper waste through recycling—a major improvement on earlier methods. AirDye® has also found new use for any dye waste, noting that it can be repurposed into tar or asphalt.[87] Companies like AirDye® are at the forefront, addressing one of the most potent concerns of this sector of the textile industry—the lack of available water, and the excessive water consumption associated with the dyeing process.[88]

Suggestions for Further Reading:

Chakraborty, J. N. (2010), *Fundamentals and Practices in Colouration of Textiles*, New Delhi, Cambridge and Oxford: Woodhead Publishing India.
Karthikeyan, K. and Dhurai, B. (2011), "New method of discharge printing on cotton fabrics using horseradish peroxidase," *AUTEX Research Journal* 11 (2): 61–5.
Slater, K. (2000), *The Environmental Impact of Textiles: Production, Processes, and Protection*, Cambridge: Woodhead Publishing.

At a glance: Indigo

The indigo plant has a long history, prized worldwide for its beautiful blue dye. Indigo, however, like most other natural dye materials, was subject to the nineteenth century quest for chemical alternatives. Unlike chemical purples and reds, for instance, it took scientists comparatively longer to develop a profitable blue synthetic. In 1893, although formulas had been developed, none was "sufficiently cheap to compete with natural indigo."[89] In the early twentieth century, however, researchers gained ground.[90] John Lindemann of the company F. Bredt & Co, reported in 1915: "There has been very little natural indigo consumed by the textile mills since the introduction of the artificial indigo." Synthetic, he maintained, gave "results superior to the natural indigo and in normal times at considerably less cost."[91] The second half of the twentieth century has seen the blue jean (once work wear for laborers) move from the clothing of rebel teenagers to an everyday fashion garment, and a democratic one at that. Nearly every closet in the Western world features at least one pair of jeans. Around the time that the denim suit in figure 4.1 was produced, James Sullivan wrote: "three hundred fifty million pairs of jeans were sold."[92] Today, the supposedly superior results of synthetic indigo fulfill our unrelenting appetite for blue jeans.[93]

Suggestions for further reading

Sullivan, J. (2006), *Jeans: A Cultural History of an American Icon,* New York: Gotham Books.

At a glance: Greenpeace

Although the primary target of her consternation was chemical pesticide, Rachel Carson's *Silent Spring* issued a caution about how we treat our earth, its waterways, and the damage that repeated and prolonged chemical exposure can wreak on animals and humans alike. "In this now universal contamination of the environment, chemicals are the sinister and little recognized partner of radiation in changing the very nature of the world—the very nature of its life," she wrote.[94] Yet, as we have seen, prior to the pesticides that so concerned Carson, we were polluting our water with a multitude of chemicals, visible and otherwise, generated in the production of clothing and textiles.

The environmental organization Greenpeace extensively investigates the link between the processing of clothing and textiles and the dye and chemical content of polluted water. Since 2011, their Detox campaign has raised public awareness, urged transparency, and pushed implicated companies and brands to respond. A number of companies have now committed to the organization's request to "eliminate all releases of hazardous chemicals from their supply chains and products" by 2020.[95] Among the numerous chemicals that Greenpeace wants out of fashion, and out of our water supply, are azo dyes and the heavy metal chromium.[96] Greenpeace has also put into practice what they preach, and have withdrawn from producing t-shirts until such time as their suppliers can do what they have asked of others.[97]

As part of the campaign, Greenpeace researchers have tested the chemical content of water and extant clothing, resulting in the publications, *Toxic Threads: Polluting Paradise* and *Toxic Threads: The Big Fashion Stitch-Up,* respectively. For the former, they chose as the subject of investigation the Indonesian textile plant, PT Gistex, and its connections to the pollution in the Citarum River. Greenpeace found chemicals in the water related to the dyeing process, as well as the production and finishing of textile materials, especially polyester.[98] They had previously conducted similar research in Mexico as well as China,[99] where the photo in plate 1b was shot. The chicly dressed model might easily have appeared in the glossy pages of *Vogue* or one of the fashion industry's other leading style publications—until you examine the rest of the image. Her high heels are perched atop a dirty yellow effluent pipe; behind her is a murky brown sea, containing who knows what. The photo was one of the striking images from a series called "Toxic Glamour" that was created to accompany the Detox campaign. To drive home their point, the organization juxtaposed the allure and mystique often associated with the fashion industry with the much uglier realities of production outlined in their reports.

Toxic Threads: The Big Fashion Stitch-Up found that a number of popular fashions had "residues of a variety of hazardous chemicals," including some originating with the dyeing process.[100] Out of the 141 garments that they bought and tested two were positive for carcinogenic amines associated with azo dyes, and both were from fast fashion retailer Zara. While two may not seem like a significant number, the organization emphasized that two is too many.[101] Furthermore, the problem is twofold; these products would almost certainly pollute at the time of manufacture, but evidence indicated that with residue present in garments, laundering was also a concern and could yield an additional pollution stream.[102]

Suggestions for further reading

Greenpeace (2012), *Toxic Threads: The Big Fashion Stitch-Up*, Amsterdam: Greenpeace International.
—(2013), *Toxic Threads: Polluting Paradise,* Amsterdam: Greenpeace International.

5
LABOR PRACTICES

Introduction

This chapter discusses the treatment of garment and textile industry workers in the nineteenth and twentieth centuries, placing contemporary labor practices in historical context, and providing an overview of the industry's checkered relationship with its labor force. Throughout the past two centuries, the industry has been criticized for disregarding the health and safety of its workers, paying them inadequate wages, and employing children. In examining the history of nineteenth- and early twentieth-century garment and textile industry labor, the chapter is first structured around the two environments where work is performed: mills, which produce textiles, and factories or shops, which produce ready-made clothing. From the late eighteenth to early twentieth centuries, textile production, like other industries, underwent rapid increases in mechanization, which triggered a shift from smaller-scale textile and garment production in the home to centers of manufacture in mill towns and urban tenements and factories, as well as a greater demand for inexpensive and unskilled labor.

Subsequent sections give an overview of the impact of unionization and reform in the United States domestic industry, as well as the resurgence of poor labor practices as production of clothing and textiles has increasingly moved overseas. With the rise of mass production and the corresponding (and barreling) increase in the speed of fashion production, standards have lowered—not merely in the quality of the product, but also the ways in which those who produce it are treated. Low standards have come to pervade the textile industry, as consumers have often chosen to purchase cheaply made products, made affordable because their creators are paid so little. A comparison of the industry's past and present demonstrates the cyclical nature of its problems, and the chapter concludes with a discussion of proposed solutions to deep-rooted labor practices.

Textile mills

Telling the history of labor practices through physical objects presents a unique set of challenges, as it is easy to view them as disconnected from the circumstances of their

Figure 5.1 Dress and spencer jacket, white cotton, c. 1819, England. Collection of The Museum at FIT, P88.28.2. Museum purchase; shown with paisley shawl, wool and silk, 1820–50, possibly Scotland. Collection of The Museum at FIT, P86.71.2. Museum purchase. Photograph © The Museum at FIT.

creation. More often than not, with historical pieces, such as the cotton dress in Figure 5.1, dated c. 1819, we cannot determine the individual who made them. We can, however, look beyond stitches and pattern pieces, cloth and thread, and think abstractly about the conditions under which those objects may have been produced. The white dress, sheer and relatively simple, is representative of the cotton dresses that were frequently worn in the earliest decades of the nineteenth century. Yet, the dress speaks not just to fashion trends, but also to the development of cotton mills, and the growth in production, during the late eighteenth and early nineteenth centuries, first in England, where this dress was produced, and then in the United States.

Both countries developed active mill industries, but our discussion focuses primarily on American mills. In the United States, cotton mills sprang up in places like Pawtucket, Rhode Island, and Lowell and Lawrence, Massachusetts. Silk mills formed as well, most notably in Paterson, New Jersey, a town dubbed "Silk City" during its peak in the late eighteenth and early nineteenth centuries.[1] Women formed the core of workers at many mills, particularly in Lowell, Massachusetts, perhaps one of the most recognizable names in mill towns. For a time, Lowell's mills had a rather good reputation.[2] Hours were lengthy and the work tiring, but efforts were made to maintain ethical standards and adequate housing,[3] and the comparatively good pay drew many well-bred farmers' daughters to work there.[4] Even so, there were problems under the surface. In the article "A Second Peep at Factory Life," which appeared in 1845, the last year of *The Lowell Offering*, a periodical organized by the mill's employees, the reader was allowed to eavesdrop on a group of fictitious workers as they complained about wage reductions.[5] The article's narrator admitted, "There are objections to the number of hours we work, to the length of time allotted to our meals, and to the low wages allowed for labor." The author hedged her criticism, however, resignedly declaring that "every situation in life, has its trials, which must be borne, and factory life has no more than any other."[6] One trial faced by the workers in Lowell during this decade was an increase of their already long working hours. As Benita Eisler noted, the women of Lowell's mills faced 75-hour weeks.[7]

By the early twentieth century, the southern region of the United States had absorbed a significant share of the production of yarn and cloth in mills that formed there after the Civil War.[8] In his 1906 study on the rapid industrialization of North Carolina, Holland Thompson summarized the benefits of southern manufacture. The "favorable" labor conditions in the development of Southern mills stemmed largely from the following: "The labor cost has been less, due partly to lower money wages, partly to longer hours, and finally to the absence of strikes and other forms of industrial friction."[9] He noted that after 1890, a number of the new Southern mills were "branch mills," opened by extant "Northern manufacturers,"[10] no doubt to profit from those very conditions.

Irrespective of location, mill conditions were worsening. Southern workers faced similarly long and strenuous workweeks. A report by D. A. Tompkins at the end of the nineteenth century put the figure at 11 hours per day in North Carolina mills.[11] In no uncertain terms, Thompson said of his state's mills, "the hours of labor … are long."[12] His statement could be more or less universally applied. Pay was also low. As compared to their counterparts in New England, Southern mill workers earned significantly less; in the case of women who spun yarn, half, at US $3 in contrast to the US $6 earned north of the Mason-Dixon line.[13] Yet, comparisons aside, Victoria Byerly and Steve Dunwell have both observed that as a whole textile workers have historically always had some of the most meager salaries.[14] Holland Thompson, however, defended industry, concluding that turn-of-the-century textile workers were not "wretchedly paid" and could earn more in mills than in agriculture.[15] Though difficult to determine because pay varied by skill of worker, Thompson estimated that a mill family, on average, could earn around US $10 or US $15 a week.[16] Nonetheless, the pay was still paltry; one reported salary around 1912 for 72 hours of work in a North Carolina mill was US $3.[17]

In addition to the lengthy workday and inadequate pay, mill conditions were often dangerous and unsanitary. Some defenders declared this to be the province of only a few unscrupulous employers. Tompkins wrote in 1899, "Every good superintendent has been trained to know that a dirty mill cannot turn out first-class product."[18] Yet, the images and the remembrances of mill workers often contradict Tompkins's rosy claim. Cotton dust, or lint, was a serious problem in mills. It covered the floors and filled the air, and its inhalation could cause mild to severe respiratory problems. Cotton dust was so pervasive a problem within the history of textile production, that it was one of the earliest concerns of the Occupational Safety and Health Administration (OSHA), formed in the United States in 1971.[19] Clara Thrift, who worked in mills during the second half of the twentieth century, recalled that the thread was the chief concern of the mill owners, not the cleanliness of the conditions to which workers were exposed.[20]

Accidents with mill machinery were also common. Maneuvering the quickly moving machinery could easily result in a severed finger, crushed limb, or worse. Women with long hair risked catching it in moving machinery, which could literally pull the scalp from their heads. Less dramatic, but of no less import, were the physical sufferings caused by excessive heat and physical overexertion. Prior to unionization and in the absence of regulatory oversight, workers in these early mills had little recourse and few advocates, so they often simply endured chronic exposure to the various dangers of their work.

Although the majority of workers were women, children also formed a large contingent of the nineteenth century and early twentieth century workforce. As others have noted, child labor has existed since the textile mill industries were burgeoning,[21] and it was not exclusive to the textile industry, or even manufacturing. "Industrialism does not create the phenomenon," wrote Thompson, "but concentrates it, and changes the form, regularity and intensity."[22] Some mill employees were as young as eight years old. Termed "apprentices" or "helpers," children often accompanied their parents to the mill, to help with small tasks. According to Hugh Hindman, author of *Child Labor: An American History*: "The 'helper system' enabled the mill to gain production from very young children and to train the workforce of the future while disavowing a direct employment relationship."[23] A. J. McKelway, Secretary for Southern States of the National Child Labor Committee in 1911, derided the hypocrisy surrounding the exploitation of helpers:

It will be evident to the most superficial observer that the injuries to a child under twelve years resulting from working a twelve-hour day or a twelve-hour night are greatly lessened if his name is not carried on the payroll![24]

In cotton mills, Thompson observed, children were concentrated in the spinning rooms.[25] Though statistics could be unreliable, "observation … shows the extensive employment of children."[26] He noted the percentage of child labor was correlated with the number of spindles operated by the mill.[27] In the autobiography, *Through the Mill, the Life of a Mill-Boy*, Frederic Kenyon Brown, writing under the pseudonym, Al Priddy, recounted the backbreaking conditions children faced in the mills during the late nineteenth century. About two years under the legal age of 13 when he began working at a mill in New Bedford, Massachusetts, Brown was at first eager and excited to work. It seemed an adventure, and even preferable to other ways of making money.[28] Initially, his work was rather light—cleaning cotton from the floors or oiling machinery.[29] It was when he was moved to the mule spinning room that "the terror of the mill began to blacken my life."[30] The conditions Brown described were abhorrent. He recalled the cruel bosses who forbade employees from speaking, sitting down, or opening a window to combat the extreme heat:[31]

> The mule-room atmosphere was kept at from eighty-five to ninety degrees of heat. The hard-wood floor burned my bare feet… To open a window was a great crime, as the cotton fiber was so sensitive to wind that it would spoil. (Poor cotton fiber!)[32]

Choked by lint, the child could also have been easily maimed—and some of his peers were—by the moving machinery they sometimes had to clean.[33]

There are perhaps no more evocative images concerning millwork and child labor than the photographs of Lewis Hine, taken under commission for the National Child Labor Committee. The somber young girl in Figure 5.2, stands stoically between machines far taller than she is. Cotton litters the floor around her. A print of this image, which probably dates to c. 1909, now resides in the collection of the New York Public Library. The handwritten text on the reverse of the image identifies the child not by name, but as a ten-year-old spinner in a North Carolina mill. During the 1980s, writer Victoria Byerly conducted interviews with Southern mill workers, the results of which are published in *Hard Times Cotton Mill Girls*. A number of the women interviewed had started working at the mills at young ages—some not much older than the child in the Hine photograph. Bertha Miller, one interview subject, began at age 11, and recalled being "so little that they had to build me a box" to reach the machine.[34] Another regretted the education sacrificed to work in the mills. Around 1911, "the biggest portion of the spinners was kids back then," remembered Bertha Awford Black, who also began work at age 11, although she noted "the girl that trained me was younger than that."[35] Some writers characterized the preference for and benefit of lowly paid child laborers in the Southern mills as merely a "phase." Said Leonora Beck Ellis in 1903, "manufacturers … are learning the lesson that it is a false economy, with expensive practical as well as ethical results," arguing that adults were simply more conscientious workers and in the long run their work was most cost effective for employers.[36]

Figure 5.2 Photograph of a ten-year-old spinner in a North Carolina cotton mill by Lewis Wickes Hine. Photography Collection, Miriam and Ira D. Wallach Division of Art, Prints and Photographs, The New York Public Library, Astor, Lenox, and Tilden Foundations.

Garment factories

In contrast to textile mill conditions, life in the US ready-to-wear industry's tenement shops and factories was often little better (Figure 5.3). The increasing mass production of clothing brought with it a host of concerns, not unlike those faced by mill workers. Much of the work of the garment industry was conducted in the small, overcrowded and often filthy tenement homes, which housed the industry's largely immigrant population, or in similarly poor, unsafe and unsanitary conditions within larger factory shops. Jacob Riis, in the influential exposé, *How the Other Half Lives*, first published in 1890, recounted that tenements in New York numbered some "thirty-seven thousand" and "more than twelve hundred thousand persons call them home."[37] Abraham Bisno, who as a young man in the 1880s worked in similar conditions in Chicago and later sought to unionize there as well as in New York, described succinctly the viciousness of industry conditions faced by garment workers. Many of these workers had:

Figure 5.3 Two women and two men working in an early garment shop. Photographer unknown, 1910 (estimated). Kheel Center, Cornell University, http://www.ilr.cornell.edu/trianglefire/

> A bare living, long periods of idleness, unreasonably hard work during the season, poor and unsanitary shops, crowded, many of them on fifth floors of buildings, with no fire protection or elevators, poorly lighted, working by gas all day with the strain of eyes, and great assault on the vitality of the workers, with lung tuberculosis pervading the trade.[38]

Unions, with advocates like Bisno, were eventually formed to combat the low wages, extremely long hours and often unsafe conditions faced by garment workers in such "sweatshops." The term has many connotations: a hot, crowded space; mistreated workers; and repugnant working conditions. Today, we could safely define a *sweatshop* as any working environment in which production of goods is done through violation of any aspect of fair labor, whether that is wages, hours, or conditions of work. The word's origin is a little more peculiar, however, and actually derives from the system of production. The term "sweater" referred to a "class of middlemen, or contractors," who acted as a liaison between the manufacturer and the "sweated" worker. These workers, explained the *New York Times*, in 1895, "did work by the piece in shops or in their own homes, and were tempted to long hours by the extra pay to be made. Out of these conditions grew up what is known as the sweat-shop system."[39] Yet, but for "perhaps … the accidental possession of two or three sewing-machines," the sweater, as Riis observed, was not so different from those whose sweat he profited from.[40] Abraham Bisno noted too that in a perverse way, the sweater, though his behavior was bad, was important in building up the trade and supporting immigrants.[41]

Although Bisno may have occasionally played devil's advocate, he recognized fully the degradation brought by such conditions. The piecework system under which so many garment manufacturers operated drove down wages through competition among desperate workers.[42] In factory shops, some limitations on child labor and working hours might exist, but not so in the tenements.[43] "The child," Riis wrote, "works unchallenged from the day he is old enough to pull a thread." Even workers in the large factory shops frequently did home work after hours to supplement their meager wages.[44]

The labor of poor garment workers made comparatively inexpensive ready-to-wear fashion accessible to greater numbers of people during the late nineteenth and early twentieth centuries. The shirtwaist, a feminized version of a masculine shirt (often worn tucked into a long, dark skirt), is an example of a popular, democratic garment, and one that was easily mass-produced. The example pictured in Figure 2.5 (Chapter 2) bears the label Stanley, and it was likely produced by the Stanley Shirt Factory, in Trenton, New Jersey in the mid–late 1890s.[45] At costs ranging from 48 cents to US $2.50, the company lauded their product as the "best fitting Shirt Waist made."[46]

While women might profit from the availability of affordable fashion, the *Ladies' Garment Worker*, a union journal, urged its readers, and the larger public to consider the origins of their fashionable shirtwaists, and their own role as consumers. "Do you ever stop to think where, how and by whom the thousands of shirt waists you see on sale all over the city are made?" it asked;

Do you know that 45,000 women and girls in New York alone are employed in making these waists? Do you realize that the conditions under which these girls work, the wages they receive, the hours they spend at their machines depend directly on YOU?[47]

One dressmaker considered these questions; shirtwaists sold for so little that they baffled her. In 1900 she went undercover to a shirtwaist factory to try to understand how these inexpensive, ready-made garments were produced, and her story was recounted in the *New York Times*. Paid by the piece, she earned some money, "but it would have been some time, even with the experience she had already obtained in the exercise of her profession, before she could have made what she would have considered living wages." Wages motivated her fellow workers, she noted, to perform their task with "wonderful rapidity," but she was unaccustomed to the pace of the work:

It did not seem possible that a human being turned into such a mere mechanical organism could live. To the dressmaker it did not seem possible that this one could exist long under such conditions. But this is the way clothing is made at such low prices.[48]

The anonymous dressmaker's account revealed that a large number of women worked in the shop, but gave no real detail about the conditions of the workplace or the number of hours that she and her colleagues worked. She mentioned no outrageous practices, aside from the low wages and accounts of workers being docked for damages to the shirtwaists.[49] Yet the brief report is telling. It is an admission that something is materially sacrificed in producing goods cheaply and quickly. This woman may have been lucky in comparison to others toiling perhaps blocks away under far worse conditions. Even in conditions presumed to be superior, there is an acknowledgment that it is not possible to produce very cheap clothing without a human cost.

In the spring of 1911, this human cost became more apparent than ever. The aforementioned shirtwaist became symbolic of the problems within the industry, as its production was implicated in one of the era's greatest industrial tragedies. On March 25, 146 people, mostly women, were killed in a deadly, fast-moving blaze at New York City's Triangle Shirtwaist Company. As numerous historians have described, the factory had a confluence of unsafe building conditions. The *Ladies' Garment Worker*, at the time the organ of the International Ladies' Garment Workers' Union, rightfully noted that a similar tragedy might have occurred in any number of factories, as "most of the garment manufacturing establishments in New York City are not any better as far as fire protection is concerned." However, they continued, "It is significant that the worst calamity happened at the Triangle, known among the workpeople in the trade as the 'prison'."[50] On the day of the fire, locked doors blocked the exits, and many women jumped in desperation—fatally—to the street below.[51] It was "an event which horrified not only the needle trades but the whole nation," recalled *Vogue*'s Edna Woolman Chase.[52] Although company owners were never convicted on criminal charges, the tragic incident became crucial to labor reform. Legal scholar Arthur F. McEvoy has noted that the fire "finally made possible the kinds of regulation over working conditions for which reformers had been struggling for some time."[53] McEvoy argued that it was the high visibility of the accident that made the difference. People could not simply ignore the dreadful sight of the fire's unrecognizable victims spread out on the ground.[54]

Unionization

In a horrible irony, shortly before the tragedy, workers at the Triangle Shirtwaist Company had been at the forefront of a strike for better conditions. The *Ladies' Garment Worker* proclaimed that as a result of the strike, "every girl employed in these waist shops, feels instinctively that she is not to be slighted or trifled with by the firm, and that there is a power outside ready to take her part."[55] For some, this was the case. When Leon Stein, the foremost researcher on the fire, interviewed survivors, blouse operator Mary Domsky-Abrams recounted leaving her machine slightly early that day to change into street clothes—against the orders of her manager—her will having been steeled by participation in the strike.[56] But others saw the results as not so very great, and the tragedy proof of that fact. In his chronicle of the fire and its aftermath, Stein quoted reporter William Shepard's remark, that "these dead bodies were the answer," to the workers' recent struggle.[57]

Union membership often did empower individuals, giving them backing, and the support of a collective of their peers. As Abraham Bisno put it, "when a union was organized, the spirit of the people rose and the price for labor was increased materially."[58] Historically, one of the most important unions within the garment industry has been the International Ladies' Garment Workers' Union (ILGWU). Founded in 1900, it merged with the Amalgamated Clothing and Textile Workers Union (ACTWU) in 1995 to become the Union of Needletrades, Industrial and Textile Employees (UNITE). Early on, the union faced the problem of how to exert widespread influence on an industry in which small shops, which took little funding to organize, sprang up continuously. As Max Meyer explained, the "union allegiance in such a shop is naturally weak," and its immigrant staff were often "only too ready to accept employment below union standards."[59] Non-union shops maintained their competitive edge in this way, and those who cooperated with the union rightly complained that their interests could suffer as a result.[60] One of the key points of debate during the 1916 meetings of the ILGWU and the Ladies' Waist and Dress Manufacturers' Association was how to address this problem. Julius Henry Cohen, counsel for the Association questioned: "What we want to know is what is the Union going to do to make the Union cover the entire industry? What does it intend to do to make the standards already existing enforceable and enforced throughout the industry?"[61] The vehemence of their disagreement on issues—wages, hours, and the relative failings of the other party—in the minutes of the conference is sometimes palpable. Yet, even if disputes were seemingly deadlocked, the existence of the forum, and the presence of discussion, bargaining and compromise, was an important step in addressing the rights of workers.

Despite the inroads made by unions, sweatshops were once again a serious problem during the financial crisis of the Great Depression. "Even the strongest unions were placed on the defensive, able to do little more than slow the downward turn of wages," wrote Joel Seidman in *The Needle Trades*. He continued, "Scarcely able to resist, they watched the emergence of sweatshop conditions in the industry comparable to those of the nonunion era a generation earlier."[62] "Women are not mean, but getting clothes cheaply has become a sort of game," wrote journalist Marjorie Howard in 1933. Consumers, she continued, "… do not realize what it means to other women working in the sweatshops." According to Howard, higher price points relieved suffering of workers.[63] By 1941, conditions seemed to have improved, as M. D. C. Crawford observed that the word sweatshop "stands for an evil condition somewhat vague in outline"—a sight unfamiliar.[64] Regulations, such as child labor legislation and the Fair Labor Standards Act of 1938, as well as the persistence of unions, helped to ameliorate the worst abuses and make sweatshops the "vague" entity Crawford had described.

"Only a Pollyanna would say that perfection had been reached," said the *New York Times* in 1939, "but the garment industry can count on at least two things: employers do not lock out their employees, and when workers decide to sit down it is not inside a factory, but around a conference table."[65] In marked contrast to tenement slums, the ILGWU of the mid-twentieth century provided cooperative housing to some of its members, in addition to health care, and regulated conditions of employment.[66] The union, too, also helped assure proper wages for the work its members performed. Nan Robertson described the union's method of bargaining in 1956:

> The labor cost of each new style is hammered out behind locked doors between manufacturers and the International Ladies' Garment Workers' Union. Every buttonhole, pleat, collar, pocket and seam must be priced. The sum of these prices is what the machine operator will receive for making the garment.[67]

Of the ILGWU's many efforts, perhaps the one best remembered by the populace is its union label campaign. Meant as a visual certification of labor standards, former ILGWU President David Dubinsky characterized it as the "signature" of union members.[68] [See "At a glance: Labels: Advocacy and awareness" for further discussion of early mid-twentieth-century labeling initiatives.]

History repeating: The resurgence of sweatshops, subcontracting, and the "runaway shop"

Of sweatshops, M. D. C. Crawford had previously noted that, "the nature of the industry is such that without a constant surveillance the evil might return."[69] Crawford's words were prophetic. Sweatshops experienced a major resurgence both in occurrence and public awareness in the 1980s and 1990s, internationally, as well as domestically, with an estimated 3,000 sweatshops in the New York area alone in 1987.[70] A decade later another source put the figure of workers in sweatshops at 100,000, with 70 percent of those in Los Angeles.[71] Targets of exposés and protests included The Gap, Guess?, Nike, and memorably television host Kathie Lee Gifford, whose Wal-Mart clothing brand was associated with child labor and sweatshop conditions in Honduras, as well as allegations of unpaid labor in a New York factory.[72] In Los Angeles, SK Fashions so grossly violated labor laws by keeping their Thai workers imprisoned in its factory that the press likened it to modern-day slavery.[73] The union journal *Justice* reported that in one Indonesian factory workers toiled for an appalling 85 hours a week but made less than $1 each day.[74]

A strong sense of *déjà vu* pervades even a cursory perusal of press coverage at this time—writers noted the similarities, as did worried union officials. The President of UNITE, Jay Mazur, cautioned against "a replay of turn-of-the-century conditions."[75] In investigations into the factories that produced for Federated and May department stores, UNITE discovered "sub-minimum wages, child labor, sexual harassment, overtime without pay, locked fire exits, and industrial homework,"[76] a list of offenses which could easily be a century old. "Good union jobs can't exist in a sea of sweatshops," wrote one article, "we'll be drowned by the competition,"[77] a statement echoing the problems of union versus non-union shops voiced by people like Abraham Bisno in the early twentieth century. Low standards were detrimental to the entire industry, foreign and domestic. New York garment worker Nelly Pacheco told the union publication, *UNITE!*: "Working conditions in my shop were fair until sweatshops mushroomed in the Garment District. Sleazy competition forced our employer to cut wages, stop paying overtime, and abuse his workers just to stay in business."[78] When UNITE formed in 1995, it included as part of its mission statement a commitment to global labor advocacy.[79] "Either workers' standards go up throughout the world," it argued, "or our own standards go down."[80]

Jacob Riis recalled that the tenement sweatshops of late nineteenth-century New York created the "economical conditions" that prompted a "manufacturing friend to boast that New York can 'beat the world' on cheap clothing."[81] Today, New York can no longer "beat the world." In search for the highest profits, the majority of garment manufacturing now takes place far outside of its limits. Factories and shops like the one in Figure 5.4, in Delhi, India, have become the new norm—or rather, a return to the old, merely a new incarnation of a persistent problem. The small and crowded shop is reminiscent of some of the conditions that Riis and others observed during the nineteenth century. The obvious youth of the worker in the foreground clearly illustrates the continuing problem of child labor in garment production. The notion of "apprenticeships" still complicates the problem of child labor in the industry. As a 1994 US Department of Labor report discussed, the word's connotation is good—"learning the skills and disciplines of an occupation, which will be his or her lifelong trade." If legitimate, apprenticeships can be

Figure 5.4 Young worker in a small factory in Old Delhi, Delhi, India, February 2008. Photograph © Paul Prescott/Shutterstock.com.

very beneficial, but it remains "one of the most controversial forms of labor" because the term can be easily used as a façade for child labor abuses.[82] Likewise, unfair, unethical and sometimes downright abusive treatment continues to plague the industry. Recent research on factories in Tamil Nadu, India uncovered severe ethical violations with regard to labor practices. Female garment workers, some of them children, contend with long hours and little earnings, often deceived by promises of a dowry payment that fails to materialize.[83] Although a century has passed, little seems to have materially changed, besides location.

While we may see this trend as pervasive now, production has been moving abroad for most of the second half of the twentieth century. High import levels were prominent in the periodic press releases on garment industry conditions published by the International Ladies' Garment Workers' Union in both the 1970s, when they noted an "erosion" of domestic apparel production and in the 1990s, by which time the pattern seemed fully established.[84] According to *Women's Wear Daily*, as of 2012, 85 percent of apparel for the US market was produced outside its borders.[85] Within the industry, however, this is far from a new phenomenon. Lower costs of production have always lured manufacturers to move. As noted earlier, mill owners moved their mills to the southern United States in the late nineteenth and early twentieth centuries in response to labor cost pressures. Manufacturers likewise followed suit in the early twentieth century, leaving cities like New York in search of more "favorable" conditions. The 1925 publication, *The Clothing and Textile Industries in New York and Its Environs, Present Trends and Probable Future Developments* discussed the trend of manufacturers fleeing the city: "The chief motive for moving … is the desire to escape from the union, and to secure cheap and docile labor."[86] Businesses that relocate for this reason are sometimes referred to as "runaway shops." According to Joel Seidman, this "out-of-town movement is a phase of the search for cheap labor that has gone on virtually without interruption since the needle trades developed."[87]

Similarly, subcontracting of work is another practice that has a long history within the garment industry.[88] In 1925, New York researchers complained of the industry's use of "contractors or sub-manufacturers" and the "intense competition … with consequent reduction in prices sometimes even below production cost" it generated.[89] The problem has been exacerbated as contractors and sub-contractors have moved farther afield. The sub-contracting from employer or manufacturer to middleman "sweater" is still prevalent. In an interview with the *New York Times,* Robert B. Reich, US Secretary of Labor under the Clinton administration, described the problems inherent in "networks of contractors and specialized subcontractors" which exist as part of the "the garment 'food chain'." A brand might contract to a manufacturing company, which in turn farms out parts of production to someone else, making the chain more and more convoluted—and harder to monitor.[90] Yet, subcontracting has endured partly because it makes it easier to pass the buck on responsibility to the contracted factories. "The inside manufacturer disclaimed all responsibility for the evils of the sweatshop," wrote Benjamin Stolberg in the chronicle of the garment industry, *Tailor's Progress*, "insisting that he was not the employer of the workers in the contract shop."[91]

Awareness and action: Combating poor labor practices

Combating the opaqueness of the garment supply chain requires effort. Writer Kelsey Timmerman went so far as to trace the origins of his clothing back to the places and people who made them. His unique endeavor "cost … a lot of things, not the least of which was … consumer innocence."[92] The loss of consumer innocence is in many ways a good thing, but unfortunately, it sometimes takes catastrophe to lift the veil. In 2013, Amy DuFault, a fashion writer covering sustainability, created a shirt to benefit a worker advocacy group, Clean Clothes Campaign, which read "Spectrum & Ali & Tazreen & Rana," with the understanding that "the shirt wouldn't make sense to most people." Those names reference factories involved in a spate of recent tragedies that have brought the plight of garment industry workers to the forefront, in much the same way as did the Triangle Shirtwaist Company fire of 1911, heretofore the industry's most notorious workplace accident. DuFault turned her anger to action, with the hope that the action begets awareness.[93]

There are many parallels between the modern-day manufacturing disasters and the Triangle fire. During the fire at Ali Enterprises, in Pakistan, which claimed the lives of close to 300 in September 2012, workers faced locked exits and barred windows. That year Pakistan had two industrial fires, in quick succession, the other killing 25 people at a shoe factory.[94] As Ali's facilities had recently been deemed safe by inspectors, the tragedy also laid bare the shortcomings of monitoring systems. According to the *New York Times*, the visit was pre-announced and workers "coached to lie about their working conditions, under threat of dismissal."[95] About two months later, a fire at Tazreen Fashions in Bangladesh claimed the lives of over 100.[96] Apparel workers at Spectrum Garments, in 2005, and Rana Plaza, in 2013, both in Bangladesh, were victims as collapsed.[97] Some writers have rightly noted the similarities of these recent tragedies with the collapse (later followed by a fire among the ruins) of the Pemberton Mill in Lawrence, Massachusetts in 1860[98]—a building that was by all accounts thoroughly "unsound," and unable to bear the load of machinery and the workforce. Shortly after that tragedy, the *London Times* issued the following caution, which is just as applicable today as it was then:

> Let the calamity be a warning to manufacturers and architects throughout the world. Too much care cannot be expended on structures in which the lives of hundreds are exposed day after day amid the unavoidable dangers of machinery and steam.[99]

With over 1,000 victims at Rana Plaza alone, figures far dwarf the fatalities associated with their historical predecessors. The recent list of fires and accidents is shocking, but they are only the *most recent*. A fire at the Chowdhury Knitwear Factory in 2000, for instance, also located in Bangladesh, killed 51 workers, some of whom were children. In another obvious parallel to Triangle, a number jumped fatally "out the windows to escape the flames."[100] A decade earlier, 80 employees of a Chinese raincoat factory met a similar fate.[101]

Events such as those described above may spur discussion—and even action—but the problem is entrenched. There are few obvious answers, much less simple ones. Labor activist and advocate Charles Kernaghan, who has been at the forefront of discussion on these topics since the 1990s, recently told *Women's Wear Daily* that when it comes to labor conditions and workers' rights "we are racing backward."[102] And it is not just regression, as Kernaghan noted, but on some levels conditions have worsened. As he pointed out, "garment workers in Bangladesh earn less than one-tenth of the wages earned over 100 years ago in New York."[103]

Awareness of these issues is crucial. Naomi Gross, Assistant Chair of the Fashion Merchandising Management program at the Fashion Institute of Technology, thinks that understanding can stem from what she called the "story-telling piece," citing the efforts of company Eileen Fisher as a good example of this approach. According to Gross, media, particularly social media, can help us connect to the manufacturing process. When you buy a garment, Gross says, "you're not just buying a garment … you're buying into an understanding of the supply chain." She encourages her students—and consumers—to "make that connection between the product you're buying and who, not even where, but *who* actually was involved in making it." Gross believes that this will make the product more meaningful to the consumer.[104] Garment labels are another method proposed to raise consumer awareness, as organizations such as the New York Dress Institute (see "At a glance: Labels: Advocacy and awareness") and the ILGWU did in the past.

Experts realize that it takes more than awareness to address the endemic poor labor practices of the garment and textile industry, but they have struggled to find lasting solutions. As Jay Mazur, then president of UNITE, lamented in 1995, we are witnessing "the growth of the global economy without global laws" with regard to labor.[105] In the 1990s, his union had a five-point plan to fight sweatshops: "retailer responsibility; stepped-up enforcement including confiscation of goods; basic labor standards for overseas production; laws that don't discourage undocumented workers from asserting their rights; and consumer refusal to purchase sweatshop goods."[106] Over a decade later, Bruce Rayner echoed similar statements to *Women's Wear Daily*.[107] Phrases like "Corporate Social Responsibility" and "Codes of Conduct" are often bandied about. In the 1990s, many apparel companies adopted such codes in response to the growing backlash against sweatshop exploitation, but even as they grew in number, experts noted the difficulty of monitoring and enforcing.[108] Many observers believe enforcement efforts are flawed and ineffective.[109] Likewise, a labor department report in 1996 cautioned not to view the codes as a "panacea."[110] Charles Kernaghan put it more blatantly: "Voluntary corporate codes of conduct do not work!" He called them "one of the great scams that allowed outsourcing to proliferate across many developing countries that have no concrete intention to respect internationally recognized worker rights and safety standards."[111]

For organizations like the Clean Clothes Campaign, which advocates for the rights of workers, and for all groups and individuals working toward reform, it is an uphill battle. There seems to be a consensus that the approach must be multi-faceted. Robert Ross, in his detailed study of historical and modern sweatshops, *Slaves to Fashion*, proposed that the industry follow "three pillars of decency," which revolve around unionization, governmental policy, and the efforts of reformers and consumers.[112]

It should be noted, however, that there does exist another point-of-view on labor issues. Some economists, such as Jeffrey Sachs and Paul Krugman, have argued that sweatshops have benefit in raising the economies of poor countries.[113] Timmerman noted a similar realization about child labor in his observations of life in developing countries. Where is the morality in outlawing child labor if it means that the child and its family starve?[114] The fact that workers are caught between starvation and a sweatshop, argued eco-fashion scholar Sandy Black, makes for a "a complex situation which is ethically unacceptable."[115] Ross, too, has refuted what he termed "the better than" defense.[116] Advocating sweatshop conditions because other options or consequences are worse is "uncivilized, unrestrained by moral boundary," Ross maintained: "'Better than' is a slippery slope."[117]

Designers and clothing companies, too, have searched for solutions that provide greater assurance of ethical treatment of workers, often settling on those that involve the building of relationships. One practice that has been adopted by a number of designers working within sustainable fashion is collaboration with *cooperatives* or *collectives* of artisans, often women, living and working in impoverished areas. There is a long-standing practice of sewing circles, in which women gather together to sew for personal or charitable purposes. Likewise, cooperatives that benefit local and artisanal labor are not new ideas. During the 1960s and 1970s, a woman's cooperative based in Appalachia, historically one of the poorest regions of the United States, rose to prominence. The Mountain Artisans, who made the patchwork skirt seen in Figure 5.5, were honored with a Coty Award in 1972 for their contribution to American fashion. Operating as a non-profit, Mountain Artisans recruited the West Virginia women and gave them "the designs, the patterns and the materials," while the women supplied their needle skills.[118] A renewed interest in traditional crafts, such as the time-honored quilting techniques practiced by the Appalachian women, was linked to the burgeoning environmentalist movement, and likely contributed to the group's visibility and success. Their clothing was sold in high-end New York stores such as Bergdorf Goodman.

Modern cooperatives were involved in the production of many of the contemporary garments featured in *Eco-Fashion: Going Green*, including the designs by Alabama Chanin, Figure 2.8 (rural Alabama); John Patrick, Plate 6 (Peru); and Kate Brierley, plate 12 (Zanzibar). Since 1999, Carlos Miele has been collaborating with the Coopa-Roca collective in his native Brazil in the making of his luxury fashion line. Miele's partnership with the women of the Coopa-Roca not only provides employment to local artisans, but also preserves traditional Brazilian crafts. The evening dress in Figure 5.6, called *Fuxico*, is named for the Portuguese word for "gossip," but the word is also used to refer to the intricate rosettes, seen over the body of the dress, that are hand-stitched by the circle of women who converse as they work.[119]

Establishing trade partnerships is another popular means of supporting sustainable practices. The cover story of the January 1993 union publication *Justice* asked, "Where in the World is Fast Buck Dress?" Framed as a board game, "The Trade Game," had players trot the globe in search of the lowest production costs. Among the game's "rules": "Players seek out the lowest possible wages regardless of labor or human rights abuses. (Use of unions by workers is considered cheating.)" "If you don't like this game," read

Figure 5.5 Mountain Artisans, patchwork skirt, multicolor cotton, c. 1968, USA. Collection of The Museum at FIT, 92.171.6. Gift of Michael Dykeman. Photograph © The Museum at FIT.

Figure 5.6 Installation shot from *Eco-Fashion: Going Green* (The Museum at FIT, 2010). Carlos Miele, *Fuxico* evening gown, tan and ivory silk, Spring 2008, USA. Collection of The Museum at FIT, 2010.48.1. Gift of Carlos Miele. Photograph © The Museum at FIT.

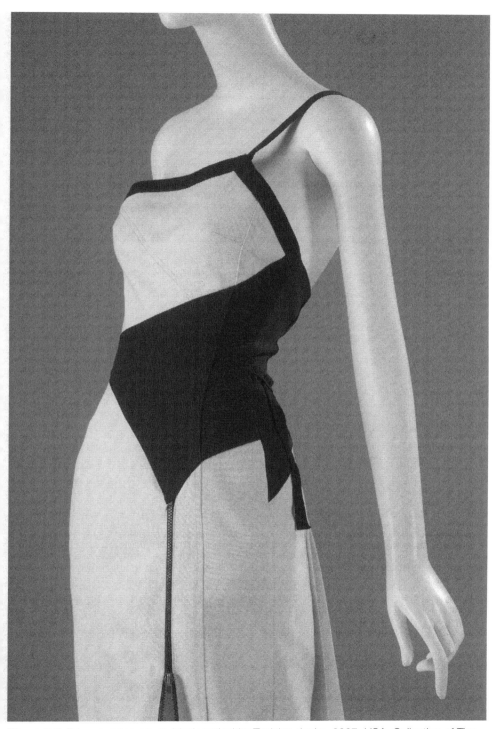

Figure 5.7 Edun, evening gown, black and white Tunisian denim, 2007, USA. Collection of The Museum at FIT, 2010.7.1. Gift of EDUN. Photograph © The Museum at FIT.

the Manufacturer's Warranty, "return in its original packaging and we'll send you our new version called 'Fair Trade.' This game differs in that workers have the right to organize for better wages and conditions, reducing the incentive for firms to move."[120] In principle, *fair trade* overlaps with concepts related to collectives, as both provide employment for workers and fair wages through an ongoing trade relationship.[121] A 2003 *Women's Wear Daily* article attempted to elucidate the meaning of fair trade to its readers, as it was often "misunderstood or unknown" to manufacturers. The trade journal summarized fair trade as follows: "in addition to wages, fair trade promotes cooperative workplaces; consumer education; environmental sustainability; financial and technical support; respect for cultural identity; and public accountability."[122]

Committed to such principles, rock musician Bono (of U2) and his wife, Ali Hewson, in 2005, formed the prominent eco-label, Edun, with the belief that they could improve the lives of African workers through trade. The one-of-a-kind Edun dress in Figure 5.7 was produced from organic cotton from Tunisia, one of the regions in Africa within which Edun still works. Central to the brand are strong ethical principles of fair trade and connection to communities that produce organic cotton. Since its founding, the brand has diversified the network of communities with which they work to include a number in South America and Asia.[123] Africa remains at the core of their business, however; according to Edun's website, only 15 percent of the brand's Spring 2014 collection was manufactured elsewhere.[124] Hewson, in 2006, explained her motivations for focusing on fair trade clothing, telling *The Times* (London), "I really don't want to wear clothes created from someone else's despair."[125]

Conclusion

Sustainability in the context of labor practices means consideration for the health and ethical well-being of workers in all stages of garment production—from the harvesting of raw material to the preparation of a finished garment. For a garment to be sustainably made, workers must have a clean and safe working environment. They should receive a living wage for the work they perform, and be treated fairly by their employers. In short, sustainable clothing is clothing that is not produced at the cost of the suffering and mistreatment of those who make it.

Child labor, sweatshops, subcontracted work, and opaqueness in the production lines, plagued the industry in its earliest days, and their continued presence demonstrates history of the very worst kind repeating. Conditions have improved at textile mills and factories in the United States and other Western countries, in large part due to regulation and the efforts of unions. At issue now, however, is that the Western world produces less and less of its own clothing. The garment industry, like many others, has increasingly moved its production overseas. Abuses, like those that plagued the American garment industry in the nineteenth century, are not uncommon at foreign garment plants. Today the low wages, long hours, and poor, unsafe, or unsanitary working conditions faced by textile workers of the past are the norm for their twenty-first century counterparts—in countries around the globe that lack stringent regulations. Conditions thousands of miles away are harder to monitor, and often easier for consumers to ignore.

All of the methods suggested by designers and experts for improving the lot of industry workers—whether by raising the wages and standards abroad, creating better monitoring solutions, supporting artisanal labor, or ensuring fair trade—will raise the ticket price of the clothing we buy. As consumers, it is necessary to acclimate to this fact. Consider the figure presented by Charles Kernaghan in 1996, that a sweatshop worker might be paid "less than 1 percent of the price of the garment in the United States."[126] Yet, if we pay more for those products, we take a step toward ensuring ethical wages and treatment for those who supply fashion for the world. "It's making people aware of the story of clothes," Ali Hewson told *Vogue* of the origins of the brand Edun,[127] but her statement could be broadly applied—to the past and the present. The story of clothes begins with people, and how they are treated matters.

Suggestions for Further Reading:

Bisno, A. (1967), *Abraham Bisno: Union Pioneer*, Madison: University of Wisconsin Press.
Byerly, V. (1986), *Hard Times Cotton Mill Girls: Personal Histories of Womanhood and Poverty in the South*, Ithaca, NY: ILR Press.
McEvoy, A. F. (1995), "The Triangle Shirtwaist factory fire of 1911: Social change, industrial accidents, and the evolution of common-sense causality," *Law & Social Inquiry* 20 (2): 621–51.
Priddy, A. (F. K. Brown) (1911), *Through the Mill, the Life of a Mill Boy*, Boston, New York and Chicago: The Pilgrim Press.
Riis, J. (1957), *How the Other Half Lives: Studies Among the Tenements of New York*, New York: Hill and Wang, Inc.
Ross, R. J. S. (2007), *Slaves to Fashion: Poverty and Abuse in the New Sweatshops*, Ann Arbor: The University of Michigan Press.
"The Sweat-Shop Problem" (1895), *New York Times*, December 17.

At a glance: Madeleine Vionnet, Elizabeth Hawes, and Max Meyer: Historical perspectives on labor practices

While the history of the garment industry is rife with bad labor practice, it is heartening to recognize that there have also been industry leaders who maintained and encouraged good practice and fair treatment of workers—whether in their own ateliers or in the industry at large.

Madeleine Vionnet

Madeleine Vionnet is one of the most lauded fashion designers in history; her name is virtually synonymous with the pioneering use of bias cut in the 1930s. The image in

Figure 5.8 Madeleine Vionnet, dress, ivory silk georgette, c. 1931, France. Collection of The Museum at FIT, P83.39.7. Museum purchase. Photograph © The Museum at FIT.

Figure 5.8, a stunning example of her work during that decade, is typical of the neutral color palette she favored, as well as her celebrated craftsmanship. Cecil Beaton recalled, "Vionnet was a genius in the way she used her materials." So fluid were her designs, that "women dressed by her were like moving sculpture."[128]

According to writer M. D. C. Crawford, Vionnet's beautiful dresses were not the only legacy for which she deserved praise. He wrote: "she had a deep and sincere interest in the welfare of her workers, and even in her greatness she remembered the conditions of those who worked with their hands for a living. She never overlooked their interests in favor of her own profits."[129] Vionnet had begun working as a seamstress at age 11, experiencing firsthand the poor working conditions that existed not only in American ready-to-wear factories, but also in the Parisian dressmaking industry. Vionnet's treatment of her employees at the atelier Vionnet et Cie was indeed as innovative as her clothing. Scholar Betty Kirke, who did exhaustive research on Vionnet, is right to call it progressive. Before others were doing so, Vionnet offered her employees the unique perks of coffee breaks and paid time off, in addition to benefits, which included complementary medical and dental care, as well as maternity leave.[130]

Max Meyer

Max Meyer worked in ready-to-wear manufacturing in New York City, where he emigrated as a child. He spent his career at A. Beller & Co., which manufactured high-style ready-to-wear based on foreign models. As was the norm in that era, Meyer began work as a boy of 14 in 1890. He later recalled one of the difficult tasks assigned to him: "one of my jobs ... was to take bundles of cut garments over to the East Side and into the filthy tenements ... I can still recall the sights of poverty, misery, and human degradation."[131]

Like Vionnet, this early experience seems to have shaped Meyer, who became a leading labor mediator and arbitrator, remaining active in such pursuits even after his retirement from industry in 1929.[132] Meyer was also an advocate of education, active in the beginnings of the Central High School of Needle Trades (now High School of Fashion Industries) and the Fashion Institute of Technology, both in New York.[133] He championed cooperation between unions and employers: "The continued existence of any agreement, new or old, is dependent on two strong organizations, a workers' union and an employers' association, each respecting the other," he wrote in an article for the *New York Times* in 1915, under the modest byline Max Meyer, One of the Manufacturers.[134]

Elizabeth Hawes

During her lifetime, Elizabeth Hawes experienced many facets of the fashion industry. She once worked for a house that made its profits copying designs from Parisian couturiers such as Vionnet. She also worked as a fashion journalist for *The New Yorker* under the pen name "Parasite." Later, she was the head of her own custom dressmaking salon in New York, Hawes, Inc. During World War II, she was a war worker and once served in the education division of the United Auto Workers union.[135] Hawes had a deep interest in economics and "labor problems," which stemmed as far back as her days as a student at Vassar College.[136]

Sharply intelligent, Hawes was as prolific a writer as she was a designer. Her book *Why Women Cry, or Wenches With Wrenches* recounted her experiences within the wartime aeronautical industry, but also pondered the subject of the balance of women's labor inside and outside the home. Her most famous book *Fashion Is Spinach* is a memorable critique of the fashion industry. In its pages, she mentions the plight of immigrant garment workers—"the skilled craftsmen and women of the American couture." On Seventh Avenue, in New York City proper, workers "are organized, that hated word"—unionization hated by the industry because it ensured higher wages and a reasonable workday. Yet, Hawes also noted the continuing problem of unfair treatment: "Out of town they are sweated and exploited, kicked and underpaid." Hawes was not shy about pointing out the flaws in an industry in which workers still "hive in cellars where they get [US] $9 a week for fifty-four hours of sewing up your [US] $4.95."[137]

Suggestions for Further Reading:

Crawford, M. D. C. (1941), *The Ways of Fashion*, New York: G. P. Putnam's Sons.
Hawes, E. (1938), *Fashion Is Spinach*, New York: Random House.
Kirke, B. (1998), *Vionnet,* San Francisco: Chronicle Books.

At a glance: Labels: Advocacy and awareness

Phrases on a label tell us little, as writer Kelsey Timmerman discovered in his modern-day investigations into the origins of his clothing.[138] For consumers, it can be difficult to have a real concept of the conditions under which a piece of clothing was produced. Timmerman's observations highlighted a contemporary need for consumer awareness, but there has long been a recognized demand for greater transparency in garment production. Consumers' leagues in the early decades of the twentieth century advocated for labeling and other measures to guide the public. They felt that consumer knowledge was key to addressing the ills that plagued the industry.

The "real manufacturer is the woman who goes shopping," proclaimed Mrs Frederick Nathan, who was in 1912 the president of the Consumers' League of New York City. A National Consumers' League had existed since 1899, and had developed a label to mark certain goods made under accepted conditions and without the labor of children under 16. But as Florence Kelley, its 1925 General Secretary, noted, the adoption of such labels was not then widespread within the industry.[139]

The "Prosanis" label, a measure of the Joint Board of Sanitary Control, in tandem with the ILGWU, was an updated version of this idea, conceived as a tool, or a guideline, for shoppers to ensure that work conditions were safe, fair, and as the name indicates, clean. It was also meant to benefit those manufacturers who maintained "civilized industrial conditions" over the cheaper sweatshop alternative.[140] The question was:

Given two frocks of equal style and value, will the shopper care enough for the working members of her own sex who have bent over whirling machines to fashion it for her, to say, "I shall take the one with the Prosanis label: I know it means that no worker has been exploited to make it for me"?[141]

Consumer advocates hoped the answer would be yes. The development of the "Prosanis" label was not just about the conditions of the workers, however. It was also imbued with the public fear of tuberculosis transmission from worker to consumer via purchased goods. "Consumers," Mrs Nathan had written some years before the introduction of the "Prosanis" label, "do not go about inculcating their fellow-citizens with tuberculosis germs but, by purchasing clothing made in sweatshops, they encourage conditions which lead directly to the same results."[142] The pulmonary infection tuberculosis was linked in the public mind to the garment industry, and its sweatshop workers and tenement dwellers were prone to the disease. By 1925, according to one article, New York City was the source of three-quarters of ready-made "dresses, coats and suits,"[143] swelling concern over the issue. The label was to be "a guarantee of protection, alike for shoppers and workers, against disease-bearing garments."[144] Sentiment related to consumer awareness and empowerment against sweatshops continued through the 1930s. It was championed by figures like Eleanor Roosevelt, who likewise supported labeling initiatives,[145] and fashion show events were organized during the 1920s and 1930s to draw attention to ethically produced clothing.

Although it did not have the connotation of consumer fear, the "New York Creations" campaign of the New York Dress Institute in the 1940s served a similar purpose to that of the relatively short-lived "Prosanis" consumer label. Funded by manufacturer and union,[146] the New York Dress Institute was at its core a promotional body for the New York garment industry, so its label and its motives were not wholly altruistic. Marketing New York's style cachet, initial advertisements emphasized high quality of craftsmanship and attractive design, facts apparent in the elegant evening dress in Figure 5.9.[147] Its symmetrical floral print is pattern matched, for instance, and hem hand sewn.

However, the "New York Creations" labels did signify that marked garments were all locally manufactured and adhered to union standards of fair labor and quality. The plan, which went into effect after July 1941, involved the cooperation of the 800 manufacturer members of the New York Dress Institute, and the International Ladies' Garment Workers' Union, who set the labor standards adhered to, and whose moniker was featured alongside the "New York Creations" logo.[148] As *Harper's Bazaar* explained:

[The label] assures you that your dress has been made under sanitary working conditions. A solid guarantee that no one has worked long hours overtime, and no one has been unfairly paid for his or her labor, no one has been gypped to turn you out so smart and pretty for Saturday night.

"New York Creations" were also "a unique step in the history of employee-employer cooperation," according the magazine.[149]

Figure 5.9 New York Dress Institute, evening dress, printed red rayon crepe, rhinestones, seed pearls, c. 1941. Collection of The Museum at FIT, 76.100.11. Gift of Mrs. Harold E. Thompson. Photograph © The Museum at FIT.

As the above implies, unions and industry do not always agree; "friendly enemies" was the way one manufacturer preferred to characterize the relationship.[150] But the fact that workers in the Western world are protected by better regulations and have unions and consumer groups to advocate for them—whether they always succeed in their efforts or not—is an advantage that many foreign workers or illegal domestic workers simply do not have.

Suggestions for Further Reading:

Bulletin: The Consumers' League of New York, 4, no. 5, May 1925.
"A Label and What It Means" (1941), *Harper's Bazaar*, September 1: 96.
Nathan, Mrs. F. (1912), "Real Manufacturer is the Woman Who Goes Shopping," *New York Times*, December 29.

6
TREATMENT OF ANIMALS

Introduction

This chapter will explore the historical use of animal products in fashion from the nineteenth century to the present, discussing arguments both for and against their use, as well as the emergence of cruelty-free alternatives. Throughout modern history, we have adorned our bodies with many animal materials such as leather, wool, and silk, as well as tortoiseshell, ivory, and reptile skins. [See "At a glance: Tortoiseshell, ivory, and reptile skins" for more on the latter.] This chapter, however, focuses on two key categories of animal product use: feathers and furs. Intriguingly, it was feathers—not furs—that sparked greater outrage during the late nineteenth and early twentieth centuries, and the chapter begins with a discussion of the debate over the use of feathers as a fashion embellishment. A subsequent section explores the wearing of fur during the nineteenth and early twentieth centuries—as the sentiment against fur slowly brewed, culminating in outcry against fur trapping in the 1920s. The discussion of fur trapping is followed by a short overview of fur farming, bringing the largely chronological discussion of fur use to the 1950s. The rise of the anti-fur movement from the 1960s through the present, and an overview of sustainable, or mediating, alternatives to the use of animal products conclude the consideration of what remains an extremely contentious issue.

Nineteenth-century feather debate

Feathers have been popular embellishments for centuries, but reached a peak in demand as millinery adornments during the late nineteenth and early twentieth centuries, alarming many ornithologists, environmentalists, and animal lovers. In 1886, the zoologist and ornithologist, J. A. Allen speculated that:

> In this country of 50,000,000 inhabitants, half, or 25,000,000, may be said to belong to what some one has forcibly termed the 'dead-bird wearing gender,' of whom at least 10,000,000 are not only of bird-wearing age, but—judging from what we see on our streets, in public assemblies and public conveyances—also of bird-wearing proclivities.

Figure 6.1 Berthe Tally, hat, woven straw, grey (possibly gull) feathers in the shape of wings, c. 1904, France. Collection of The Museum at FIT, P84.14.3. Museum purchase. Photograph © The Museum at FIT.

Even with a conservative estimate of only one bird per woman, "'made over' so as to do service for more than a single season," he continued, "still what an annual sacrifice of bird-life is entailed!"[1]

In February of 1886, an oft-cited letter from ornithologist Frank M. Chapman appeared in the publication *Forest and Stream*. Based on observations conducted during two walks in New York City, Chapman calculated that 77 percent of hats were decorated with feathers. While Chapman's "appended list of native birds" contained 40 types of bird, including the common tern (a seabird) and songbirds, such as the robin and blue jay, he noted that many feathers or bird parts could not be identified.[2] Part of the difficulty in identifying which birds had been used was the popularity of "composite plumes" in the late nineteenth and early twentieth centuries. "Composite plumes," read an 1907 article in the *New York Times* (via the *London Chronicle*), "are the most fashionable, and wings are of such remarkable size and hue that it is obvious that no birds could have supplied the plumage."[3] The decoration on the hat shown in Figure 6.1, from the collection of the Museum at FIT, is likely a variation on the idea described above. While the feathers may be derived from the same bird or type of bird, liberties have been taken in forming the dramatic arrangement on a built wing base.

An article appearing in *Science* described the complexity involved in determining "the actual statistics of bird-slaughter for millinery purposes." Although "everywhere where women are seen" is "evidence of its enormous extent," they could provide only limited estimates from various parts of the country, primarily the East Coast. The figures, while hard to substantiate, were high. Of herons or egrets, whose slaughter by and large seemed to attract the most publicity during this period, they noted: "the statistics ... could they be presented, would be of startling magnitude. We only know that colonies numbering hundreds, and even thousands, of pairs, have been simply annihilated."[4] The article continued: "But scarcely a bird can be named ... that is not to be met with as an appendage of the female head-dress."[5] Millinery advertisements, they noted, also attested to the volume of the bird materials on the market. Hat makers and vendors were plentiful, and so too their advertised goods.[6] Millinery manufacturer and importer Thomas H. Wood and Co., for instance, included in its offerings for 1897–8 "a full and attractive line of ostrich tips, plumes, and boas, birds' wings, quills, fancy feather novelties."[7]

Throughout the late nineteenth and early twentieth centuries, *Vogue* and other fashion magazines, as well as trade publications, readily covered shifting style trends in millinery, and corresponding shifts in demand for different types of bird. A "novelty" for fall of 1897, for instance, was pheasant bodies "placed in a position of such natural repose that one is almost afraid to approach it lest it might take its flight from its nest of velvet."[8] The cavalier descriptions of plumage trends—the variations on wings, beaks, and bodies—made these "fashion journals ... not altogether pleasant reading to bird lovers or to persons of refined or humane instincts," according to *The Auk*.[9]

Noting the dwindling numbers of many varieties of bird, concerned citizens began public appeals to stop, or at the very least, reduce the use of these feathers. Their outrage, the formation of the Audubon Society in the latter half of the nineteenth century, and attempts at state and federal legislation to regulate the use of domestic plumage birds, and later the importation of foreign birds, all factored into a large-scale, widespread campaign for animal protection. Some of the loudest voices in opposition to the wearing of bird feathers belonged to members of the Audubon Society, whose name was derived from that of naturalist John James Audubon. However, the Audubon Society was not alone in its efforts. The American Ornithologists' Union (AOU), whose Committee on the Protection of North American Birds was organized in 1886, sought to "awaken public interest on behalf of birds, by giving information as to the extent of their destruction for millinery and other needless purposes." The Audubon Society, they categorized as "an outgrowth of the Committee's work" and a "most efficient co-worker."[10]

The organization of the first Audubon chapter was under the auspices of the nature periodical, *Forest and Stream*. In February of 1886, the editors ventured their idea for the new organization. Three goals were listed:

These objects shall be to prevent, so far as possible (1) the killing of any wild birds not used for food; (2) the destruction of nests or eggs of any wild bird, and (3) the wearing of feathers as ornaments or trimming for dress.[11]

Forest and Stream later elaborated some of the ways in which they strove to meet the goals outlined in their formation. One important means was to educate and sway public opinion.[12] However, by 1888, this first society, initiated by George Bird Grinnell, was for all intents and purposes defunct.[13] The Audubon Society successfully reorganized in the late 1890s, starting in Massachusetts and moving forward to a number of other states.[14]

The motivations for their campaigning probably varied from person to person, but several refrains echoed in the discussion. The ethical quagmire, which saw species facing elimination at the cost of decoration, was an overriding factor. Those who studied nature also pointed to the crucial role that birds played in many eco-systems. Birds fed on insects, which in turn helped protect local crops.[15] One article described birds as "indispensible friends of agriculture."[16] According to conservationist T. Gilbert Pearson, however, it was their beauty that was loved best: "our affection springs rather from an appreciation of the aesthetic influence on our lives."[17] Those things considered, Frank Chapman, an active member of the Audubon Society, once conceded that: "This society recommends, as far as it recommends any feathers, the use of those belonging to edible birds,"[18] a category that perhaps seemed justifiable if it preserved so many others.

The Audubon Society and AOU worked not just to educate, but also to push forth legislative efforts. The AOU, for instance, as early as 1886, concerned itself in the legal aspect of the movement, by drafting and promoting a model law for bird protection at the state level.[19] They concerned themselves with fashion, as well. If women wore feathers because they were fashionable and beautiful, perhaps providing alternatives that met both qualifications would stem the trend? The ornithologist J. A. Allen argued that the milliners' livelihoods would not be materially injured if other materials were sold instead of birds.[20] Witmer Stone, in his report to the AOU in 1899, was pleased to report that "the milliners in many of our large cities have joined gladly with the Audubon Societies in exhibiting 'birdless hats' and some, notably Gimbel Brothers of Milwaukee and Philadelphia, have advocated in circulars and advertisements the abandonment of wild birds."[21] "Audubon Hats" were likewise promoted in New York City. Saks Fifth Avenue advertised them in October 1913.[22] Of some styles of "Audubon Hat," claimed one review, "The ribbon imitations of feather effects are said to be so clever that the hats lose nothing in stylish appearance by the lack of plumage."[23] Unfortunately, as Frank Graham, Jr. has noted, these hats had only marginal impact.[24]

Importantly though, the larger public was being made aware of the debate surrounding bird preservation. Much of this had to do with the coverage the movement received in the popular press, in magazines widely distributed and read by women. In 1875, *Harper's Bazar* published the seminal and stirring anti-plumage article, "The Slaughter of the Innocents," which railed against those who "decorated themselves with the spoils of the forest." Birds were beautiful creatures, but there was little beauty in them as hat adornment; they were "only ghosts of birds, mute warblers, little captives deprived of life and light and song." *Harper's Bazar's* notice is markedly earlier than many others in the popular press,[25] but the publication had by no means a perfect track record on this subject. It was at different junctures the source of criticism for its endorsement of feather fashions, and praise, for favorable coverage of the bird movement, by the ornithology publication, *The Auk*.[26]

Although *Vogue* actively reported on feather fashions, the publication did occasionally address the controversial nature of feathers, and the battle with bird lovers. Reporting the content of a humane society circular, and citing the *Boston Herald* as its source, the article "Woman's Cruel Folly," appeared in *Vogue* in March 1896. Its focus was on the white heron or egret, and the manner in which its feathers—the "*aigrettes*"—were obtained. The article described the end result in strong, graphic terms. "When the killing is finished and the few handfuls of coveted feathers have been plucked out, the slaughtered birds are left in a white heap to fester in the sun and wind, in sight of their orphaned young, that cry for food and are not fed."[27] Hunters desired the "feathers on the sides of the back" which were at their peak during its nesting time.[28] According to one source, 400 to 600 birds might be killed in one day's hunting.[29]

Egrets also attracted the attention of Edward Bok, editor of the *Ladies' Home Journal*, which by the end of his tenure in 1919 had circulation figures of over one million.[30] In his third-person autobiography, *The Americanization of Edward Bok*, he detailed his horror in discovering the manner in which the aigrette feather—as he called it, the "the most desired of all the feathered possessions of womankind"—was obtained, and printed damning photographs and descriptions of the cruelty in his magazine.[31] But instead of motivating their abandonment, the market continued to increase.[32] Bok wrote that a "truest woman-friend" told him: "A woman will regret that the mother-bird must be tortured and her babies starve, but she *will* have the aigrette. She simply trains herself to forget the origin."[33]

It was women wearers, consumers of fashion like the one cited by Bok, who often bore the wrath, criticism, and mockery of feather opponents and fashion writers. Were women fools, and inconsistent ones at that? In an 1887 *Good Housekeeping* article, an anonymous New York milliner ridiculed his clients who exhibited qualms about the heads of the birds that appeared on hats, but not other parts of the bird, or its feathers. "What geese women are," he was quoted: "Now, this very hat will be put aside by half a dozen women in succession because it has got the head and beak of a bird of paradise among its trimmings ... And then they turn around and buy a hat with a pair of wings or a bird's back or a breast on it."[34] Some writers were kinder to the female sex; women were ignorant, but not unfeeling. Their crime was committed "unwittingly."[35] Such writers wanted to believe the best of women, that "love of 'style' blinded their eyes."[36] Or perhaps they were indeed heartless, as claimed a brief article appearing in *Vogue* in 1897: "the case of birds versus woman is damning evidence of woman's inhumanity." In spite of the outcry against the wearing of feathers, "woman has continued to strut about in borrowed plumes."[37]

One feather that a woman could reportedly wear without compunction was that of the ostrich. Ostrich feathers were another common trim for hats throughout this period. "Women, civilized women, new and 'advanced' women, are all bitten with the craze, and show no satiety so far," wrote *Vogue* in 1895 of the demand for the plumes.[38] The ostrich feather was to remain in demand for nearly two more decades. Unlike many of the birds hunted to supply the millinery industry, ostriches could be farm-raised for feather harvesting. The birds were native to Africa, and farms there accounted for most of the feather volume, estimated in value at around $7,000,000.[39] By the beginning of the twentieth century, however, a number of the animals, albeit comparatively fewer, were being farmed in the United States, in places like Arizona and California.[40] As the ostrich was not killed for its feathers, it was removed from much of the controversy and legislation surrounding wild and songbirds, and even leading bird preservationists condoned their use. Their feathers, it was claimed, could be extracted without death or excess pain. "The Audubon societies," wrote *Vogue* in 1906, "regard ostrich feathers as legitimate as well as beautiful decoration, and approve them."[41] A 1907–8 souvenir catalog from California-based Cawston Ostrich Farm went to great pains to present its ostrich farm as humane. Ostriches were treated kindly over their 40 to 50 year approximate lifespan, claimed the farm's proprietors. The catalogue includes a full double page spread entitled, "Kind to Our Ostriches: Feathers from California May be Worn Without Compunction by Humane Women." It reprinted a communiqué to the *Los Angeles Times*, in which Mary E. Lovell, of the Pennsylvania SPCA, announced: "I can vouch for these feathers for I have visited the ostrich farm in California and found that there was no cruelty practiced there."[42]

According to Cawston's, feathers were not taken until the bird reached nine months of age, and then every nine months from then on—they were "plucked, or rather cut, for there is no pulling, merely a clipping of the quill about an inch from the body." The dried remaining quill was later removed from the bird, and the catalogue assured "there is no pain caused to the bird during the whole process of feather removal."[43] Yet, as Sarah Abrevaya Stein has pointed out, many women failed to differentiate between ostrich feathers and those feather varieties actually under legislation.[44] The Retail Millinery Association, concerned over this matter, printed a bulletin in 1917 hoping to educate women accordingly. Quoting Dr William Hornaday, a leading voice in the bird movement, the bulletin read: "There is no ban on any kind of ostrich feathers, and even the best bird conservationist may wear them in good conscience."[45]

In the early twentieth century, letters from both sides of the feather debate peppered the *New York Times*, and illustrate the polarizing nature of this argument.[46] The millinery industry, through outlets like trade publication *The Millinery Trade Review*, was persistent in its defense against what it characterized as persecution. Their words, sometimes eloquent and quick-witted, sought to portray the Audubon campaigns as at best, sentimental hogwash, and at worst, hypocritical and destructive. Noting the derivation of the society's name, they wrote: "Our fair friends who make much ado concerning the cruelty in the trapping and killing of birds for millinery adornments forget that it is equally cruel to kill and trap birds for illustrations in books on bird life …"[47] referring to Audubon's practice of killing birds as models for his now-famous tome *Birds of America*.[48] Although they tended to mock the society, they warned their constituents not to be blasé about its "efforts … to interfere with their business." Speaking of the Audubon Society's influence as malignant, they told readers, "the disease is spreading, the cankerous growth must be cut out of the millinery body politic."[49] At the mercy of fashion, the milliners "must supply what is demanded."[50] Plus, they noted, many popular trimmings were not from songbirds or exotic species, but from food animals: "It will interest those who have humanitarian scruples to know that the gayest plumage … comes from the humble barnyard, the poulterer's shop, and sportsmen's guns."[51] That the industry also provided work to many men and women was another touted point. Yet, said a writer in the *New York Times*:

> The pathetic tale of innumerable poor but honest girls who would starve if the egrets and the paradise birds were protected has lost its force because of the frequency with which folks have been reminded that even when feathers are not in style the trimming of hats continues.[52]

In its reports, *The Millinery Trade Review* played down threats to the aforementioned egret, a subject that gripped public attention. In 1899, *The Millinery Trade Review* published the opinion of a British consul on the subject of the hunting of Venezuelan egrets. He warned that at current rates, the population would decline rapidly: "He estimates that the number of birds killed in 1898 for this purpose was 1,538,738. No less than 870 birds have to be killed to produce less than two and a quarter pounds of the smaller feathers." This, scoffed the trade paper, was just "the usual Audubon 'scare' that the trade can use with profit to itself."[53] They also tried to assuage readers by discussing attempts to farm the egret, sometimes citing the ostrich as an example. If the egret could be successfully farmed perhaps women would have no compunction in wearing its feathers.[54] Scholar Robin Doughty, who has written extensively on the subject of bird feathers, has noted industry claims were "admixtures of fact and fiction." A marginal number of farms and the collection of dropped egret feathers did not stop hunters from killing the birds to obtain the best quality feathers.[55] Doughty has also noted that the trade's line of defense with regard to the egrets ultimately backfired, serving only to injure its cause.[56]

Indeed, some of the statements printed, and presumably endorsed, by *The Millinery Trade Review* were not just inconsistent, they were illogical. The publication reprinted an essay by feather worker Wanda Travis, the factory foreperson at the firm Wurzburger & Hecht, who argued that since fashions shift, "what is worn to-day will not be worn next year, which gives the birds ample time to multiply; and, since no one species is used continually, how can they become extinct?"[57] Walter Goodfellow, in an essay for *Feathers and Facts*, said he had heard similar statements with respect to the bird of paradise (Figure 6.2), whose numbers were grievously threatened by its popularity in fashion, but concluded, "we cannot delude ourselves that this will be so."[58]

Figure 6.2 This bird of paradise body was intended for millinery trimmings. Collection of The Museum at FIT. Photograph © The Museum at FIT.

"There is very little that fair woman wears that does not cost life, and if these Audubon notions were to be carried to extremes, we blush to think of the possibilities of her future appearance," argued *The Millinery Trade Review* in 1897.[59] Those extremes (of "vegetarianism") could include relinquishing not just feathers, but silk, leather, and fur.[60] It was a line of defense they carried back even earlier, when an 1886 article questioned whether those materials, and also tortoiseshell, reptile skins, and ivory, were any less cruel than feathers.[61] [See "At a glance: Tortoiseshell, ivory, and reptile skins.] "Why discriminate and be filled with sentimental concern for one and not for all?"[62]

It was to this point that the arguments of the millinery industry and its sympathizers often returned. If feathers were cruel, were not all animal products equally so? Why did a fur coat trouble a person's mind less than a feathered hat? And if we eat them, why shouldn't we wear them? In a letter to the editor of the *New York Times*, a writer identified as J. H. H. asked: "Do the Audubonites think it hurts a skylark more to be killed for adornment than it does a chicken for eating? Consistency, isn't it? And how about the fur-bearing animals, the seals, minks, and all the others—doesn't it hurt them to be killed for adornment?"[63]

Within the millinery industry, fur, too, was not an uncommon trimming for women's headgear. The December 1897 issue of *The Millinery Trade Review* discussed in detail the use of fur trimmings on hats for the winter season. Modish styles that year incorporated trim of heads and tails, and even composite animals—"... A fancy in some instances mounting a tiny lambskin head on a mink, or on a sable tail."[64] Was this less gruesome or vulgar than a bird's head or what the trade termed "made birds," of feathers and parts cobbled together?[65]

Unsurprisingly, the trade organization, the Millinery Merchants' Protective Association, and *The Millinery Trade Review*, as a soapbox for the industry, lobbied hard against all attempts at legislation, but eventually the parties tried to reach some kind of bargain, however tenuous. The Lacey Bill was enacted by the US Congress in 1900. A notable provision of the act regulated the "interstate traffic in birds killed in violation of State laws," but exempted barnyard fowl.[66] According to *The Millinery Trade Review*, Senator Lacey and the Millinery Merchants' Protective Association collaborated on the law that bore his name. Although the trade presented it as a cooperative effort, G. O. Shields, of the League of American Sportsmen, claimed in a letter to the *New York Times* that Lacey conceded on some terms because of the "bitter fight" the trade groups presented.[67] *The Millinery Trade Review* acknowledged the "powerful influence" of the bird preservationists, who "kept the trade in constant agitation and caused it no little expense in its efforts to deny untrue statements and offset wrongful influences."[68] The milliners would agree to stop using North American birds, if the Audubon Society and its sympathizers would cease legislative attempts against barnyard and other edible and seasonal game birds, as well as non-native imported birds, which would also be exempted from the agreement.[69] Such an accord would show that "the birds have no better friends than those engaged in the millinery trade."[70] It was a provision to turn the other cheek on imported birds that made this settlement difficult for the activists to stomach.[71] No agreement was reached; "the idea of the societies seems to be that they will be looking out for the birds of this country at the expense of those of others, and it is not in accordance with their tenets to do so."[72]

The millinery industry in 1903 proposed to extend their compromise to include the much-contested egret, though hardly gracefully. Charles W. Farmer of the Millinery Merchants' Protective Association was quoted in the *New York Times*:

> Fashion demands the aigrette, but we have decided to stop selling it, if that will satisfy the Audubon Society people, though why they should be so interested in a swamp bird which no one but the hunter ever sees, is more than I can understand.[73]

Overall, agreements between the two sides, were, as Robin Doughty has noted, "partial and short-lived."[74] Business coverage in 1904 reported that the Millinery Merchants' Protective Association would not make further attempts to challenge restrictive legislation. Their position had not changed, but the public, they felt, supported the laws to a degree that "further agitation of the subject will only tend to injure the trade."[75] Legislation in 1913 later supplemented plumage law by regulating imported feathers.[76] Feathered fashions would eventually wane with the changing of fashion, as well as the decline in hat-wearing in the latter half of the twentieth century. Yet the failure to reach any substantive agreement is indicative of the divisive nature of this debate over the use of an animal product in fashion, providing a thought-provoking preface to the twentieth and twenty-first century disputes associated with the wearing of fur.

Fur in the nineteenth and early twentieth centuries

The primary use of feathers in fashion has been decorative, but one can make the argument that the use of fur is a practical choice. "To be warmly clad," advised C. C. Shayne's, a fur manufacturer in the late nineteenth century, "is not only an absolute necessity, but it is also a fact that many a doctor's bill and many a human life may be saved" by its wear.[77] Fur has long been worn in the harshest cold-weather climates, yet it is also worn in more moderate areas of the world—and not just in winter weather—so practicality cannot be the only explanation for its popularity. Fur garments, as undeniably warm as they may be, have in fashion functioned equally as often as a status symbol. The fur trimming on the collar and hem of the dressing gown in Figure 6.3, for instance, would provide some warmth, but served mostly as a display of wealth. At various points during history, furs have been presented as the ultimate covetous luxury.

Fur for apparel is obtained by one of two methods: trapping, which is the traditional practice, or farming, which developed during the nineteenth century. Breeding animals specifically for their fur is now the more prevalent means of supplying the fur industry, and at points in history, it was lauded as the far better alternative to the barbarism of the trap. However, neither practice has been exempt from criticism for cruelty in its methods.

As was the case with feathers, conservationists' concern was piqued by the depletion of animal populations, and how this trend might be tied to the shifting popularity of

Figure 6.3 Dressing gown, silk faille, fur, 1870s, USA. Collection of The Museum at FIT, 82.22.1. Museum purchase. Photograph © The Museum at FIT.

particular furs in fashion. Among the animals whose populations were depleted at various points in the nineteenth and early twentieth centuries were the beaver, chinchilla, sea otter, and fur seal—each with a corresponding link to fashion. The nineteenth-century "rage for chinchilla swept the world of fashion ... furriers soon swept the Andes bare of the little animals," recounted one source.[78] Agnes Laut, a writer who scoffed at the idea that fur animals would become extinct, conceded the sea otter to be an exception. Her claim, however, was that intervention by the fur industry could have saved it from its precarious position during the 1920s.[79] Government involvement in sealing practices was often cited as an example of this. A 1911 treaty was enacted against the hunting of seals in the open sea, referred to as pelagic sealing, a thoughtless hunting practice which had decimated fur seal populations.[80]

The fashion industry rationalized the decline of wildlife populations. C. C. Shayne's, around the 1880s, advised that "fashion has been as busy in dictating styles for furry garments as in the other garments pertaining to a lady's wardrobe." Cavalierly they continued, "As different races of animals become extinct before the merciless hunter's path, the fashions in skins are necessarily changed."[81] Who was to blame: capricious fashion, its female adherents, or the "merciless hunter" striving to meet the demand? In addition to fashion, the open-air automobile, posited *Vogue* in 1913, was responsible for an upswing in demand of furs, so dramatic that the publication even issued an uncharacteristic warning:

> This demand has resulted in a depletion of fur-bearing animals, and, as in all cases where man has discovered that he can convert natural resources into gold, it will eventually cause their complete extinction unless more restrictive measures are introduced.[82]

Concern for animals was a moral and philanthropic issue of note during this period. During the nineteenth and early twentieth centuries, humane societies were formed, many initially campaigning against vivisection, a practice of medical dissection on live animals. The American Society for the Prevention of Cruelty to Animals (or ASPCA) was founded in 1866.[83] However, an 1891 article in the *New York Times*, observed that attentions toward wild animals had to that point been insignificant. "Until, however, the Society for the Prevention of Cruelty to Animals takes wild animals under its protection," they wrote, "along with the Harlem cats and tenement-house rats, gentle woman, whose name is synonym for tenderness, will continue to adorn herself with all the furs she can pay for."[84]

Around this time, *Vogue* magazine devoted significant space to animal-related columns and articles. Edna Woolman Chase, a former editor-in-chief of *Vogue*, was employed at the magazine during its nascence. In its earliest years, *Vogue* differed from its current form and focus on fashion. Chase noted, "the editorial thinking was that it was a magazine for ladies and gentlemen, not just a woman's fashion magazine."[85] *Vogue*'s first editor, animal lover Josephine Redding, was responsible for the coverage of wildlife. Chase recalled: "During [Redding's] regime the pages of *Vogue* barked, meowed, cheeped, and roared with accounts of animal life."[86] Redding authored a recurring column, "Concerning

Animals." She continued to do so, and thereby exert some influence, even after dismissal as editor-in-chief in 1900. The column was suspended at the end of 1910.[87] One article during Redding's tenure urged that part of the ethical teaching of children should include kindness to animals. *Vogue* spoke of the burgeoning humane movement: "Not yet so widespread, but still well-grounded and constantly growing, is a sentiment born of this very humaneness (that has done and is doing so much to make the race civilized), of love for animals and a perception that the human being has duties toward his humbler brothers of the kennel and stall, cage, jungle, field, forest and sea."[88]

Some began to equate the killing of animals for medical purposes and the killing of animals for fashion as similarly cruel. Towards the end of the nineteenth century, *The Animals' Friend*, an early animal rights magazine, published a letter from "A Repentant Sinner." Its author, a supporter of the anti-vivisection movement, described the realization that the numerous fur garments in her wardrobe made her a "vile hypocrite": "All these badges of cruelty I wore with as little thought of *how they were obtained* as I should wear a lace scarf without troubling myself as to who made it … I blamed *others* for cruelty, I called myself a 'lover of animals.'" The thought of the tortured trapped animal made her recoil: "All this … at the instigation of woman, that she may strip a tiny piece of fur from the back of the innocent victim. What difference is there between the victim of this fur-clad woman and the victim of the Vivisecting doctor?"[89]

One of the millinery industry's chief defenses in response to the heavy criticism it received for feather use was that the same complaints were not made about fur. Certainly, the case for cruelty can equally be made for fur as it was for feathers. Hints of a growing awareness of this fact appear sporadically in the popular press during the late nineteenth century. Although it primarily concerned fur trends, an 1891 article in the *New York Times* did note that: "It would seem that the charge of cruelty preferred against the ladies for their bird decorations might with equal justice apply to the wearers of furs."[90] Fur animals, the anonymous author noted, used to be overabundant—to the point of nuisance and threat—but by 1891 the trade was supported by "the wholesale slaughter of inoffensive animals like the seal and the beaver and the Eastern lambs."[91] That the author makes mention of these points is unusual, and certainly contradictory if his purpose is recommending and selling furs. He even goes so far as to say that although no woven cloth is "comparable in warmth … there is but little justification for overloading with furs in a climate like ours."[92]

Such opinions appear to have been the exception rather than the rule. Fur was more commonly discussed in terms of its fashionability, with little to no qualms about the animal. Discussing "the extent to which fur is to be used," *Vogue*, in 1897, described the great "quantities" of fur being used as trimmings on hems, bodice revers, muffs, boas, shawls, and opera capes: "as far as the fashion goes you may trim with much or little."[93] The same article claimed that the "splendor and sumptuousness" of opera cloaks "verges on the barbaric."[94] The term barbaric, rather than connoting the cruelty or brutality that is its very definition, as used here, seems almost praiseworthy of the decadence of fur fashions.

It was the use of heads, tails, paws, and claws, features prevalent during the late nineteenth and early twentieth centuries, which seemed most upsetting to observers. Perhaps those features made it more difficult to dissociate the fur from its former state, a living animal. "As with the birds," the aforementioned 1891 *New York Times* article noted, "the use of the heads, though usually in furs only 'play' heads made in miniature, gives an added aspect of cruelty to many of the fur garments." The article went on to describe some of the fashions in graphic detail:

> Heads with wide-open mouths and lolling red tongues lurk at every vantage point … The cravattes just take the little mink or sable, head, tails and feet, and twist him, writhing round fair throats. To heighten the barbarity, sometimes his eyes are punched out and jewels set in their place.[95]

Another writer was so discomfited by the styles that she urged women to only buy furs without heads: "Its absence gives one a kinder feeling toward the world, for there is nothing pleasant in looking a dead animal in the face and realizing that some one either shot or trapped it to appeal to woman's vanity." Preferring a state of willful obliviousness, she wrote: "If we must wear furs, don't let us be reminded of the way in which we got them by attaching the head of the animal to its hide."[96] Another writer agreed, "There is nothing artistic about the head, glassy eyes, and feet of a dead animal hanging below a woman's live face."[97] To describe the inclusion of the heads, appendages, tails, or paws, the *American Album of Fur Novelties* was fond of using the more innocuous terms "animal effect" or "animal style."[98]

Many furriers and fashion writers remained unabashed. In *Les Belles Fourrures*, a 1913 book of fashion plates from furrier Felix Jungmann, the illustrations celebrated the sacrifice of the fur animal for the benefit of fashion. Side by side are plates that depict,

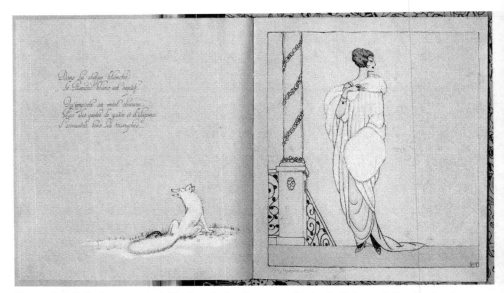

Figure 6.4 Felix Jungmann et Cie, *Les Belles Fourrures* (Paris: A. Colmer et Cie, September 1913), plate 1. Image courtesy of the Fashion Institute of Technology|SUNY, Gladys Marcus Library Department of Special Collections.

at left, the live fur animal and, at right, its ultimate fate. The plate in Figure 6.4, shows a white fox, trapped and bleeding. Its text, translated from the French, reads: "In the white steppe, the white fox is captive … Who cares for his obscure death? By gestures of grace and elegance, he will know all triumphs."[99] That his triumph is through fashion is asserted by the accompanying image of his pelt transformed into a chic fur coat. Another plate in the collection shows frolicking karakul sheep, known for broadtail fur, which has a distinctive moiré pattern. The sheep "will only begin life by becoming an ornament" like the fur wraps and coats modeled by the women in its accompanying illustration.[100] *Vogue* was almost flippant in describing the pervasiveness of rabbit fur in the 1916 collections. "Lo, the Poor Rabbit," they wrote, "is there no one who will found a Society for the Prevention of Cruelty to Bunnies?"[101] Despite some observations of these "aspects of cruelty," there was not yet strong sentiment against furs—although it *was* brewing. The controversy over furs and cruelty would pick up steam in the 1920s, sparked by the public's new awareness of trapping practices.

Fur trapping

Furs remained popular during the 1920s. The 1926 *Year Book of the Fur Industry* reported that it was "fifth among the huge industries of New York, and throughout the nation has more than two million souls devoted to its calling."[102] In the pre-crash 1920s, they cited "prosperity" as one major reason that furs were now "almost a necessity among those of moderate, or even small means, where, formerly, furs were the privilege of wealth alone."[103]

In the 1920s, fur fashions shifted as readily as anything else. "Gone, apparently, are the days when a fur coat lasted a lifetime," wrote *The New Yorker*'s Lois Long in 1926, attributing the new disposability to "the use of novelty furs, most of them lightweight and perishable, and the cuts [which] place them definitely in one season."[104] Additionally, "fur fashions … have never been so extravagant as they are now," said Long.[105] *Vogue* concurred: "One 'sealskin sacque' once used to be the height of any woman's ambition, but the wardrobe of to-day which contains but one fur coat or one set of furs, is poor indeed."[106] Extravagance in furs was not the sole province of women; indeed, men, particularly collegiate ones, indulged in the expensive luxury of full-length raccoon fur coats during the 1920s, although the trend did not outlast the decade. (See Figure 6.5.)

The fur industries even actively promoted furs for summer wear. The 1919 *American Album of Fur Novelties* told its readers that the "summer fur is a necessity of the well-dressed woman's wardrobe."[107] Women were determined to wear summer furs "no matter how great may be the incongruities," wrote Janet Duer in the 1919 publication *Art & Life*.[108]

What significance did trans-seasonal fur coats and trimmings have for the industry— and the animal? Agnes Laut, who chronicled the fur industry in 1921, spoke to two experts about the fashion for summer furs. One believed it nothing to worry over, but another viewed it as a detrimental trend. "Of all the accursed follies of fashion, this whim

Figure 6.5 Installation shot from *Eco-Fashion: Going Green* (The Museum at FIT, 2010).
Left: Man's coat, raccoon fur, wood toggles, c. 1920, USA. Collection of The Museum at FIT,
P88.78.1. Museum purchase. Right: Opera coat, blue silk velvet, metallic sequins, bugle beads,
raccoon fur, c. 1925, USA. Collection of The Museum at FIT, 2002.78.1. Gift of Elinor Toberoff.
Photograph © The Museum at FIT.

for summer furs is the silliest and the most destructive of wildlife … If it lasts for ten years, there will not be left a fur-bearing animal in its natural state."[109]

The enormous popularity of fur did, however, run concurrent with increasing sentiment against trapped fur, particularly caught by steel leg-hold traps, which are today banned in numerous places. Dr Edward Breck, president of the Anti-Steel Trap League in Washington, DC, cited a figure that if true is egregious. In a letter to the New York Times in 1925, he claimed that of the approximately 100,000,000 animals killed for the fur trade annually, "nine-tenths … are used for summer furs and fur trimmings."[110] According to one source, six million steel traps were sold per year.[111] Such traps would often maim, trapping an animal by the leg or foot, but not immediately kill. Critics argued it was patently inhumane to leave the wounded animal writhing in the trap until it ultimately died or was later killed by the trapper. Some terrified animals managed to escape only by chewing off a limb.

The fur industry had its vocal defenders, chief among them writer and self-professed nature lover Agnes Laut, author of the The Fur Trade in America. It was her belief that trapping by the fur industry was far from cruel, and indeed, trappers performed a service, providing population control and eliminating superfluous males. Predatory fur-bearers, she claimed, demonstrated that "natural life is crueler by far than the most careless, thoughtless fur hunter."[112] One of her main arguments was that the industry had to use good practice to preserve its supply of material. It was counterintuitive to trap animals until the fur was prime, or if a female animal was pregnant, because such poor practices would limit yields and profits.[113] Laut also called a woman who cared well for her furs "as great a conserver of wildlife as the most ardent lover of game."[114]

The 1926 edition of the Year Book of the Fur Industry claimed that the industry was working to develop better traps, but felt that "the suffering of animals in traps has been grossly exaggerated by many misguided enthusiasts."[115] Frank G. Ashbrook, of the United States Department of Agriculture, contributed an essay to the aforementioned publication in which he observed that: "the steadily diminishing supply of fur animals tends to prove that the 'fur wearer' is increasing faster than the 'fur bearer'."[116] However, he also claimed that pollution and land development were likewise to blame because they damaged and destroyed the habitats of animals. Conservation practices—"conservation with use"—he maintained, should take a multifaceted approach, factoring in the concerns of the game hunters and fur industry, with laws that were more thoughtfully designed.[117] Ashbrook also put forth an additional argument in defense of the fur industry: the numerous people who depended upon it for their livelihoods.[118] "An industry," Ashbrook wrote, "the finished product of which is so much in demand, scarcely needs to apologize for its existence. So far as members of the fur trade are concerned, it is unreasonable to believe that they are not interested in perpetuating a natural resource which is the backbone of their business."[119]

On the other side, Minnie Maddern Fiske, a prominent theater actress, emerged as an early animal rights activist and as an outspoken opponent of such steel leg-hold traps.[120] Although she can be classified as an early celebrity activist on the subject of animal cruelty and fur wearing, her contemporary counterparts would criticize the stance she took on fur farming. Fiske was not entirely anti-fur, but instead advocated farms in which animals were purpose-raised and killed "humanely" by methods such as asphyxiation.[121] "I want no one to get the idea that I am a sentimentalist ... We approach this subject from the practical viewpoint."[122] The consumer had influence, she claimed; women's refusal to buy inhumanely trapped furs would compel the trade to change its trapping practices.[123] According to Fiske, "if women determined to buy furs produced only under these humane conditions, obviating atrocities of trapping in the wilds, the more serious objections to furs would be removed."[124]

Fiske likened her cause to the battle over the hunting of egrets and the wearing of aigrette feathers. "People are pretty decent. As soon as they found how horrible was the method of obtaining aigrettes they stopped buying aigrettes," she declared. "And now that something is known about the cruelty of fur-trapping, farms are being established on which fur-bearing animals are bred and humanely destroyed."[125] In this Fiske overstates, as even exposés and graphic descriptions did not hold as much weight as dictates of fashion. However, as has been noted, her comparison of the two causes has merit. Surprisingly, it was reported by the *New York Times* that the ASPCA likewise supported fur farms, and was unequivocally "not starting a campaign against the wearing of fur." Said the paper, "we may soon become accustomed to the idea of certain animals being as generally raised for their fur as other animals are for their wool or their flesh."[126] Agnes Laut also praised fur farming as a great development in the industry. Pelts of silver foxes bred on farms could be so lucrative, she wrote, "It doesn't need telling that the pups get the care of millionaire babies."[127]

Fur farming

The first successful fur farms were started on Prince Edward Island in 1894, and initially foxes were the only animals raised.[128] According to *Vogue* magazine, the first US farm was founded in 1910.[129] The idea of raising animals for fur may have existed earlier, in theory, if not in widespread practice. In 1866, the *New York Times* profiled a New York State farmer by the surname of Stratton. Stratton had achieved some success in the raising of elk, and had since diversified into farming of mink, with an eye toward otter and beaver. The article praised Stratton's ingenuity in finding profit in farming "animals we have been accustomed to consider untamable." Its conclusion:

> We trust he may go on and prosper ... we see no reason why mink and otter and beaver may not be raised by the thousand, greatly to the delight of those who want their furs, and to the profit of those who raise them.[130]

While Stratton may have been an anomaly, the practice of fur farming took off after its early successes in the late nineteenth century. Sources claim that by 1933, there were apparently 4,500 farms in the United States and Canada, comprising 20 percent of the fur market.[131] According to Lois Fenske and Dwight Robinson, most minks were trapped up until 1943, the turning point.[132] In 1954, Frank Ashbrook wrote that the number of mink skins from farms had grown steadily between the years 1946 and 1951.[133] The *New York Times* reported that fur retailer Gunther Jaeckel had its own associated farms during the mid-1950s "where 11,000 of these little beasts were pelted last year [1954]."[134] By this time, fur farmers had also developed ways of breeding mink to ensure specific colors—colors that would occur naturally only occasionally, but which could be cultivated through careful breeding. According to a 1944 *Time* magazine article, the color possibilities were so varied that "fur men are already quipping: 'Have a mink to match your hair'."[135] Mink was to become the fashion fur of the 1950s.

Figure 6.6 Sketch of a Ben Thylan coat to be rendered in mink or sable. Image courtesy of the Fashion Institute of Technology|SUNY, Gladys Marcus Library Department of Special Collections.

In *The Little Dictionary of Fashion*, couturier Christian Dior reserved some of his highest praise for midcentury status symbol mink. Mink is "the best and nicest of all the furs," he wrote, noting also, "a mink coat in certain countries is synonymous with a certain standard of life and of social standing."[136] According to Cedric Larson, "fur coats made of the rarer types of mink retail today [1949] for as much as [US] $3,000 and even more, although [US] $1,000 to $2,000 is considered standard."[137] *Vogue* concurred, a mink, like the one illustrated in Figure 6.6, "will, and should, cost you several thousand dollars."[138] In the film, *The Lady Wants Mink*, the sapphire blue mink coat owned by the character Gladys Jones cost US $7,000 and was comprised of 82 skins.[139] It is a figure matched by *Time* magazine, which wrote, "a full-length mink coat takes up to 80 carefully matched and graded pelts."[140] If her husband had not been able to buy her a mink, Gladys told her best friend, lead character Nora Connors, then she would have taken matters into her own hands. "I'd have a mink coat if I had to stalk it in the forest with a slingshot," she says, "or have my own mink ranch," inspiring Nora to start one in her own backyard.[141] A mink coat is presented as the aspirational garment for women of the middle class. *Vogue* asserted that women could "rightfully expect rewarding years of flattery, euphoria, elegance—and incidentally—warmth" from a mink coat.[142] Status, then, very clearly is posited as the more important aspect of fur ownership. In December 1952, *Time* reported that mink was outselling all other fur varieties, but that "most mink-hunting women have little idea of how or where the coats come from," not fully understanding that the animal must be killed for its fur. According to the article, "at a mink ranch not long ago, a woman visitor asked: 'How many times a year do you pelt the animals?'"[143]

Rise of the anti-fur movement

During the 1960s and 1970s, furs got more experimental, as trends like mink miniskirts and exotic colors held sway.[144] Said *Time* magazine, "the fur is flying as usual, but now the animals are coming from every corner of Noah's ark in colors, forms and designs that would make the old sable set roll over and play possum."[145] These unconventional "fun furs" would be revisited during the 1990s. But as one writer once asked, fun furs—"fun for whom?"[146] One fur trend in the late 1970s echoed the "animal style" of the 1910s. Calling it the "untamed look," Kathy Larkin for *New York* magazine, wrote of the style for "unlined, jagged pelts" and "dangling rows of tails."[147]

During this period, public sentiment also began to turn. At issue was the use of a number of endangered cat species, such as leopard and tiger, which had been hunted to disturbingly low levels. Although this certainly was not the first time that animals had been hunted to near-extinction, rising concern led to federal and state legislation, agreements from trade organizations, and an international embargo by the International Fur Trade Foundation.[148] Eight years earlier, *Time* magazine had observed a "recent wild trend to leopard," but now the industry was feeling the backlash.[149] Poaching of those animals had become a serious problem for African officials. In the face of mounting pressure by environmental and animal protection organizations, wrote Angela Taylor, "the fashion press has toned down its display of spotted furs, and it takes a defiant woman, indeed, to wear a leopard coat."[150] But Taylor noted: "there is … confusing disagreement about which animals must be protected or who is to blame if a cheetah coat, say, winds up on a fashionable woman. Governments, poachers, hunters, furriers, stores and customers are all blaming each other."[151]

The list of endangered animals in the "Red Data" book—a resource produced by the International Union for the Conservation of Nature and Natural Resources—was cited as a guideline for some furriers as to what furs were off-limits. This approach was faulty, claimed William G. Conway, the General Director of the New York Zoological Society. In an editorial to the *New York Times*, he argued that the publication was not the "sole arbiter," nor a comprehensive account.[152] *Vogue's* editorial in its September 1, 1970 issue was titled, "Furs, Fashion, and Conservation." The magazine assured its readers that they recognized the dire threat to many species of wildlife. "We are deeply concerned about preserving animals threatened with extinction, and we have made and will continue to make every effort not to publish photographs showing the skins of such animals." They would show furs that were "ranch-raised," as well as those under conservation management programs. There was "no reason why women should not wear, and enjoy" the latter.[153] The month before, in August 1970, *Harper's Bazaar* noted "the threat" to wild cats "has been so real, we haven't put a genuine spot before your eyes in three years." What the accompanying spread of fashion illustrations celebrated were "leopard spots, jaguar spots, tiger dashes—patterns of the great cats exchanged for their lives, printed on the furs of non-endangered animals to create new and splendid species."[154] "The Animal Kingdom Out of Danger," they cried, "Great Fashion Has a Heart."[155] In the same issue, the magazine ran a spread on fake furs, "Furs of Man's Invention."[156]

For their part, furriers asserted that they were not "villains." Depleting the fur supply was bad business practice. Isadore Barmash wrote: "Instead, [furriers] claim, they have for years advocated conservation legislation, in order to sustain the wild animal supply and preserve the endangered species."[157] With anti-fur voices prominent in the discussion, the fur industry launched the Fur Conservation Institute of America as an organ to communicate its point-of-view in the debate. The industry had been cooperative, according to fur manufacturers like Oliver Gintel, who reminded the *New York Times* that "the industry stopped using such skins as those of spotted fur animals, ocean otter, and polar bear … following rising outcries against looming extinction of such species."[158] Furrier Jacques Kaplan of the firm Georges Kaplan publically announced the list of furs he would refrain from using.[159]

By 1976, said fashion writer Angela Taylor, "furriers [had] made their peace with conservationists." She declared that in a roundabout way, "the conservation movement was a blessing—it forced furriers to be more ingenious, and, as a result, techniques such as fur dyeing and fur treating have improved."[160] While the promises with regard to endangered furs may have eased the conscience of some, they did little to placate those who opposed the use of any and all furs on ethical grounds. Although there was a seeming peace on the cats issue, the fur industry, in conjunction with the meat production industry, simultaneously worked to "promote high-fashion in furs and also to combat anti-fur forces."[161]

Despite the uproar by conservationists, and the ups and downs in demand for furs during the previous decades, the fur industry ended the 1970s on a high note with reported sales of US $613 million.[162] During the 1980s, sales surged among young, middle-class women, who treated furs as a status symbol—and an indulgence.[163] According to the New York Times, the stigma was attached only to the wearing of endangered animals, and not purportedly to the use of farmed furs such as mink. "Fur industry analyst" Edward B. Keaney asserted that "wearing a farm-bred fur has become as socially innocuous as eating a hamburger at McDonald's."[164]

Since the 1980s, the fur industry has made a concerted attempt to actively rebut attacks from anti-fur activists.[165] Their industry, asserted the International Fur Trade Federation, was "the victim of manipulated public opinion."[166] The fur industry has long sought ways to justify the cost and the use of fur garments. One of its earliest arguments was that quality furs were investment pieces, meant to last for many years and which could be repurposed. C. C. Shayne's argued during the late nineteenth century that furs were expensive, but "a handsome sealskin sacque or dolman may be worn for many successive winters, and when it has finally lost its pristine beauty, it may still be utilized by cutting it over the little folks or making it up into trimmings."[167]

Many industry supporters asserted that farm-raised fur animals were treated well, so that they would produce high-quality pelts.[168] Not only that, they argued, unlike synthetic fabrics, fur was sustainable. Furbearer populations could renew each year, and as a product of nature, fur would return to nature and biodegrade. It is the use of synthetics in faux furs, which even today, generates the criticism that the product receives. Some of the industry statements—that trapping is a necessary, even kind, conservation method— also echoed those of decades earlier. Sandy Blye, a fur industry representative, was quoted in the New York Times as saying, "if animals aren't trapped they fall victim to overpopulation, starvation, and disease."[169]

The fur industry positioned the debate as an issue of freedom of choice. According to the Wall Street Journal, campaigns in the early 1990s from both Saga Furs and the Fur Information Council of America were centered on that point.[170] Fur industry executive Maria Cattallonitti told the New York Times that just as anti-fur proponents have rights, so too do fur-wearers—"but no one has the right to impose their choice on others."[171] Fur wearers have also decried the hostility they face on the street and other public places; "it seems ironic that the champions of animal rights show so little regard for human rights," wrote Yona Zeldis McDonough.[172]

One of the most outspoken champions of animal rights over the past three decades has been the organization People for the Ethical Treatment of Animals, or PETA, which was founded in 1980. It is now probably the most familiar name in animal rights activism. PETA's role in the fur debate is prominent, and they were a major player as animal rights activism gained steam in the early 1990s. At its core, PETA believes that we should not use any animal products and advocates vegetarianism. The central tenet of their organization is, "that animals are not ours to eat, wear, experiment on, or use for entertainment."[173] PETA has run campaigns on numerous issues, from factory farming to circus animals. Speaking in terms of fur, however, they maintain that all methods of obtaining fur are cruel, exposing conditions related to fur farming, as well as fur trapping,

Figure 6.7 Models with the Janice Dickinson Modeling Agency showing their support for the PETA "I'd Rather Go Naked Than Wear Fur" Campaign, Hollywood and Highland, Hollywood, CA, August 20, 2007. © s_bukley/Shutterstock.

which although less prevalent, still remains an issue. As writer Dirk Johnson pointed out in 1990, not all animal breeds were farm-raised, so if their pelts were on the market at all, it was through trapping.[174] Conditions on farms have been a large concern for animal activists. Small, cramped pens (in use since at least 1938[175]), reports of mistreatment, and inhumane methods of execution have been the subject of reports by PETA and other organizations. Some mink farms, for instance, have used gas exhaust or lethal injection.[176]

PETA is well known for its provocative activism, although the organization is not associated with the type of militant and violent protest that often characterizes the behavior of fringe groups such as the Animal Liberation Front.[177] In his autobiography, Dan Mathews, who now works as PETA's Senior Vice President of Media Campaigns, wrote that the group had to push the envelope largely because of a media-saturated culture that "helped mold an escapist society hungrier for entertainment than education."[178]

PETA's members have thrown vegan pies,[179] red paint and dead raccoons, among other objects, and they have used nudity in their advertisements. In the early 1990s, model Christy Turlington posed unclothed for a now-iconic shot with a now-iconic slogan, "I'd rather go naked than wear fur."[180] The slogan has been recurrent in PETA campaigns and protests, as seen in Figure 6.7, from a 2007 protest in Hollywood by the Janice Dickinson Modeling Agency. PETA protesters have also leaped onto fashion runways—the first apparently being an Oscar de la Renta fur show in 1991.[181] They have occupied offices, such as *Vogue* magazine and Calvin Klein, achieving success with the latter. His fur contract, it was later reported, was dormant, but according to some sources he credited PETA's occupation with helping spur his final decision not to renew.[182]

With *Vogue*, PETA has had less success. Anna Wintour, the magazine's editor-in-chief, has been open about her support of the fur industry, which has garnered her unwanted attention from animal rights groups. As a *Newsweek* article once described it, "she's PETA's pet target."[183] During a notorious incident in 1996, a PETA member interrupted Wintour's meal at the Four Seasons in New York by dropping a raccoon carcass on the table.[184] The following year, fur was still well represented in *Vogue*'s advertisements—the autumn issues contained a reported 28 pages.[185] Despite the antagonism between the two groups, Wintour's stance has never wavered. In her editorial letter in the May issue of 1998, Wintour noted the prevalence of fur on international runways. "The PETA people have probably sabotaged themselves with their attention-seeking vandalism. It does attract attention, but to furs rather than their cause."[186] When Teri Agins of the *Wall Street Journal* questioned her about fur, Wintour replied, "I think *Vogue*'s support of fur absolutely helped the fur industry ... We totally supported it and will continue to support it."[187] Like Wintour, others in the industry have spoken out against some of PETA's methods. In a statement to *New York* magazine, designer Marc Jacobs wondered whether PETA would appreciate the tables turned: "They wouldn't want anyone to spray paint their offices. What if someone threw paint on their vinyl coats because they didn't believe in chemicals?"[188]

More recently, PETA has changed some of its tactics. In 2002, they backed the fur-and-leather-free fashion show of Marc Bouwer. Bouwer told *Women's Wear Daily*, "I'm not telling people not to wear fur. I'm telling them how fashion has evolved today ...

There are amazing new fabrics and technology to create imitation fur and leather that a lot of people don't know about."[189] For its part, PETA recognized that working within the fashion system might help them achieve their goals.[190]

Sustainable alternatives

In the twenty-first century, the use of fur and other animal products is still hotly contested, but they remain very much a part of fashion. Throughout this study several options for the sustainable use of animal materials have emerged: ethical sourcing, the use of byproduct materials, buying vintage, and cruelty-free products.

For those who wish to continue the use of materials such as fur, ethical sourcing presents an alternative that at least brings transparency to the process. At the end of the 1980s, when his friend Bill Blass publicly quit furs, Oscar de la Renta told *Women's Wear Daily*: "Right now, I am under contract to Wagner Furs, but I am concerned about how animals are killed for the furs to be acquired. I care a lot for nature. I really want to investigate it further and see what I will do."[191] In the past, he had experimented with faux furs, such as the faux leopard skin in Figure 6.13. Today de la Renta uses only Origin Assured™ furs, which since 2007 has set standards for sourcing.[192] The converse viewpoint, however, is that such measures are lacking. As scholar John Sorenson wrote, "since all fur is taken from animals that are deliberately killed by the industry to obtain it, the meaning of 'ethically-sourced' sounds at best like a euphemism."[193]

Another way to mediate the use of animal products in fashion is by subscribing to the belief that by-product materials, such as leather (from beef production) or shearling (from lamb production) are acceptable because animals are killed for their meat first. Fur by-products are sometimes referred to in the industry as "foodie" furs. A Macy's West fashion executive was quoted in the *Wall Street Journal* in 2004 as saying, "If you can eat it, we can buy it."[194] That distinction appeases some; but "if that's the difference," one article quipped, "it suggests a new billboard slogan for the fur industry: 'Let them eat mink'."[195] The idea of by-products is long-standing; it was also the primary rationalization for the use of certain bird feathers during the nineteenth century. In his research, Sorenson likewise provided an important critique on the use of by-product materials, articulating the strong problems of cruelty and "assembly line killing" associated with the meat industries.[196]

Leather is perhaps the most significant by-product material. While the exploitation of by-products from leather production provides an ethical answer to some, their use raises other questions. First, as PETA has noted, many leathers are sourced from countries with lax standards for treatment of animals.[197] Second, leather processing is notoriously dirty and its effluent must be carefully monitored. Leather products are often treated with hazardous chemicals, notably chromium, a non-biodegradable heavy metal, and sulfides, which must be filtered from wastewaters, though in some instances, the chrome solution can be reused.[198] Tanning with vegetable material is a method favored by some eco-conscious designers as a way to reduce harmful waste. In general, the processing of hides also generates waste in the form of organic matter and hair, which must be dealt with, as well as copious amounts of salt utilized in the process. While it may seem innocuous, salt can be very challenging for leather manufacturers, as the release of excess saline in wastewaters can damage surrounding ecosystems.[199]

The wearing of vintage is often touted as an eco-friendly alternative to purchasing new animal products. When it comes to animal materials such as fur or leather, it may offer some consolation to consider that the animal was killed long before. Abstaining from the vintage product will not resurrect the animal, but its purchase in principle may prevent an animal's death in the future. One woman, interviewed for a 1998 New York Times article, said of a fur that had been bequeathed to her: "I guess I feel like it's already dead and gone, so it's better not to waste it."[200]

Materials whose harvesting and manufacture do not harm animals are generally termed cruelty-free. The term describes all synthetic fibers, as well as organic cotton. Included in this category, if broadly applied, could be tussah (also known as wild or "peace") silk and organic wool. Tussah is favored by eco-designers as an alternative to conventional silk. Cocoons are collected after the silkworm has abandoned them, as opposed to cultivated silk, which is boiled to harvest the fibrous cocoons, thus killing the silkworm inside.[201] Organic wool (see Figure 6.8, left) while less common than organic cotton follows similar principles. Sheep that produce wool are often treated with pesticides by injection or immersion baths—methods that are noxious to the animals as well as the environment. The pesticide-free production of organic wool is by contrast carefully monitored for non-toxic and compassionate cultivation.[202]

Synthetic leathers have also emerged as an important alternative for vegan consumers, particularly with regard to accessories. Stella McCartney is a lifelong vegetarian who eschews the use of animal products in her collections. As accessories are frequently made from leather, McCartney's beliefs are especially pertinent to her chic designs for bags and shoes (Figure 6.8). Fashion writer Chioma Nnadi has noted that "McCartney's strategy for success is simple: Create eco-fashion that is utterly irresistible, and you can nudge a stylish woman into reducing her carbon footprint without her even noticing."[203]

However, the paradox of cruelty-free is something with which eco-designers must contend. Early synthetics, such as "pleathers," or plastic leathers were often considered inferior to the real thing. Many of these modern imitations have been derived from petroleum, meaning they require energy-intensive manufacturing processes, and do not biodegrade as a natural fiber would. Unquestionably a humane alternative to real fur, especially to those for whom animal welfare is the overriding concern, faux materials present real environmental challenges. This point was understood during the surge of faux fur use in the 1970s. Said Time magazine in 1975: "Rising concern about industrial pollution has enabled many ecology-minded buyers to rationalize that the purchase of a fake fur made with chemicals produced in a pollution-prone plant may be a greater environmental sin than buying the real thing."[204] "The real thing," however, might also contain a fair share of chemical components, applied as part of processing and preservation treatments,[205] a fact which calls into question fur industry claims that fur is a natural commodity (a tactic Sorenson characterizes as "greenwashing fur").[206]

Figure 6.8 Installation shot, *Eco-Fashion: Going Green* (The Museum at FIT, 2010). Left: Stella McCartney, sweater dress, grey organic wool, alpaca, 2009, England. Collection of The Museum at FIT, 2010.46.2A. Gift of Stella McCartney; Shoes and bag: Stella McCartney, faux patent leather, 2009, England, The Museum at FIT, 2010.46.2BC, 2010.46.3. Gift of Stella McCartney. Photograph © The Museum at FIT.

Figure 6.9 Charmoné (Lauren Carroll and Jodi Koskella), *Cezanne* pumps, tan and red multicolor faux leather, 2010, USA, The Museum at FIT, 2010.8.1. Gift of Lauren Carroll and Jodi Koskella of Charmoné. Photograph © The Museum at FIT.

Yet there is room for innovation in the arena of faux alternatives, and new ways to minimize the trade-offs are welcome. For example, cruelty-free shoes by Charmoné are manufactured from microfiber faux leather, which is breathable and does not use contain the compound PVC (Figure 6.9). There are also faux leathers made from cellulose products such as Lorica on the market.[207] Designers, such as Leanne Mai-ly Hilgart of the vegan label Vaute Couture (see figure 6.10), address this paradox by designing clothes that are investment pieces, purposefully made to last, in much the same way that high quality wool or fur pieces have long been touted as lifetime purchases.

Conclusion

Of the various topics related to ethics and sustainability in fashion, the use of animal products is perhaps the most polarizing, lacking any sort of middle ground. As is noted by examining the histories of feather and fur use in the nineteenth and twentieth centuries, compromises are often tenuous at best. From one perspective, sustainability in the context of the treatment of animals can refer to the responsible, humane use of animal products. Yet, for some there is no such thing as responsible and humane use of any animal product. In that view, forswearing all animal products is the only true interpretation of sustainability. Scholar John Sorenson rightly notes

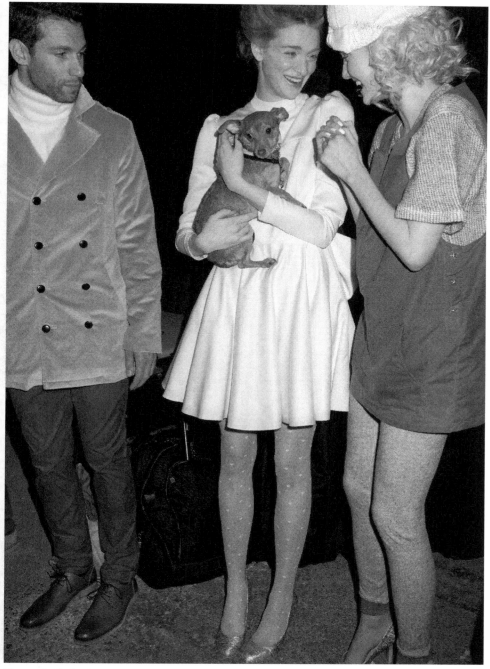

Figure 6.10 Backstage at Vaute Coutre, New Yorj Fashion Week Fall–Winter 2013. Photograph by Gregory Vaughan and Leanne Mai-ly Hilgart.

that this discussion is underrepresented in the literature on sustainable and ethical fashion.[208] His research adopts an animal rights perspective,[209] as he argues that "the fashion industry's use of nonhuman animals is a 'theatre of cruelty,' one that hinges on the industrialization of exploitation of animals which essentially turns them from living beings to mere products, or raw materials."[210] Sorenson's work points to the need for scholars to further examine, carefully and critically, this controversial issue, as animal products will almost certainly remain in use by various industries, including fashion, for the foreseeable future. Today's warring factions are no nearer to agreement than they were over a century ago, nor are they likely to resolve their differences anytime soon, but the consideration of fashion's past disputes regarding the use of animal products brings an interesting frame of reference to the ever-inflexible debate.

Suggestions for Further Reading

Doughty, R. W. (1975), *Feather Fashions and Bird Preservation: A Study in Nature Protection*, Berkeley, Los Angeles and London: University of California Press.
The Fur Trade Library: Answers (1985), International Fur Trade Federation.
Graham Jr., F. (1990), *The Audubon Ark: A History of the National Audubon Society*, New York: Alfred A. Knopf.
Laut, A. C. (1921), *The Fur Trade of America*, New York: The Macmillan Company.
Mathews, D. (2007), *Committed,* New York: Atria Books.
"The Slaughter of the Innocents" (1875), *Harper's Bazaar*, May 22: 335.
Sorenson, J. (2011), "Ethical fashion and the exploitation of nonhuman animals," *Critical Studies in Fashion & Beauty*, 2 (1–2): 139–64.

At a glance: Tortoiseshell, ivory and reptile skins

Today the tortoiseshell patterning on our eyeglasses and accessories is usually rendered in plastic. As we seldom see the real thing anymore, it might be easy to forget that historically the material was harvested from sea turtles, primarily the Hawksbill turtle, known for the extraordinary patterning of its shell. Although it was possible to harvest from living turtles, many were killed during the process. During the nineteenth and early twentieth centuries, tortoiseshell found wide use in decorative fashion accessories, such as the hair comb in Figure 6.11.[211] International trade legislation now protects the Hawksbill turtle, whose numbers were decimated by high demand during this period.[212]

Like tortoiseshell, elephant ivory could be intricately carved, and was considered an ideal material for delicate accessories, like the handle of the fan shown in Figure 6.11. Fashion's demand, too, had a devastating effect on elephant populations.[213] Although all ivory trade is strictly regulated now, poaching remains a significant problem, boosted by black market trade.[214]

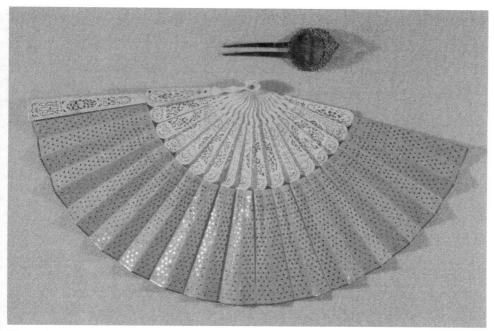

Figure 6.11 Fan, ivory, paper, metallic foil, c. 1895, France. Collection of The Museum at FIT, 69.160.42. Gift of the Estate of Elizabeth Arden; Hair comb, tortoiseshell, c. 1880, USA. Collection of The Museum at FIT, 2007.63.3. Gift of David Toser. Photograph © The Museum at FIT.

The uses of reptile skins, including those belonging to alligators, crocodiles, and snakes, have also been contested. All methods of obtaining snakeskin are cruel, not the least of which is live skinning,[215] which some dealers believe improves the quality of the saleable skin.[216] Reptile skin is most commonly used for small accessories, but consider the copious amount of the material needed to cover the full-length Donald Brooks coat, circa 1971, shown on the right in the installation image, Figure 3.9 (Chapter 3). The handbag in Figure 6.12, c. 1938, used not only the skin, but also the body of a small alligator. The alligator head wraps around the front flap, and its legs are affixed to the back of the purse. Its appearance may also seem jarring, not unlike the "cruel aspect" attributed to heads and tails on furs and bird bodies on hats.

Suggestions for further reading

Ivory: An International History and Illustrated Survey (1987), New York: Abrams.
"Status of trade in Hawksbill turtles," *Convention on International Trade in Endangered Species of Wild Fauna and Flora (CITES)* http://www.cites.org/eng/prog/hbt/bg/trade_status.shtml [accessed August 4, 2013].
Warwick, C. (1988), "Reptiles—Misunderstood, Mistreated, and Mass-Marketed," in International Wildlife Coalition (ed.), *Skinned*, North Falmouth, MA: International Wildlife Coalition.

Figure 6.12 Handbag, alligator, c. 1938, USA. Collection of The Museum at FIT, 2010.33.1. Gift of Rene Resnick Gratz. Photograph © The Museum at FIT.

At a glance: Faux furs

Faux furs have long been a viable alternative to real furs. Although we think of the end of the twentieth century as the heyday for fake furs, they have, in fact, existed for far longer. In the fashion press, they are referred to by a variety of names: faux furs, imitation furs, simulated furs, or fabric furs. As part of the American World Humane Conference in 1923, there was a display of such "fabric furs, which, it was said, had reached such an advanced state of manufacture that only an expert could detect the difference from real furs."[217] In the collection of The Museum at FIT, a 1942–3 brown wool coat by Madame

Figure 6.13 Madame Grès, coat, brown wool faux fur, 1942–3, France, The Museum at FIT, 2004.16.1. Museum purchase. Photograph © The Museum at FIT.

Grès mimicked the look of the fur Persian lamb (Figure 6.13). The coat offered a chic alternative to coats made from traditional furs, which were quite rare and prohibitively expensive for the average Parisian woman during the German occupation of Paris in World War II. The coat's dense wool pile is probably as warm as the fur it imitates, and it precedes the more common use of simulated fur by nearly 30 years. Real Persian lamb, also referred to as karakul, has long been a controversial fur as it is taken from newborn or fetal lambs. Frank Ashbrook, in 1954, defended the industry's use of Persian lamb, writing, "Lambs are prematurely born as a result of accident or exposure. There is a widespread misconception that the ewes are maltreated or killed."[218]

Post-war, fake fur was the subject of fashion editorials: "Frankly artificial, plush-soft, pleasant to watch and to wear, fake furs are a natural to a hearthside role," wrote *Vogue* in 1949, showcasing "mock" broadtail and moleskin.[219] By 1950, wrote one newspaper account, fake furs were meant to be discernable as such: "'Frankly fake' furs ... not only imitate the animal kingdom, but poke fun at it. They have been dyed in fanciful colors and made with exaggerated markings."[220] According to *New York Times* fashion editor Virginia Pope, who chose fake furs as the subject of her recurrent home-sewing column, "Patterns of the Times," in November 1950, the "frankly fake" fabrics were composed of wool, cotton, or rayon, or blends thereof.[221] During the 1960s, synthetic fibers, such as acrylic, were increasingly utilized in the production of fake furs.[222]

In 1968 the *New York Times* reported that sales of faux furs, as well as leathers, were thriving.[223] Not only were sixties youth shunning the "minks that mother wore" in favor of fun furs, the wearing of "synthetic fur garments" was becoming more prevalent. According to Isadore Barmash: "These coats and jackets made of fur-like fabrics from man-made fibers, are priced considerably lower than the natural furs and have tended to siphon off some of the sales that natural furs would have had."[224] Some fabric manufacturers also capitalized on the public sentiment against endangered skins during this period. E. F. Timme & Sons, Inc. ran an advertisement in *Vogue* in July 1970, in which they marveled that "one woman ... is actually wearing 1/60 of the world's tiger population on her back." Certainly, the widespread adoption of fakes was in their financial interest, but the company claimed to espouse an ecological point of view. Real furs, they said, were "unnecessary because modern technology has made the wearing of animal skins virtually obsolete."[225]

An article in *Time* characterized the trapper—then a dying breed—as "a victim of the fake fur."[226] Barmash also claimed that many furriers were shuttered by the combination of "industry neglect of other furs [besides mink], the advent of synthetics known as 'fake' furs, [and] by antifur forces seeking to stem the killing of fur-bearing animals."[227] Conversely, however, some, such as Arnold Perlbinder, a fur industry executive, argued that fake fur was not really a true substitute for fur; this "nonsense of fake fur being an alternative to fur has to stop. A lot of people now realize that. If a customer wants a real fur, I could stand on my head and show her a fake fur, but she won't buy it."[228]

According to Anne-Marie Schiro, during the late 1980s and early 1990s, some in the industry referred to fakes as "ecological fur."[229] Although it was possible to make faux furs that looked deceptively real, a number of designers in the late 1980s and early 1990s embraced obvious imitations, as some had several decades earlier. "Fun fur"

Figure 6.14 Installation shot from *Eco-Fashion: Going Green* (The Museum at FIT, 2010). Leftmost ensemble: Oscar de la Renta, coat and hat, green wool, faux leopard skin, Mongolian lamb fur, Fall 1995, USA. Collection of The Museum at FIT, 96.81.2. Gift of Oscar de la Renta. Second from left: Dolce and Gabbana, coat, tiger print faux fur, 1992, Italy. Collection of The Museum at FIT, P92.58.16. Museum purchase. Photograph © The Museum at FIT.

colors and exaggerated styles and motifs were techniques used then; the latter was likewise adopted by Dolce & Gabbana, whose 1992 printed "tiger-stripe" coat (Figure 6.14) typifies this look. Linda Wells wrote, "obvious fakes are certainly more appealing" in light of the "current concern about wildlife preservation."[230] Still, designers had mixed views on the subject of fake fur, as a *Women's Wear Daily* article noted, questioning also whether fakes might provide "the real thing a big boost." Some designers used it, they acknowledged, more as a fashion choice than an ethical one.[231]

Suggestions for further reading

Koshetz, H. (1964), "Imitation Fur is Flying High as Fabric for Women's Coats," *New York Times*, June 17.
Schiro, A. (1989), "Fake Furs are Saving More Skins," *New York Times*, September 5.

CONCLUSION

This book is part of an ongoing discussion on the sustainable fashion industry. While it is the first publication to focus on the history of the relationship between fashion and the environment, it was designed to provide context for the current challenges being faced by the fashion industry. Within each of the topics discussed, there remains room for further exploration. We hope that this text provides a framework for future study by others who are interested in the field. The authors are indebted to those who laid groundwork for our own research, many of whom are cited within our text.

As the sustainable fashion industry continues to evolve and expand at a rapid pace, the true experts are those who are immersed in its day-to-day operations. The following pages feature six interviews that were conducted between the authors of this book and leaders in sustainable fashion practice. While designers are clearly of great importance to the sustainable fashion industry, educators and entrepreneurs also play a crucial role in the development and dissemination of ideas. Their combined knowledge will drive the future of sustainable fashion.

Interview with Adam Baruchowitz, Wearable Collections

Wearable Collections is a clothing recycling business based in New York. Entrepreneur Adam Baruchowitz founded the company in 2004, after he noticed a bag of unwanted clothing waiting for pick-up in the hallway of his apartment building for three weeks. In an effort to make clothing recycling as convenient and efficient as possible, he began negotiations to place clothing recycling bins in buildings all over New York City. Wearable Collections has since expanded to become a fixture at many of the city's popular green-markets. Baruchowitz estimates that his company has now picked up nearly seven million pounds of unwanted clothing, shoes and textiles that may have otherwise ended up in landfills. While Wearable Collections is a for-profit agency, a portion of its proceeds goes to charities, including The Miami Project to Cure Paralysis and Habitat for Humanity.

Colleen Hill: *What inspired you to begin Wearable Collections?*
Adam Baruchowitz: I have a friend who has a sorting facility based out of New Jersey. He has a [textile] sorting facility, and he was always telling me about the

opportunities in used clothing. It seemed like a good business opportunity. I would consider myself more of an entrepreneur than an eco-entrepreneur, and if there was an opportunity that availed itself I was interested in it.

CH: *What type of work had you done prior to textile recycling?*

AB: I was a stock day trader for ten years. I managed both jobs concurrently when I started Wearable Collections. This really started as a project. The other part of the story is that one of my day trading partners at my firm was hit by a car and paralyzed. These two things were running concurrently in my mind—my friend's accident and the opportunities in used clothing. My friend was paralyzed from the chest down, and we wanted to do anything we could to raise funds for spinal research. We had a large group of friends that were wholeheartedly behind supporting our fallen friend.

I was living in the Village, in a building that had about 250 units in it. Someone left a bag of used clothing to be picked up in the hall. That was my "light bulb moment." It doesn't really make sense for the Salvation Army or Goodwill to come and pick up one bag at a time. There's a reason it was sitting in the hallway for three weeks. I thought it would make sense to put a collection bin in a building—my building was a whole community in itself.

I'm from Long Island [New York], and the way it works there is that either they call you or someone drops a flyer in your mailbox. They'll basically cover a whole neighborhood with flyers that tell homeowners which day to leave their used clothing out. It's a more labor-intensive system. First of all, you need guys running around putting materials out, or you need a call center. It takes a lot of time. But in one building in New York, you could probably reach the same amount that it takes people to go around all day in the suburbs.

CH: *And everyone in New York needs to get rid of things, because very few people have storage space.*

AB: Yes, there are all of these ancillary things that come together and make sense. I thought that one building would basically be enough to make it worthwhile. As an entrepreneur, I'm the type of person who comes up with an idea and just attacks it. I don't come up with a business plan or anything like that. We just engaged some of our friends and asked them to put bins in their buildings. That was the beginning.

CH: *So it was really just reaching out to friends first?*

AB: Yes, it started off simply as a project. We were just getting to every building we could. This was not easy. We had three partners at that time, and we had no experience. What it really is, when you're dealing with buildings, is waste management. You want to put a garbage bin in a building, basically. As much as you can glorify what this actually is, to the superintendent and the people that manage buildings, you're a waste management solution. It's keeping items out of the garbage. We got into ten to fifteen buildings to start with, and realized the difficulty of handling the logistics of just a few accounts in NYC.

CH: *How many bins are there now?*

AB: Now we have over 200 bins in buildings throughout the city. Really, to tell you the truth, the bins aren't necessarily our focus anymore. They're just one of the verticals of what we do. We've made an amazing partnership with the people who run the greenmarkets. We collect a lot of clothes at these markets. Right now we're doing 26 markets weekly.

We're trying to organize this so if we have a bin route on the Upper West Side on a Thursday, we handle a couple of greenmarkets there that day—we're just trying to figure out ways to maximize volume per trip. We get paid per pound, basically, for the stuff that we collect. I know what my costs are going to be—the truck, gas, employees. So we need to collect enough clothes to cover those costs.

CH: *How many employees do you have at the moment?*

AB: We have about 15, and most are part-time. If you break down what we do, I think one of the most impressive things we do is efficiency. I think from the outside, people think that we're a lot larger business. People will see me on a video, then they'll call to inquire about a bin and say, "wait, I just saw you!" I'm the person who answers the phone, too. We're a small business.

We keep trucks in Redhook [Brooklyn], but our base is basically just a tractor-trailer. The trucks drive around the city through the routes and then we empty it out into the back of a tractor-trailer. When that trailer is full, it goes to a sorting facility. There's no warehouse. We only really handle it from the point of collecting these bags, putting it in the bag, putting it in the truck. So we don't sort it at all really. As much as Wearable Collections promotes itself as a recycling organization, we've only been able to do that because my partner is the guy who runs the sorting facility. I know the ins and outs of the people we're dealing with. But really once we collect it and sell it to them, it's off our hands.

CH: *And sorting is a whole other endeavor.*

AB: Yes. I have experience with it just because of my proximity to my partner. I spent some time devoted to understanding his operation. I'm very interested in running a transparent company, so I wanted to know the whole stream of what I was dealing with. Wearable Collections is focused on keeping the textile items from entering the waste stream, while the sorting facility's job is to distinguish different types of grades of materials and distribute them to their proper destination.

CH: *Your website helps, too. You have an FAQ page on which you clearly state how Wearable Collections operates.*

AB: I want to be honest. Sometimes I sit at the Farmer's Market and I have discussions with people. I know how to answer their questions as well as anyone, and still people take their bag out and tell me they'd rather take it to the Salvation Army. Some people have their imbedded views, and that's part of the green movement. We're trying to change some of those imbedded views, raise consciousness a little. I'm pretty proud of that.

CH: *Do you feel that for textile recycling to be feasible on a large scale, it does have to be a business rather than a charity?*

AB: That's the way for anything to be successful. Large charities are run like companies. Some are very mission-based, obviously, and they're not really fundable with anything other than donations. But when it's something that's operational and actually producing goods, they're run like large businesses—the difference is more of an accounting thing.

People are often so happy with what [large charities] do, but those guys are first trying to resell the clothing back to Americans, because that's where they can make the most money—rather than packaging it en masse and selling it abroad. And after that what doesn't sell just enters the same chain of the stuff that we [Wearable Collections] sell for the most part. It enters the international used clothing market. Because they're dealing with such volume, they can keep the price at a certain level. They're the ones who are dominating. I always compare it to Target and Walmart—some of these organizations are huge. They have good missions and I'm sure they do a lot of good things with the capital that they generate, but once you get so big, you're subject to any of the issues that happen with large organizations.

CH: *I think that most people don't think about the organization of large charities.*

AB: I think things are changing now. A lot of these solutions aren't permanent; they're just working right now. But I think it's important to raise consciousness of [textile recycling]. I always think about how we started this before *The Inconvenient Truth* came out. That was an interesting turning point, really. When *An Inconvenient Truth* came out, I thought, "well, we are green. We are keeping items out of landfills. We are maintaining these resources that someone worked really hard on." Growing the cotton, sending it to China—it's already gone all that distance to be produced, so I think that it only makes sense to keep things in circulation once they're made. So we began using "green" in our marketing and literature. I think we were really early on that tip.

CH: *Have you found that the textile recycling industry has noticeably changed and grown over the past decade?*

AB: For sure. The sell has gotten easier and easier. But as the sell gets easier for me, it also gets easier for other people. [New York City] has started a textile-recycling program, for the most part copying exactly what Wearable Collections has done, but not really allowing us to participate, because we're a for-profit.

When I said we're not really focusing on buildings, maybe that's part of the reason. It's hard for me to compete with Housing Works. They're the ones who won the bid [for City of New York textile recycling]. They have these really beautiful bins, whereas we're doing this really efficiently, so we have used bins that we wrap in a canvas material. When it comes to luxury buildings in the city, people really care about these things. Housing Works has a sales force, whereas a lot of our business has simply come from having a decent website, having decent media exposure, and being out there in the greenmarkets is a key part of it. The partnership with the greenmarkets for NYC has been important for the amount of clothing we get.

Our marketing is: hopefully you hear about us, and hopefully you request a bin for your building. Whereas the first thing [the city] does is spend a million dollars to get flyers about recycling in every mailbox across the city. In the past week, I've seen two buildings leave me for the city program. But I saw their numbers for the year, and they're nowhere near ours—so even though they're a large organization, with all this money, it's still hard to get a lot of clothes.

CH: *Do you have any idea of how many pounds of clothing you've collected since Wearable Collections began?*

AB: I would say we're close to seven million pounds collected now. Over the past two or three years, numbers have been at 1.2 million, 1.75 million, and we'll probably pass two million this year. We're starting to generate a good amount of clothing now. And even then it's a small percentage of New York City residential waste. As per the 2004/05 Waste Characterization study, New Yorkers discarded 386 million pounds of textiles per year. That's including curtains and carpets, and shoes.

CH: *And you accept everything except carpets, right?*

AB: Yes. And 386 million pounds of waste was in 2004, so I imagine that's probably growing per year as well. Two million pounds is a small percentage of the actual total. People ask if we'll be expanding to other areas, but there's plenty of growth potential in New York alone.

CH: *So you don't plan to expand to other cities?*

AB: Probably not. We've done collections as far as Boston and Washington, DC, so we will do that if it makes sense. I'm not going to say we won't expand to cities in different ways. We're starting a shoe recycling division of Wearable Collections. Shoes can potentially be taken national instead of just local. If people pack enough shoes in a box, and they ship it to us, I can pay for the shipping. Working with shoes may allow us to reach more people, and that's really exciting to me, to try to attack from another direction.

The way you get paid, for the most part, is on loose credential clothing. There's a certain expectation of a percentage of shoes in this. So we do accept everything, and that's because everything is going to be part of any bag that you're not looking at. When you go to a store, and they're accepting it for resale, they're going to be more particular about what they're accepting. When it comes to the bin business, you have no idea what people are putting in there. From any untouched bag, as a general rule across the industry, maybe 50 per cent is going to be used as secondhand clothing, 20 percent is going to be used as rags, and the rest will be broken down, shredded to be used for low-grade fiber products. There's very little money in the textile waste that's not reused as secondhand clothing.

We do accept everything, but some companies want to be green and they want to use Wearable Collections to get rid of their scraps. Sometimes I have to say I can't come and pick that up. I could be inundated with scraps that have no value to the people I'm bringing the items to. Sometimes I pick up 20 or 30 bags of scraps—I've done it, many times. As a small business, you never know where the relationship starts. If it's a [large clothing company] and they want you to pick up their scraps, you do it with the hope of getting better items in the future. A lot of this is trial and error.

Interview with Bob Bland, Manufacture New York

Bob Bland has an important mission: to bring clothing manufacturing back to New York City. Ms. Bland—a fashion designer, entrepreneur, and community art advocate—founded her locally made clothing line, Brooklyn Royalty, in 2006. Consistently inspired by the creativity and aesthetic innovations of her fellow Brooklyn residents, Bland has since spearheaded a number of innovative projects. In 2010, for example, she opened Kingdom, a unique concept store that served as a bar, boutique, and gallery space for the local creative community.

More recently, Bland set her sights on her largest endeavor yet: Manufacture New York, "a fashion incubator/factory hybrid dedicated to providing independent designers with the resources and skills to streamline their production processes and transform local manufacturing into the most affordable, innovative option for all." With Bland's astute understanding of New York's fashion industry (she has worked as a menswear designer for Rugby Ralph Lauren and Triple Five Soul, among others), Manufacture New York has developed into a superbly planned model for local fashion production. Many of its participants are also interested in other aspects of sustainable design.

Colleen Hill: *You have design experience with major labels like Ralph Lauren. What inspired you to shift focus to your own label, and to local production?*

Bob Bland: I went into the corporate world specifically because I wanted to see how they do it in big business—what works, what doesn't work. It's important that we don't shun the corporate world, but rather take a look at it, to get involved. Their design processes, product development, the ways they structure their businesses are very relevant to what's going on in the rest of the industry—whether you plan on starting your own line eventually or not.

Certainly in terms of sustainability, there's no way that we're going to be able to affect major change without working with major labels. A lot of that can come from inside changes—little things that designers can do from within their organizations to make their lines more sustainable. For me, one of the best and most positive impacts that we can have is bringing production back to the United States, and preferably as local as possible. Most major labels are making their goods overseas, whether it be in India, China, or southeast Asia. It's very difficult to be connected to the production process when the only contact you have is over the phone, through tech specs, and through email correspondence.

CH: *What are some of the biggest problems with overseas production?*

BB: Working with manufacturers overseas can lead to major errors. If manufacturers were closer in and working directly with product development teams, maybe the quality of the clothing produced would be much better. Certainly you can then go into how wasteful it is to be boating a huge amount of goods. It's wasteful in time, it's wasteful in money, and it's wasteful ecologically. Businesses that have the opportunity to support the local economy should do that. It's a matter of bringing infrastructure back here to New York, but there are a lot of challenges involved. It would be very expensive to move operations. It will take a lot of time to reorganize the current manufacturing system. For big brands, it's something that would have to be done gradually. For as much money and time was spent moving production overseas 20 or 30 years ago, it would take just as much time at least to bring it back here. That would have a huge economic impact on a company for multiple years.

But before anyone starts pointing fingers at anybody for not bringing manufacturing back to the US, they've got to remember that these are businesses. They are employing people currently. If they would have to lay off their entire work force to be able to bring it back, is that worth it? I just want to clarify that I considered all of those things, and certainly I don't blame companies who are hesitant to bring manufacturing back to the US. I think it makes sense to first bring back capsule lines and try that out, lay the inroads for a structure, and then bring back as much as you can as quickly as you can.

CH: *Tell me more about starting your brand, Brooklyn Royalty.*

BB: Because I was starting a line fresh, I made a conscious decision from the beginning to make it all in the US, and to use as many local materials as possible. That was the complete intention of the line—to show my love of Brooklyn. When I moved here, it inspired me so much to see the incredibly creative, passionate community. I'm originally from Northern Virginia, right outside of Washington, DC. I grew up with a real sense of public service and social responsibility, because of growing up right outside of the capital. Coming into fashion I felt really uncomfortable on the corporate side, only having to think about design, and being asked to only consider design decisions versus the most holistic idea of "what am I making here, and what impact does it have?" It was so fun with Brooklyn Royalty to actually know the makers of my clothes, and to get to see them on a regular basis—as difficult as that was, because there's currently not a lot of infrastructure for finding manufacturers.

When I was starting Brooklyn Royalty, not only did nobody care whether things were made in the USA or not, a lot of people thought it was strange. I knew it was what I wanted to do, but I had to just make my own way. Nobody would tell me anything about where I could get this done, or what to do, or what the path was really—and they don't teach that in a school. I know a lot of schools are just now starting to address that more, and to integrate sustainability into their regular curriculum.

CH: *Do you feel that things are picking up speed in terms of interest in local manufacturing?*

BB: Undoubtedly. I'm incredibly positive and happy to be a part of the future of local manufacturing. I received unprecedented—really completely unanticipated—support of Manufacture New York. People's minds have changed throughout the industry. It's incredibly encouraging. I think it's important, just in terms of perspective, to know where we came from with this. Every era wonders how they got to the point they're at. I always like to preface talking about now with talking about the past—because I did actually live that. So I think it's valuable to know what it was like in the early 2000s. Now we're in a place where we're collaborating on novel ideas without fear of people stealing them.

CH: *What were the steps involved in starting Manufacture New York?*

BB: I founded Manufacture New York by myself. It turns out there's a lot of people who have had ideas similar to this, but I think what makes MNY different is that I am a designer, and I need this for my own brand. We're not a professional organization, coming down and doing something for designers. We're not an academic institution—we're designers creating this for designers.

I had a dream and then I just woke up and wrote it all down. I truly believe that my entire career and every experience I've had both on the corporate and independent design side of fashion has been leading up to this. By doing Brooklyn Royalty over the last seven years, I met a ton of other designers who were interested in the same thing. That community was supportive of each other and we shared resources whenever we could. We just didn't have something like this—this will be a central location where people can get support, mentorship, and training on both the business and design side of things. For instance, one of the keystones of this is helping designers to recognize that their line can be their business. They shouldn't have to have another job in retail or restaurants—that's not the way it should be. We're going to have mentors who are on staff to help with sourcing. It's going to be a real incubator. The classes that we're going to offer are going to be offered to everyone—including the public.

We're going to offer legal, accounting, business development classes, co-working space with industrial sewing machines and also with actual desks. You'd be amazed how much having something like a copy machine changes your business. Having one place where all of that is streamlined and together just makes sense. Then we take it one step further and say "well, why should the manufacturing be separate from that?" What I've seen is that some of the most successful, well-received, innovative lines have failed—and it's always been the manufacturing that really kills it.

What we're also bringing to the table is not just a fashion incubator with classes—we're also going to have a production facility in-house. We're only going to work with someone who is committed to transparency and sustainability and bringing innovation to the production process. The designers will get assigned a product development manager that will help them through the process. We'll also be teaching them the best practices with how to communicate with factories. That's one of the biggest things—most designers don't learn that in school, so they never learn it. Just having those tools and knowing what you need to have to place an order, when to place orders, how to get that ready, how to prepare those materials so that you can come to your production manager and have it all ready to go—that is a huge hurdle for designers. Apparel manufacturing is an industrial process; it's more than just a design education that is needed to do the work. But once you have that skill, you can take it to any factory in the world, and it's pretty similar.

Manufacture New York wants to begin working with small runs specifically, but our factory is open to everybody. So if bigger brands want to try bringing some manufacturing back, and want to try to do it with us, that's great. If more established, made in NYC brands want to try something that's more transparent, we're here for them. For designers who are already participating in the incubator, everyone has two opportunities a month to place an order—set times—and then we're going to establish the production schedule based off of that. That will mean predictable lead times, predictable pricing—a lot of these things are huge hurdles for small designers. There's an enormous amount of waste that happens when designers aren't able to meet their lead times, and there can be whole orders that can be wasted and sold for pennies when deadlines are missed.

CH: *Was it more difficult to work in a sustainable way when you began designing for yourself?*

BB: Eco-fashion wasn't part of our awareness at first. My friends and I just considered ourselves indie designers, and our clothes were made in NYC. What we found out, though, was that what we were doing was already sustainable. My main concern is that people need to do what makes sense for them. If we want to move toward sustainability, people need to be in business to do that. You have to have it integrated into a fiscally sustainable business plan. So that's the really great thing about doing it locally. Are we paying people more? Yes. Can we save money? Yes, we can, because there's a lot of waste and a lot of overhead that comes from doing a global supply chain.

There are a lot of sustainable options that are just plain practical. We have a tribe of designers in MNY who do low-waste or no-waste fashion. They initially did it because they were able to go dive at textile factories in the area and get huge plastic bags filled with scrap fabrics. And that was free! By doing that, they happened to be contributing to a more closed-loop product. But they never thought about it that way. They just thought about its practicality.

I always used old leather that I got at the Salvation Army to cut up to make bags, for example, or I would take the cuttings from a moto jacket and make all of my leather trims out of that. Once again, it's a closed loop. That was cheaper, and it had the aesthetic I wanted. I wanted a used look to the leather, but it seemed stupid to enzyme wash it, etc. if I could find leather that was old and looked old. Also, the idea of making products that look authentic is really important to a lot of our designers. A way to achieve an authentic look was to use old materials. I would go diving at these insane old army/navy warehouses to get my camo material because it was dead stock—it was just sitting there rotting. And I could get it for two or three dollars a yard instead of one hundred dollars. That's how we did things. It wasn't just my brand. We weren't buying a whole lot of new materials because we couldn't afford to. But it turned out that not only was it a better looking product, it was also better for the environment.

This was before the food movement happened. I look at the food and tech movements all the time. Those are reference points of industries that I think are doing it right. The same way that I've been looking at music since 2008 for cues on how to *not* run my business as a fashion designer. There are some real changes happening globally, in various industries, that are beneficial to observe.

CH: *What are some other benefits of local production?*

BB: Local production is sustainable *anywhere*. It makes sense globally. It helps retain culture, it helps retain artisanal practices that are specific to your community, it's vital to helping economic development into communities that have been depressed for years. That's all over the world—the recession has affected everyone. It's great for creating sustainable economies where everyone is being uplifted, and everyone is getting some sort of enrichment from that. That's what MNY is—we're paying people good, steady, livable wages, and we're also going to help people in local communities to come and learn these skills that haven't been available to them otherwise. We hope that all sorts of people come up with ideas like this. It's not just for our industry, but also for a lot of industries. Overall, we need to bring more manufacturing and more jobs back to the US.

If we do things locally, there's going to be much less waste, in different ways— waste of money, waste of materials, waste of energy resources—it hits everywhere.

Interview with Kate Brierley, Isoude

Designer Kate Brierley combines her sophisticated aesthetic with a thoughtful approach to design. Brierley launched her line, Isoude, in Newport, Rhode Island in 2008, with a focus on quality—from the construction of her clothes to the building of relationships with the women who wear them. At the core of her business is the creation of beautiful, artistic, and enduring products—a system that has brought dividends and earned customer loyalty.

Jennifer Farley Gordon: *What is your company philosophy?*

Kate Brierley: Our philosophy is very much based on a concept of long-term, meaningful relationships, and creating quality pieces. There's a quote on my website, and I talk about creating garments and clothing for women that they'll collect over a lifetime. ["To purchase clothing is a transaction, to build a wardrobe that ages with you through life, is enrichment—we design for the latter."[1]] It's kind of the opposite of fast fashion that we're really interested in…

I'm very passionate about dressing women. I want to know them for a long period of time; I want them to have a relationship with us, and with the clothing for a long period of time. I want to know their daughters. I want to know their mothers. And that's what happens. We sell to these multi-generational families, and we've known them now for years.

JFG: *That's great.*

KB: It's special. It's a real relationship. There's give-and-take, and we are so supported by this kind of tribe of women. We are very fortunate. To get back to the philosophy, it has to do with integrity, with building meaningful relationships, and creating things that people will carry with them through their lives.

JFG: *What was it that got you started along this avenue of sustainable design? Was it as a student, or once you were out in the industry?*

KB: The seeds of it were planted when I was younger. I grew up riding horses and I was literally in the same uniform day in and day out. I had custom-made Vogel boots, I had a beautiful Hermes saddle, and I had these wonderfully made British riding jackets. It really created in me an indelible respect for well-crafted pieces. You know it's kind of strange, when you first get something, like a piece of equipment, or a jacket, or your boots in the equestrian world, it kind of takes you a year to break it in and really appreciate it. I don't know, maybe that was it, but I still have my pieces and I still wear them …

I think that the values of the sustainable vision and my values, there's a lot of overlap. I asked myself what is worth spending your time, and money, and effort on. That's how it started; it wasn't so specific.

I was originally styling people, and I was shopping for people, and I really wanted to find pieces that I felt were in harmony with a female sensuality—not an over exaggeration of female sexuality, and not ignoring it either. I just wanted pieces that were beautiful and feminine and strong, like the women that I knew.

JFG: *One of the things I wanted to talk about with you was natural dyeing—how you got involved, as well as your work with your mentor, Cheryl Kolander?*

KB: When I was 19, I went to study abroad, telling my parents I was on a tour, but instead touring through Southeast Asia by myself, and spending time with hill tribes in Thailand. I don't know why I was drawn to them, but they have an incredible sense of style and the colors were unbelievable in their costume and in their dress. The colors were very rich and very vibrant, but in no way an assault to your senses. I loved these colors and I wasn't sure if I had seen them before.

Fast-forward eight years ... I was painting my own fabrics ... and then, I kind of remembered those colors. I thought, oh, they must dye them naturally. Because you know when you look at antique oriental rugs—how beautiful the colors are? The colors—they're so rich and very different than synthetic colors. That led me to want to study how to naturally dye fabric, and honestly, the pursuit is for artisanal production only ... I went out and I studied with Cheryl Kolander, and there's absolutely an element of alchemy to it. You have to understand that when you're working with natural dyes, you're working with living organisms, and it's kind of ... have you ever made bread?

JFG: *I haven't ...*

KB: You're kind of subject to how the yeast is reacting with the environment and all of that. It's very similar. It's complicated, and you have to be willing to roll with it. Cheryl really a master in this genre, and she has spent her whole life studying this. So there I was in her basement, in Portland, for days, just going over the different methodologies. Then I began experimenting on my own, and I was working out of these massive pots. They were 10, 15, 20 gallon pots. The process is to heat the silk and mordant and then boil down the dyestuffs. It's a very tactile process, and very physically challenging, but the colors that you get are great, and not something that you can derive from a synthetic process. I got better at it as I went along. There's something about that process that is very moving, a little shamanistic—my desire to do this work comes and goes for me as a designer. There are periods where I'm really into it. Then I go through periods where I'm more into painting and now I've gotten more into making our own prints. But I know I'm going to go back to it.

Materials are one part of the equation. Process is another part of the equation. There's so much that goes into what sustainability really is ... You can't try to make something that's an artisanal process for a mass market. Not only will you ruin the supply source, but also then it's not so special anymore ... it's good that things are special. I think waiting lists for products are great. Wait! Create demand for it and create excitement, just do it that way.

JFG: *We should have fewer things, but what we do have, should be special.*

KB: Yes! Just make them great, and collect them. I love the idea of collecting things in your life. Collecting experiences, collecting clothing, collecting jewelry, whatever it is. It's so rewarding.

JFG: *Do you find that your clientele actively seek you out because of some of the practices of sustainability and quality, or is it initially that they are drawn to your design style—your aesthetic—and then you're kind of bringing sustainability to women who might not have been exposed to it before?*

KB: I think that they're drawn to quality. I think that they sense without knowing all the specifics … when they look at our clothes … even if they don't have a lot of experience with fashion, they see something that registers to them as quality. That brings them in the door. What makes somebody make a purchase is that they look good. Really, no one is going to spend $2000 on something unless they look and feel great. That's OK. That's my job as a fashion designer to take these materials and to execute it in such a way that it becomes very sophisticated and very appealing to a client. I think that people come back because of the product and the atmosphere …

JFG: *You can tick every box of sustainability, but no one will buy it because it doesn't look good …*

KB: Unless people are going to purchase it and use it, it's kind of a waste. I hate to say that, but it's true. We have very little waste; we sell everything that we make.

JFG: *That's fantastic. I'm wondering what kind of advice you would give to students or others who'd like to emulate what you do, and incorporate practices that are sustainable into their work.*

KB: I think the first and most important step is "to thine own self be true." You have to be very clear about what your skill set is. If you really love the fashion industry, recognize that there are many different parts of it. It's just as important to be a great patternmaker as it is a seamstress as it is a textile designer as it is a fashion designer. So I think the first step is what do you love, what do you really love to do?

I think the next step is to have real life experience before you run your own company. If you're coming out of school look to companies that have shared values, and do everything you can to make yourself important to those companies. It's not about you. It is *not about you* at all, at that point … You have to learn how to listen to the market, learn what your company needs are, and what your client's needs are …Then I think the final step if you really want to go out on your own—what is that crossover between what you're good at, what you love, and what there's actually a market for? I think if you overlap those things you can be very successful. I think the last piece is your definition of success … Success is different to different people … Is success coming into a downturn economy and creating a community around your product? Is getting into Bergdorf Goodman your success? Is selling a billion dollars of clothes your definition of success? Everybody's different.

You really have to be honest about who you are and what your own path is. And stick to it. And work really, really hard …

JFG: *What are your future plans for Isoude?*

KB: I think the plan is to keep growing at a very sustainable rate. Our growth rates have been very strong. We're profitable … What I would really love … is for us to keep doing what we're doing. We've got this great little store/atelier, and now I've begun to hire girls, women who have graduated from RISD and FIT fashion schools, that are really passionate about quality construction and the integrity of the process … I just want to keep putting the highest quality people and product in front of the highest quality customer … When you have that, wonderful things come from it … It's a miracle that our company is working as well as it is … I mean not a miracle, but it is really unusual …

JFG: *You've hit something that appeals to people—that appeals to their value systems.*

KB: I think there's a certain way we approach our clients. Our clients are really smart, honestly. They're smart, dynamic women, and they want to be treated with respect. And they want quality. It's not about the price; it's really about the value. They feel like, for whatever reason, this is a good value for them …

JFG: *Do you have final thoughts?*

KB: I believe in the power of beauty … That's what I care about … that's what I'm going to think about on my deathbed. Did you create beauty? Did you put something worthwhile into the world? And I did, I went for it … for better or for worse. You have to try …

Interview: John Patrick of Organic by John Patrick

Organic by John Patrick was founded in 2003, when the idea of making high-fashion clothing that was also sustainable was nearly unheard of. John Patrick's interest in sustainability goes well beyond design: he learned how cotton is planted, for example, and how color cotton is grown. He has also lived and worked in Peru, where he gained firsthand knowledge of what goes into creating, developing and producing high quality, organic garments.

In 2007, John Patrick's essay on the origins of his business and its relationship to organic fibers was featured in a book entitled *FutureFashion White Papers,* which highlighted numerous designers, scholars and businesses that were making an impact on the burgeoning sustainable fashion movement. The following year, the designer was nominated for the prestigious Council of the Fashion Designers of America/*Vogue* Fashion Fund award—proving that best practice and great design need not be mutually exclusive. Today, John Patrick is a fierce advocate for non-GMO farming. His label continues to thrive.

Colleen Hill: *You worked within the traditional fashion industry before beginning your Organic label in 2003. What inspired you to focus exclusively on sustainable design?*

John Patrick: It was a personal decision to go out of the box and start to truly understand all of the components and elements within the manufacturing supply chain to make a difference and be true to my own beliefs. I read a speech that William McDonough had written and read at St. John the Divine[2] in the 1990s, called "Ethics and Design." It became a roadmap for me and how I began to relate architecture to fashion in my process. It was not only how I made and designed my collections, but where. The choice of an abandoned building as the physical home of the brand was critical because I was forced to look within myself and decide—what did I truly stand for? What were my beliefs?

The core basics of the Organic brand have always stayed true to these ideals. While widely copied and imitated my essentials are made in a very unique way with both the materials and the fit. They are the heritage now of the Organic by John Patrick brand and are sold worldwide in specialty stores and on the web. Customers have come to both trust and depend on us to supply them with clothing that has both integrity and soul.

CH: *Of the many sustainable practices you incorporate into your work, the sourcing of fabric seems especially crucial. Can you tell us about your fabric choices, and how options of eco-friendly materials have increased and evolved over the past decade?*

JP: Sourcing was a real issue when I started in 2002–3. I had already been gathering research and learning about how vast the textile universe is, but it was not until I saw firsthand organic cotton being grown on small plots of land, and processed by a farm collective in Canete, Peru, did I truly understand the potential of the movement. People all over the world were thinking and doing work in the sustainable manufacturing movement, but it was very piecemeal—you really needed to work to dig and find out what the different certifications meant from both a soil perspective and then a processing perspective. I chose early on to focus on organic cotton and the different byproducts that also come from cotton.

CH: *The name "Organic" obviously refers to many of your fabric choices, but do you feel it describes your overall approach to design?*

JP: Yes of course. I famously embrace mistakes. It was one of the decisions early on to accept the natural way that things go. Let it go! As far as the designing of a collection goes, it is a long and arduous process that is extremely slow and methodical. I want to design and produce collections and individual garments that are both collected and cherished.

CH: *How do you contend with the paradoxical nature of the sustainable fashion industry—specifically, the continued desire for creative output versus the need to manufacture and consume less?*

JP: Brands such as mine address these by being true to our DNA and really producing ethical garments. If you read the speech I wrote that was read at Fordham this spring—*before* the disaster in Bangladesh—I am actually discussing this also. Design and fashion have the power to transform the world and make it a much better place but we need to rethink what it is that we really need. Growth for the sake of growth is very detrimental to many businesses—and should be avoided until one ascertains the effects.

CH: *How did you begin working directly with farmers and cooperatives?*

JP: I met a woman in Peru whose name is Zenaida Cespedes. Her family has been farming in the Amazonian jungle for many years. We met at an Organic Exchange conference in Peru, and her knowledge of both the jungle and cotton inspired myself and my assistant to work on a project with her. From a group of 200 farmers we worked with ten, and paid a 30 percent higher price for their cotton output. It had the effect of pushing the entire area's price up to the price we were paying. Again, small efforts gain good results. Unfortunately, the world economic collapse did not help us to grow this project. Bankers don't have much interest in collective farmers—at all. Zenaida and I are still great friends and talk often, and one day we will again start up our project—only this time on a very small scale, and keep it small. The little piece of land that the community gave me in the jungle (Selva) is proof that we started there!

CH: *Your interest in sustainability goes beyond the realm of fashion. We've heard you mention a "Green Revolution"—what does that entail?*

JP: It is happening now. The industrial food supply is both tired and worn out, and not very nourishing in any aspect. The small food growers and providers and processors are both now the backbone and the engine for the new world order. Eating, living, wearing, spending less is the new ideal. We work with what I call the new "Mom and Pops"—the little stores that really understand us and support us. We will no longer be available for purchase in any department stores from January 2014 onward. Adaptive creativity and community are the future for the enlightened. Shopping in a hollow box owned by a corporation that doesn't care about you or your community is pointless. Sadly, even the design schools are stuck in twentieth-century mode— tired twentieth-century ideas that are both damaging and ineffective. Students barely have any idea of fashion or design history, nor the connectivity between agriculture and fashion. Rather pathetic actually—much of this is due to very lazy academic structure and fear of the future. Young creatives have now actually rebelled against the old formalism—see the creation of new areas of design and interdisciplinary cross-pollination. What is very old is now new again, and what is new is no longer *relevant* —this is also key to the Organic design philosophy always.

CH: *What's next for Organic?*

JP: We have established a new concept (www.communitie.org). COMMUNITIE fosters revolutionary ideas by promoting sustainable projects and education, and supporting social and artistic exchange. We believe that togetherness results in real "community" when its people are educated and inspired. It's great—it's a 501k directly tied to new ideas.

Interview with Naomi Gross, Assistant Chair, Fashion Merchandising Management, Fashion Institute of Technology, SUNY

Regarding fashion and sustainability, it is important to consider not just design, but the whole process of production, which includes things like sourcing, shipping, and management of retail establishments. Naomi Gross brings to her role as Assistant Chair of the Fashion Merchandising Management program at the Fashion Institute of Technology (FIT) many years of experience as a buyer for major retail organizations, such as Dress Barn and United Retail Group. During her career in the industry, she was involved with initiatives that helped her companies' bottom-lines, but also saved fuel, energy, and materials.

"When I was working in the industry," she recalled, "I had to focus on my company, my role, and I didn't really have a lot of time to take a look at what was happening in the big wide world, outside from what my competitors were doing." She relishes the 14 years she has been teaching, as it provides her with "the luxury of a much more global view of what is happening in the industry." Several years ago, she developed FM326: Sustainability in Fashion Merchandising, now an elective in her department's curriculum. Gross is enthusiastic about the many and varied sustainable measures taken by retail organizations. For her, making connections to the people and processes involved in fashion production is one of the most crucial aspects of sustainability.

Jennifer Farley Gordon: *I was wondering what sparked your interest in sustainability.*

Naomi Gross: When I worked in industry, I made decisions related to the bottom line that also had far-reaching implications for sustainability that we didn't even consider back then. Dress Barn is a really good example. We imported a lot of garments. A lot of the product was made in India and China, and we worked with many freight forwarders. We filled many containers but often containers would not be filled to capacity. That affected our freight charges per garment because you rent the container and the cost is then divvied up based on the number of garments shipped in each one. I was a large size buyer. I worked with a missy buyer who had a much bigger pencil than I did … We both bought suits—in some cases the same style and same fabrication, but we did not always plan for the same deliveries. So our CFO came to both of us, and said … "do you think we can start doing some consolidation of your deliveries, so that we can fill the containers to capacity and therefore reduce the freight charges per garment?" We were talking about cost savings … but as I now know we were also taking about sustainability. Other things that we did with cost savings in mind included finding ways to fit more garments into cartons and change the carton sizes to maximize how many we could fit into a container … We started by having lots of discussion about reducing the packaging inside the cartons. How could we minimize the packaging, including poly bags, pins, and plastic clips, to make each carton more productive and in turn make each container more cost effective?

I've been attending the National Retail Federation's (NRF) Big Show in January almost every year since I began teaching at FIT. For a number of years, the NRF Big Show included a track on sustainability. It was really at a time when the conversation was just beginning on the retail side. Everyone equated sustainability with added expense. It was a real game changer when Wal-Mart did a presentation for the track. The presentation focused on some of their sustainability initiatives which had resulted in huge cost savings. One initiative included adding wind flaps on the sides of their trucks, improving the aerodynamic quality, and therefore improving the mileage and reducing the fuel needed for each trip ... you can do something that's sustainable, that saves resources, and guess what, it saves money. A win-win. Think about how many trucks Wal-Mart engages to move their product—it was a huge cost savings ...

I really feel like the industry is moving in that direction in small ways, in big ways. I don't really think that there's any turning back at this point.

JFG: *In the description for your course, there is a sentence ... that ties to what you were just talking about with Wal-Mart doing the small things that saved money. You teach about "the fiscal implications of implementing sustainability initiatives, illustrating that sustainability and profit are not mutually exclusive." I wonder is it, for some companies ... fiscal uncertainties that prevent them from changing certain practices that they've had in place for a long time?*

NG: One of the things that really struck me in the past year's Retail Industry Leaders Association (RILA) report ... was that they looked at what the most forward-thinking companies are doing, how they're doing it, and what kind of returns they are looking at. How far down the road are they expecting to see a return on their investments? And it's not tomorrow. I think the companies that are really incorporating this into their mission, their vision, into their strategic planning, are looking at returns up to ten years down the road.

JFG: *Interesting, so taking ... the long road.*

NG: Companies that feel like they need to get a big return tomorrow are not setting themselves up for success. They may have some incremental improvements. I can give you an example of an incremental improvement ... there was a company that I had approached to do a collaboration with my class ... What we really wanted to do was find a few areas where we could see some small improvements, successes, return on investments that hopefully [would] keep the dialog going internally and generate momentum ... We picked paper as one of the areas to focus on ... They knew how much they were spending on paper, but ... they had never really evaluated how much paper they were using, and they were shocked. They also never considered color versus black and white. They were just doing business as usual ... The students found an existing initiative on the web where reducing the font size by one can save you, over time, significant amounts of paper ... and cost.

JFG: *Not things you would necessarily think about.*

NG: In terms of the course, I can tell you initially what led to the course.

JFG: *That would be great.*

NG: I wanted to create a special topics course in fashion merchandising … I decided since it was going to be special topics … so it was going to be changing all the time … I would use what I had just learned at the NRF Big Show about sustainability as the example for course development. As I was fleshing it out, I thought to myself, well, sustainability is a course that we should offer all of our students! It's an exciting course to be involved in, because no textbook could ever really fit the bill … it's all based on current information making the class extremely dynamic with so much new information bubbling to the surface each month and year. In addition, there are so many different facets of the industry that relate to the fashion merchandising degree in terms of career paths … the physical store, product development, buying, planning, entrepreneurship, and more.

JFG: *It sounds like, too, what you were just talking about—partnering with that company—that they're actually getting the chance to apply these principles in real world situations.*

NG: There are two things that really strike me in teaching this course. Some of the students who take the course are very interested in this already … I've found in the last few years … more and more of the students are really interested in working for a company that shares their values and core beliefs … They want to work for a company that is responsible; that does care about the environment; that does want to give back … For those students, this course helps them identify some of those companies that they will probably want to work for … I just think there's more awareness on the side of the students that they want to work for companies that are more transparent, that are doing the right thing, or are trying to as much as they possibly can.

Allison Parris was a guest speaker in my class this past semester. She graduated from FIT in Fashion Design. She's an eco designer … She came with David Dietz, who is one of the co-founders of a web-based company called Modavanti [which] sells sustainable fashion. Modavanti does not produce any of their own product, but do a lot of the vetting, representing many different designers. So if somebody is interested in buying something that was made in the USA, say, or only made from repurposed materials, they can search for that type of product easily using Modavanti's badge system.

[Allison] talked about having to make decisions. Not everything that she does is sustainable—it's impossible. It's still the fashion industry! And I think that was an important moment for my students—to hear from a designer …

For other students, the course is simply the elective that fit into their schedule. They may not know much about sustainability or it may simply not be something on their radar screen before enrolling in the class. Some of these students shop at fast fashion retailers to get something new to wear for the weekend. These retailers react to new trends quickly and the retail prices are generally low. For these students, the course is really eye opening ... experiencing some the biggest aha moments of their lives ... Moving sustainability forward is all about education. There's that old Faberge Organics shampoo commercial ... "you tell two friends and they'll tell their friends and so on and so on ...."

JFG: *I'm sure it's rewarding to teach both categories of student.*

NG: It really is ... I think one of the most important things we cover, which is not even necessarily associated with sustainability *per se* ... is finding a way to educate, inform and engage other people ... If you don't do that, you're not going to gain buy-in within an organization, you're not going to generate buzz, you're not going to get people excited, and whatever it is that you're interested in is going to die on the table ...

And I think the companies that are doing the best job in getting the word out, in terms of marketing, are the ones that do those things. They're telling a story ... they're engaging ... all of their stakeholders are involved, from their employees to their customers to their trading partners.

In the 2013 RILA report one of the things that they reported was, the most successful companies have dedicated people working on this topic. These companies have buy-in from upper management; they're the ones that are able to engage their stakeholders the best and most effectively ...

JFG: *My last question ... you sort of already answered it early on: your view on the future of sustainability? I think you said something to the effect of, that's the way we are going, and there's no turning back.*

NG: I really think that it's manifold. As more and more companies participate ... H&M taking back product for recycling whether the goods are theirs or not [or] shwopping at Marks & Spencer. Kohl's has recharging stations in some of their parking lots for people with electric cars .... There's so much positive reinforcement at this point. It's creating jobs that didn't exist before and new opportunities for collaboration and partnerships.

So I don't think there's any going back ... For me, if [the course] makes [the students] think just a little bit about where they see themselves as they consider careers after graduation, and the impact it may have on the environment, I feel like it's a win.

Interview with Leanne Mai-ly Hilgart, founder, Vaute Couture

There is a heavy dose of practicality in the way that Leanne Mai-ly Hilgart approaches sustainability, but it also stems from a deep-seated compassion for animals. She has a vivid recollection of how troubled she felt when a neighborhood child—one of the then six-year-old's school age peers—received a rabbit fur coat as a Christmas gift. At the time, she lacked knowledge of fur farming and trapping practices, but says, "What I did know was that there were rabbits that died, so that this fur coat could exist and that, to me, was inherently wrong." As Hilgart's understanding grew, so did her activism. A social studies project on the fur industry, factory farming, and vivisection led to her first foray into fashion, when the now-defunct Wild Wear environmental line purchased her project's title, "Being Cruel Isn't Cool" for use as a t-shirt slogan. Since then, her path has been somewhat circuitous—the former model, marketing associate, and MBA student did not set out to become a fashion designer. Her priority was to create a business that could positively impact the lives of others, one that strove for ethical integrity at each stage of production. She launched vegan label Vaute Couture in 2008, and presented her Fall/Winter 2013 line during New York Fashion Week.

Leanne Mai-ly Hilgart: I've always known that who I am is someone who wants to make a difference for the animals of earth … I had no idea what I was going to start, but I knew that [the business] would be a great megaphone for spreading awareness and creating positive change …

Jennifer Farley Gordon: *So, the plan came first, and the product second?*

LH: Exactly. Fashion is not my end. Fashion is my vehicle. Awareness, and activism, and change in an industry are my mission. That's my goal … [I'd] always wanted a beautiful winter dress coat that was warm enough for the winter, but that fit my ethics. But I thought … there's no market for that. How many vegans are there in the world, anyway? I googled it, and actually there were a lot of vegans looking for it … More importantly, I realized that no one had ever tried to reinvent the winter dress coat. It was always wool with a silk lining. So I had a reason, an impetus, to design and innovate how a winter dress coat is made. We can make things better than what already exists—and if we do that it doesn't matter if people care about animals and the environment. It matters that we are innovating for the future of fashion …

I come from a standpoint … of problem solving. How do I create something that has all of these criteria—strength, warmth, hand, eco, vegan, and accessible price-point?

I started 80-hour weeks, eight months of them, of fabric research and product development … [For] the first line of four styles, we ran the entire first production line off of pre-orders … hundreds of people pre-ordered their coats in the middle of July. They spent hundreds of dollars each to order their coats, and that—them believing in me—funded my entire first production.

JFG: *That's amazing.*

LH: When you do custom fabrics, you can't just do a few, you have to do hundreds … People were like, why wouldn't you just use fabrics that already exist? But there's no point. Anybody can do that. I need to create something that's actually innovating.

JFG: *Can you speak more about your research and development—the kinds of fabrics and the process?*

LH: It's really just a lot of hard work and research—and a lot of testing. I try to look at it as a moving target. There are all these different aspects to it, like I said—strength, feel, warmth and function—so you just have to keep trying all these things. I work with high-tech mills (that also work with Patagonia and North Face). So the idea is that, for people who don't care about the ethics behind it, what they're getting is something innovative. It's the warmth and protection of a sports coat, like a Patagonia or North Face, but the look and feel of a dress coat.

JFG: *In a February 2013 interview with CNN, you noted that being cold is often used as an excuse to wear animal products. I've found that historically—digging back into old magazine articles and things like that—that this is a common refrain. I'm wondering how you combat an idea that is so entrenched.*

LH: If you look at Arctic explorers, and people who are exploring in space, in the coldest climates that there are—they're wearing synthetics. They are the ones that are wearing the high-tech materials, so those must be the warmest. In terms of function, they're probably the best too … I think sometimes people get ideas and they just stick with them, and it is just tradition, how it works. I realized that as far as a winter dress coat, something that was pretty and slimming and all of that, people thought that wool was the only option. I knew that if I created something that was better than wool, I would leave no excuse left to wear animals.

JFG: *In terms of your fabrics, is it entirely R&D of new fabrics, or do you source at all?*

LH: Both. For Spring/Summer … obviously we'll use organic cottons and things like that … We have this satin that is 100 percent recycled clothes, with zero waste, produced in a closed loop … The great thing about a closed loop is that when they make a mistake, they just put it right back in … Our new satin is a great fabric. A silk alternative that's eco-conscious, vegan, beautiful—and luxurious. I'm actually planning to develop a gown line that would be the first completely eco and vegan gown line for red carpet and weddings. That would be launched for spring 2014.

   The first vegan fabrics were "accidentally vegan." They were vegan for cost-effectiveness, and therefore, sometimes people have an association with vegan fabrics, where they think that they're not as good quality … People were using "accidentally vegan" fabrics to make shoes and things like that because they wanted a cheaper alternative. It's different to create fabrics with the intention of them being high quality, ethical fabrics. Sometimes we'll use fabrics that maybe a mill had invented—a new texture, new composition—but they didn't know what to do with. I look at a lot of those fabrics, and then figure out how to construct them and combine them.

JFG: *One thing that we have looked at, historically, in the development of pleathers and faux fur substitutes, was that they had their own kinds of environmental* *impacts—especially a lot of the early ones. Petroleum-derivative and they don't biodegrade, etc. That was one of the choices that you had to make, having to balance between two different categories of sustainability.*

LH: That's an issue of scaling, too. If the intention is to lower costs and increase profits … where the intention is not at all to be ethical, there's going to be detriments in other ways.

JFG: *If you're making something that is not high quality, it's going to fall apart, and it's going to end up in a landfill. But you're making something that is made to last. It's interesting—almost everybody we talk to bridges different categories [of sustainability].*

LH: Of course, you kind of have to … it makes no sense to be doing one and not at least intending to do all of them. It's not possible to do 100 percent for everything, but the intention is always to keep moving forward. Kind of like, a hybrid car is still a car, but at the same time, it gets you closer to that future of having a sustainable transit.

   I used to shop a lot with my mom, and I always just made sure that it was "accidentally vegan." But now I've gotten to a point where it's really fun to curate my closet—to do it really thoughtfully. My closet is mostly thrift and vintage … or stuff that my friends made, so I know that it's an ethical company. But those are investments. People always say ethical fashion is so expensive, but actually those people are being paid fairly. If you invest your money in someone else being paid fairly, and then at the same time, combine that with secondhand, thrift, recycling and reusing of fabrics and clothing, then it creates a whole closet that probably costs the same amount of money as buying all of that throwaway fashion every season. Except that it's now a closet of stuff that represents who you are, your style, and your values.

JFG: *You've said before that it is Vaute's role to help make ethical and vegan fashion options more accessible. How do you go about this?*

LH: In terms of accessibility, it is so important how you price something. While I'm an artist, and it's really important to create art, it's more important to me to create something that is wearable and that is at a price point that is manageable. And it's not going to be cheap … people are used to throwaway fashion being made at slave wages. When I'm creating something, I do look at price points of similar lines at Bloomingdales or Macys … For innovations to work, they have to be sustainable and scalable … It needs to be something that people can live with, and that we can sustain as a business. We've been bootstrapped, but we are just about at the edge point right now where we are talking to investors. Great investment firms … that see the future innovations being in animal-free and compassionate lifestyle … this is going to make it more accessible.

JFG: *That was one of my questions too … about translating your business to a larger scale.*

LH: Obviously I'd like to be producing on a much larger scale, creating a much larger collection, and innovating more and more in fabrics … We want to do shoes, we want to do accessories—stuff that's again not just vegan, but vegan, high design, high performance, and sustainable … I'd love to tour all over the world … We have a lot of plans for ways to collaborate all over the country. That's a big part of what we do too, to say how can we create win-win situations, how can we get more people in the community … I feel like the world has sort of lost that sense of being with other people …

My Fall/Winter 2013 collection was inspired by Sailor Moon … I love Sailor Moon for the design aspect—hearts, and stars, and all of that—but when I looked at the story, I was kind of blown away. Basically it's these earth girls … the first one tries to save a cat on the street from being abused by local kids, and it turns out the cat is magic and turns her into her superhuman self. So her superhuman self bands together with other girls to save the universe … the story is a story of finding your superpowers through helping others. It's because she helped that she was able to find her strength …

JFG: *Do you have anything else you'd like to add?*

LH: I think the biggest thing is that living compassionately is not a sacrifice, that it is an empowerment. I'm saying I'm not allowing a larger structure in society or a corporation or an industry to decide how I impact the world. Instead I'm choosing what I purchase, what my time and energy do, what I wear, what I eat—that's a conscious decision on my part, so that I can impact the world the way that I would like to. I think a lot of people look at ethical fashion as an alternative lifestyle, but it's not—it's the future. It's the way it should be.

[All interviews have been edited and abridged]

NOTES

Introduction

1. Sandy Black, *Eco-Chic: The Fashion Paradox* (London: Black Dog Publishing, 2008), p. 46.
2. Kate Black, "Consumers Want to Shop and be Responsible to Society/Environment," magnifeco.com. Available from http://magnifeco.com/consumers-want-to-shop-be-responsible-to-society-environment/news/ [accessed March 1, 2013].

Chapter 1: Repurposed and recycled clothing and textiles

1. Karen Tranberg Hansen, "Secondhand Clothes, Anthropology of," in Valerie Steele (ed.), *Encyclopedia of Clothing and Fashion* (Detroit, MI: Charles Scribner's Sons, 2005), p. 151.
2. Beverly Lemire, "Shifting Currency: The Culture and Economy of the Second Hand Trade in England, c. 1600–1850," in Alexandra Palmer and Hazel Clark (eds), *Old Clothes, New Looks* (Oxford: Berg, 2005), pp. 41–2.
3. Beverly Lemire, "Developing Consumerism and the Ready-made Clothing Trade in Britain, 1750–1800," in Peter McNeil (ed.), *Fashion: Critical and Primary Sources* (Oxford: Berg, 2009), vol. 2, p. 254.
4. Celia Marshik, "Smart Clothes at Low Prices," in Ilya Parkins and Elizabeth M. Sheehan (eds), *Cultures of Femininity in Modern Fashion* (Durham, NH: University of New Hampshire Press, 2011), p. 71.
5. Alexandra Palmer has given lectures on the significance of altered historical dress, which often specifically reference remade objects in the fashion collection of The Royal Ontario Museum.
6. *Reticule* is the term used to describe the pouch-like bags popular in the eighteenth and nineteenth centuries. Reticules usually had a drawstring closure.
7. Pockets were not integrated into the design of women's clothing in the eighteenth and early nineteenth centuries. They were entirely separate from other garments, and were attached to a tape that was worn around the waist. Pockets were accessed through slits on the sides of women's skirts. The bulk they created made them better suited for wear with dress styles with heavier fabrics and fuller construction than those that were fashionable in the early nineteenth century.
8. Avril Hart and Susan North, *Historical Fashion in Detail: The 17th and 18th Centuries* (London: V&A Publications, 2008), p. 100.

9. Elizabeth Sanderson, "Nearly new: the second-hand clothing trade in eighteenth-century Edinburgh," *Costume* 31 (1997): 38.

10. Linda Baumgarten, "Altered historical clothing," *Dress* 25 (1998): 48.

11. Alexandra Palmer, *Couture & Commerce: The Transatlantic Fashion Trade in the 1950s* (Vancouver: UBC Press, 2001), p. 194.

12. Baumgarten, 49.

13. Anne Buck, *Dress in Eighteenth-Century England* (New York: Holmes and Meier Publications, Inc., 1979), p. 160.

14. Michelle Maskiell, "Consuming Kashmir: Shawls and Empires, 1500–2000," in Peter McNeil (ed), *Fashion: Critical and Primary Sources* (Oxford: Berg, 2009), vol. 3, p. 207.

15. Ibid. $2,000 is the equivalent of nearly $51,000 in 2013. Source: United States Department of Labor, Bureau of Labor Statistics, CPI Inflation Calculator. Available from http://www.bls.gov/data/inflation_calculator.htm [accessed].

16. Madeleine Ginsburg, "Rags to riches: the second-hand clothes trade 1700–1978," *Costume* 14 (1980): 129.

17. Most dresses from this period had a separate bodice and skirt.

18. Carol Vogel, "Valerian S. Rybar, 71, Design of Lush Rooms and Lavish Parties," *New York Times* (June 13, 1990), p. B20.

19. Ibid.

20. Baumgarten, 46.

21. $100 in 1971 was the equivalent of $575 in 2013. Source: United States Department of Labor, Bureau of Labor Statistics, CPI Inflation Calculator. Available from http://www.bls.gov/data/inflation_calculator.htm [accessed]

22. Angela Taylor, "For One-of-a-Kind Fashions," *New York Times* (July 26, 1971), p. 14.

23. Marin F. Hanson and Patricia Cox Crews (eds), *American Quilts in the Modern Age, 1870-1940* (Lincoln, NE: University of Nebraska Press, 2009), p. 5

24. Rebecca T. Stevens and Yoshiko Iwamoto Wada (eds), *The Kimono Inspiration: Art and Art-to-Wear in America* (Washington, DC: The Textile Museum, 1996), p. 109.

25. Penny McMorris, *Crazy Quilts* (New York: E. P. Dutton, 1984), p. 16.

26. Ibid.

27. "Advance Trade Edition of Vogue," *Vogue* (April 1, 1933), supplement, p. III.

28. *Dyeing, Remodeling, Budgets* (Scranton, PA: The Woman's Institute of Domestic Arts and Sciences, 1931), p. 2.

29. Studs Terkel, *Hard Times* (New York: The New Press, 2000), p. 46.

30. Ibid., p. 85.

31. Angela Taylor, "There's Something New at Altman's: Shop That Has Authentic Old Clothes," *New York Times* (July 9, 1970), p. 40.

32. Deadstock is a term that refers to merchandise that was not used or sold at the time of its making. It is sometimes also referred to as "new old stock."

33. Bernadine Morris, "Two Contemporary Designers for the Modern Generation," *New York Times* (January 11, 1977), p. 48.

34. Ibid.

35. The Museum at FIT, object accession record.

36. Ellen Weiss, *Secondhand Super Shopper: Buying More, Spending Less, Living Better* (New York: M. Evans, 1981), p. xii.

37. Jennifer Craik, *Fashion: The Key Concepts* (Oxford: Berg, 2009), p. 242.

38. Suzy Menkes, "The Shock of the Old," *New York Times* (March 21, 1993), p. V8.

39. Kaat Debo and Bob Verhelst, *Maison Martin Margiela "20": The Exhibition* (Antwerp: MoMu Fashion Museum, 2008), p. 9.

40. Mary Rourke, "An Activist Autumn: Paris Defines Trendy Issues in Statements of Black and White," *Los Angeles Times* (March 23, 1992). Available from http://articles.latimes.com/1992-03-23/news/vw-3189_1_black-tights [accessed June 21, 2013].

41. Debo and Verhelst, *Maison Martin Margiela "20,"* p. xx.

42. Caroline Evans, "The golden dustman: a critical evaluation of the work of Martin Margiela and a review of Martin Margiela: exhibition (9/4/1615)," *Fashion Theory: The Journal of Dress, Body & Culture* 1 (February 1998): vol. 2, 81.

43. Maison Martin Margiela has shown unique "garments remodeled by hand" as part of its Artisanal Collections since autumn/winter 2005–6. Clothing from these collections is perceived as the Maison's form of couture.

44. Nicole Phelps, "Maison Martin Margiela," style.com. Available from http://www.style.com/fashionshows/review/S2013CTR-MMARGIEL [accessed 21 March 2013].

45. Ibid.

46. Menkes, "The Shock of the Old," p. V8.

47. Victoria L. Rovine, "Working the Edge: XULY.Bët's Recycled Clothing," in Alexandra Palmer and Hazel Clark (eds), *Old Clothes, New Looks: Second-Hand Fashion* (Oxford: Berg, 2005), p. 216.

48. Ibid., p. 224.

49. William McDonough and Michael Braungart, *Cradle to Cradle: Remaking the Way We Make Things* (New York: North Point Press, 2002).

50. Sandy Black, *Eco-Chic: The Fashion Paradox* (London: Black Dog Publishing, 2008), p. 46.

51. Alexandra Palmer, "Vintage Whores and Vintage Virgins: Second Hand Fashion in the Twenty-First Century," in Alexandra Palmer and Hazel Clark (eds), *Old Clothes, New Looks: Second-Hand Fashion* (Oxford: Berg Publishers, 2005), pp. 198–9.

52. Nathaniel Dafydd Beard, "The branding of ethical fashion and the consumer: a luxury niche or mass-market reality?" *Fashion Theory* 4 (December 2008): v. 12, 457.

53. Jessica Hemmings, "Rebecca Earley upcycles style," *Fiberarts* (January/February 2009): 41.

54. Jana Hawley, "Economic Impact of Textile and Clothing Recycling," in Janet Hethorn and Connie Ulasewicz (eds), *Sustainable Fashion: Why Now? A Conversation Exploring Issues, Practices, and Possibilities* (New York: Fairchild Books, 2008), p. 212.

55. Jacky Watson, *Textiles and the Environment: Special Report no. 2150* (London: The Economist Intelligence Unit, 1991), p. 71.

56. Kate Fletcher, *Sustainable Fashion & Textiles: Design Journeys* (London: Earthscan, 2008), p. 35.

57. Ibid.

58. U.S. Environmental Protection Agency, "Textiles." Available from http://www.epa.gov/wastes/conserve/materials/textiles.htm [accessed May 23, 2013].

59. Hawley, "Economic Impact," p. 144.

60. This Directive was a continuation of two earlier versions: one from 1975, and another from 1981.

61. "Landfills Continue to Rule Despite EU Recycling Target," European Union Information Website. Available from http://www.euractiv.com/sustainability/landfills-continue-rule-despite-news-518229 [accessed July 1, 2013].

62. Jozef De Coster, "Green textiles and apparel: environmental impact and strategies for improvement," *Textile Outlook International* 132 (November–December 2007): 146.

63. Jana M. Hawley, Pauline Sullivan, and Youn Kyung-Kim, "Recycled Textiles," in Valerie Steele (ed.), *Encyclopedia of Clothing and Fashion* (Detroit, MI: Charles Scribner's Sons, 2005), p. 90.

64. Heike Jens, "Secondhand Clothing," The Berg Fashion Library. Available from http://www.bergfashionlibrary.com/view/bewdf/BEWDF-v8/ED.C.h8035.xml [accessed January 2, 2013].

65. Hawley, Sullivan, Kyung-Kim, "Recycled Textiles," p. 91.

66. U.S. Environmental Protection Agency, "Textiles."

67. Black, *Eco-Chic,* p. 158.

68. Fitzwater, "Secondhand Clothes," p. 153.

69. Hawley, "Economic Impact," p. 221.

70. Samuel Jubb, *The History of the Shoddy Trade: Its Rise, Progress, and Present Position* (London: Houlston and Wright, 1860), p. 40.

71. Ginsburg, "Rags to riches," p. 128.

72. Jubb, *The History of the Shoddy Trade*, pp. 2–3.

73. Ibid., p. 23.

74. Ibid., p. 2.

75. "History," The Woolmark Company. Available from http://www.woolmark.com/about-woolmark/history [accessed July 1, 2013].

76. Susan Diesenhouse, "Polyester Becomes Environmentally Correct," *New York Times* (February 20, 1994), p. 9.

77. Suzanne Loker, "A Technology-Enabled Fashion System", p. 121.

78. "10 Most Wanted: Techno," *Vogue* (January 1, 1998), p. 176.

79. Loker, p. 157.

80. Veronique de Terrene, "Pop Bottles Recycled as Yarn for Patagonia Sweaters," *The Free-Lance Star,* Fredericksburg, VA, (October 13, 1993), p. C10.

81. 'Patagonia Outdoor Clothing". Available from www.patagonia.com/us/home [accessed July 1, 2013].

82. Timo Rissanen, "Creating Fashion without the Creation of Fabric Waste," in Janet Hethorn and Connie Ulasewicz (eds), *Sustainable Fashion: Why Now? A Conversation Exploring Issues, Practices, and Possibilities* (New York: Fairchild Books, 2008), p. 186.

83. Stephanie Hirschmiller, "Shwopping is the New Shopping, Darling: Joanna Lumley Launches Clothes Recycling Initiative for M&S," *Daily Mail* (April 26, 2012). Available from http://www.dailymail.co.uk/femail/article-2135431/Shwopping-Joanna-Lumley-launches-clothes-recycling-initiative-M-S.html [accessed June 12, 2012].

84. Phong Luu, "Joanna Lumley Launches Marks & Spencers Shwopping Campaign," *Telegraph* (April 26, 2012). Available from http://fashion.telegraph.co.uk/news-features/TMG9228252/Joanna-Lumley-launches-Marks-and-Spencers-Shwopping-campaign.html [accessed June 12, 2012].

85. Robin Anson, "Can the shift of textile and clothing production to Asia be reversed?" *Textile Outlook International* 159 (December 2012): 6.

86. Alexandra Palmer, "Vintage Whores," p. 202.

87. Mary Ann Crenshaw, "Looking Back to Dresses for Today," *New York Times* (January 26, 1975), p. 298.

88. Diana Funaro, *The Yestermorrow Clothes Book: How to Remodel Secondhand Clothes* (Radner, PA: Chilton Book Co., 1976), p. 55.

89. Mitchell Owens, "Couture Shock: Vintage Clothes as Collectibles," *New York Times* (January 5, 1997), p. 25.

90. Angela McRobbie, "Second-Hand Dresses and the Role of the Ragmarket," in Angela McRobbie (ed), *Zoot Suits and Secondhand Dresses, an Anthology of Fashion and Music* (Boston: Unwin Hyman, 1988), p. 29.

91. Pamela Soohoo, "Fashions for Victory: Innovation, Improvisation & Innovation in American Women's Fashion, 1940–1946" (master's thesis, Fashion Institute of Technology, 2004), p. 2.

92. Celia Marshik, "Smart Clothes at Low Prices," p. 82.

93. The Board of Trade by the Minister of Information, *Make Do and Mend* (1943; repr., Sevenoaks: Sabrestorm Publishing, 2007), p.19.

94. "Style Inspiration Seen in Rag Bag And 'Make-Do Fashions' Prove Chic," *New York Times* (April 29, 1943), p. 24.

95. The Board of Trade by the Ministry of Supply, "How to 'Make-Do-And-Mend'." Available from http://www.youtube.com/watch?v=f4RpJcVs1Vl [accessed June 28, 2013].

Chapter 2: Quality of craftsmanship

1. Suzanne Loker, "A Technology-Enabled Fashion System", p. 67.

2. Lorna Wetherill, "Consumer Behavior, Textiles and Dress in the Late Seventeenth and Early Eighteenth Centuries," in Peter McNeil (ed.), *Fashion: Critical and Primary Sources* (Oxford: Berg, 2009), vol. 2, p. 164.

3. Translated to *Encyclopedia, or a Systematic Dictionary of the Sciences, Arts and Crafts.*

4. Philipp Blom, *Enlightening the World: Encyclopédie, The Book That Changed the Course of History* (New York: Palgrave Macmillan, 2004), p. 45.

5. Ibid., p. 46.

6. The Haute Lisse is a particular type of tapestry loom in which the warp threads are stretched vertically before the weaver.

7. James Essinger, *Jacquard's Web: How a Hand-loom Led to the Birth of the Information Age* (Oxford: Oxford University Press, 2007), p. 17.

8. Linda Welters, "The Fashion of Sustainability," in Janet Hethorn and Connie Ulasewicz (eds), *Sustainable Fashion: Why Now? A Conversation Exploring Issues, Practices, and Possibilities* (New York: Fairchild Books, 2008), p. 13.

9. Also referred to as a "sack back" gown, the *Robe à la Française* was distinguished by wide, loose pleats of fabric that hung from the shoulders at the back of the gown.

10. Ibid., 8.

11. Janet Arnold, "'The Lady's Economical Assistant' of 1808," in Barbara Burman (ed.), *The Culture of Sewing: Gender, Consumption and Home Dressmaking* (Oxford: Berg, 1999), p. 225.

12. Beverly Lemire, "Developing Consumerism and the Ready-made Clothing Trade in Britain, 1750–1800," in Peter McNeil (ed.), *Fashion: Critical and Primary Sources,* (Oxford: Berg, 2009), vol. 2, p. 242.

13. Janet Arnold, "The Cut and Construction of Women's Clothes in the Eighteenth Century," in Jean Starobinski, *Revolution in Fashion: European Clothing, 1715–1815* (New York: Abbeville Press, 1989), p. 127.

14. Ibid., p. 133.

15. Beverly Lemire, "Developing Consumerism," p. 242.

16. Essinger, *Jacquard's Web*, p. 17.

17. Richard Marsden, *Cotton Spinning: Its Development, Principles, and Practice* (London: George Bell and Sons, 1903), p. 202.

18. Ibid., p. 206.

19. There are two types of yarn necessary to weave textiles: a warp, which runs lengthwise, and the weft, which is the traverse thread. Weft threads are usually made of strong fibers, since they have to be woven through the stationary warp threads.

20. Essinger, *Jacquard's Web,* p. 37.

21. Ibid., p. 38.

22. Essinger, *Jacquard's Web,* p. 12.

23. E. A. Posselt, *The Jacquard Machine Analyzed and Explained* (Philadelphia: Dando Printing and Publishing Company, 1888), p. 8.

24. Ibid., 42.

25. Sandy Black, *Eco-Chic: The Fashion Paradox* (London: Black Dog, 2008), pp. 46–7.

26. A Lady, *How to Dress on £15 a Year* (London: George Routledge and Sons, 1874), p. 75.

27. Ibid., 55.

28. Susan Kaiser, "Mixing Metaphors in the Fiber, Textile, and Apparel Complex: Moving Toward a More Sustainable Fashion," in Janet Hethorn and Connie Ulasewicz (eds), *Sustainable Fashion: Why Now? A Conversation Exploring Issues, Practices, and Possibilities* (New York: Fairchild Books, 2008), p. 155.

29. Joann Gregory Ritter and Betty L. Feather, "Practices, procedures, and attitudes toward clothing maintenance: 1850–1860 and 1900–1910," *Dress* 17 (1990): 161.

30. Adjusted for inflation, $3,000 in 1846 was the equivalent of over $75,000 in 2012. Source: United States Department of Labor, Bureau of Labor Statistics, CPI Inflation Calculator. Available from http://www.bls.gov/data/inflation_calculator.htm [accessed].

31. James Parton, *History of the Sewing Machine* (May 1867; repr. New York: International Ladies' Garment Workers' Union, 1967), p. 10.

32. Ibid., p. 9.

33. Ibid., p. 22.

34. Grace Rogers Cooper, *The Invention of the Sewing Machine* (Washington, DC: The Smithsonian Institution Press, 1968), p. 57.

35. Parton, *History of the Sewing Machine,* p. 23.

36. Cooper, *The Invention of the Sewing Machine,* p. 58.

37. Lemire, "Developing Consumerism," pp. 252–3.

38. Ellen Leopold, "The Manufacture of the Fashion System," in Juliet Ash and Elizabeth Wilson (eds), *Chic Thrills: A Fashion Reader* (Berkeley: University of California Press, 1993), p. 103.

39. Claudia Kidwell, *Suiting Everyone: The Democratization of Clothing in America* (Washington, DC: Smithsonian Institution Press, 1974), p. 63.

40. Ibid., p. 39.

41. Cooper, *The Invention of the Sewing Machine,* p. 59.

42. H. Kristina Haugland, "Blouse," The Berg Fashion Library (2005). Available from http://www.bergfashionlibrary.com/bazf/bazf00079.xml [accessed June 22, 2013].

43. "Macy's: The Great 'White' Sale will Reach its Height this Week" advertisement. *New York Times* (January 9, 1899), p. 3.

44. Ibid.

45. Kidwell, *Suiting Everyone,* p. 15.

46. Ibid., p. 15.

47. Madeleine Ginsburg, "Rags to riches: the second-hand clothes trade 1700–1978," *Costume* 14 (1980): 128.

48. Leopold, "The Manufacture of the Fashion System," p. 105.

49. Kidwell, *Suiting Everyone,* p. 137.

50. Elizabeth Wilson, *Adorned in Dreams: Fashion and Modernity* (Berkeley: University of California Press, 1987), p. 79.

51. Helen Goodrich Butterick, *Principles of Clothing Selection* (New York: Macmillan, 1924), p. 148.

52. Leopold, "The Manufacture of the Fashion System," p. 113.

53. Wilson, *Adorned in Dreams,* p. 89.

54. Christian Esquevin, *Adrian: Silver Screen to Custom Label* (New York: The Monacelli Press, 2008), p. 118.

55. Women's Home Companion Readers, *Women's Clothing: A Survey of Selection, Sewing and Spending* (New York: Crowell-Collier Publication Company, 1948), p. 10.

56. Esquevin, *Adrian,* p. 121. Adjusted for inflation in 2013, $125 was the equivalent of approximately $1,800. Source: United States Department of Labor, Bureau of Labor Statistics, CPI Inflation Calculator. Available from http://www.bls.gov/data/inflation_calculator.htm [accessed].

57. Karen De Witt, "Smithsonian Unearths 42 Adrian Designs," *New York Times* (July 2, 1978), p. 35.

58. Enid Nemy, "Those Vintage Dresses That Defy All the Whimsies of Fashion," *New York Times* (January 9, 1970), p. 24.

59. Ibid.

60. Women's Home Companion Readers, *Women's Clothing,* p. 4.

61. $186 amounted to just over $1,800 in 2013. Source: United States Department of Labor, Bureau of Labor Statistics, CPI Inflation Calculator. Available from http://www.bls.gov/data/inflation_calculator.htm [accessed].

62. Women's Home Companion Readers, *Women's Clothing,* p. 9.

63. Vance Packard, *The Waste Makers* (New York: David McKay and Company, Inc., 1960), pp. 71–2.

64. "Fashion: Up, Up and Away," *Time* (December 1, 1967), online archive, available by subscription only.

65. Angela Taylor, "Fashions to Buy, Wear and Then Throw Away," *New York Times* (August 19, 1966), p. 41.

66. Jennifer Feingold Kibel, "Pulp Fashion: The History of Patented Paper Clothing" (master's thesis, Fashion Institute of Technology), p. 1.

67. Ibid., p. 2.

68. Ibid., p. 6.

69. Angela Taylor, "An East Side Boutique Dedicated to Disposability," *New York Times* (June 10, 1967), p. FS24.

70. Caterine Milinaire and Carol Troy, *Cheap Chic* (New York, Harmony Books, 1975), p. 9.

71. Karl Aspelund, *Fashioning Society: A Hundred Years of Haute Couture by Six Designers* (New York: Fairchild Books, 2009), p. 10.

72. Dana Thomas, *Deluxe: How Luxury Lost its Luster* (New York: Penguin Press, 2007), p. 323.

73. Lucy Siegle, *To Die For: Is Fashion Wearing Out the World?* (London: Fourth Estate, 2011), p. 89.

74. The CFDA/Vogue Fashion Fund Award provides funding for emerging designers. It is awarded to three recipients annually.

75. Hazel Clark, "SLOW + FASHION—an oxymoron—or a promise for the future...?" *Fashion Theory: The Journal of Dress, Body & Culture* 4 (December 2008): vol. 12, 427.

76. Natalie Chanin, *Alabama Studio Sewing + Design: A Guide to Hand-Sewing an Alabama Chanin Wardrobe* (New York: Stewart, Tabori & Chang, 2012), p. 4.

77. Clark, "SLOW + FASHION," 436.

78. Chanin, *Alabama Studio Sewing*, p. 137.

79. Ibid., p. 4.

80. Slow and Steady Wins the Race. Available from http://www.slowandsteadywinstherace.com/ [accessed July 5, 2013].

81. Urban Outfitters, "UO Features." Available from http://blog.urbanoutfitters.com/features/slow_and_steady [accessed July 5, 2013].

82. Ibid.

83. Slow and Steady Wins the Race.

84. Cynthia Leung, "Reflections on 'meta design' with Mary Ping," *Fashion Projects* 1 (2005): 14.

85. Dorothy K. Burnham, *Cut My Cote* (Toronto: Royal Ontario Museum, 1973), p. 3.

86. Richard Martin, "Energy and Economy, Measure and Magic," in John S. Major (ed.), *Yeohlee: Work* (Peleus Press, 2003), p. 152.

87. Ibid.

88. Yeohlee, Fall 2009 press release. Available from http://yeohlee.com/archive/fall2009pr.html [accessed May 1, 2010].

89. Holly McQuillan, "Zero-Waste Design Practice: Strategies and Risk Taking for Garment Design," in Alison Gwilt and Timo Rissanen (eds), *Shaping Sustainable Fashion: Changing the Way we Make and Use Clothes* (London: Earthscan, 2011), p. 85.

90. Save the Garment Center, "About." Available from http://savethegarmentcenter.org/about/ [accessed July 5, 2013].

91. Bernard Roshco, *The Rag Race: How New York and Paris Run the Breakneck Business of Dressing American Women* (New York: Funk & Wagnalls, 1963), p. 18.

92. Ibid., p. 28.

93. Ibid.

94. Black, *Eco-Chic,* p. 182.

95. Roshco, *The Rag Race,* p. 47.

96. Jana Hawley, "Textile Recycling Options: Exploring What Could Be," in Alison Gwilt and Timo Rissanen (eds), *Shaping Sustainable Fashion: Changing the Way We Make and Use Clothes,* (London: Earthscan, 2011), p. 153.

97. Joshua Williams, "Geoffrey B. Small," *See 7* 1 (Fall 2010), p. 28.

Chapter 3: Material origins

1. Marie O'Mahoney, "Sustainable Textiles: Nature or Nurture," in Alison Gwilt and Timo Rissanen (eds), *Shaping Sustainable Fashion: Changing the Way We Make and Use Clothes* (London: Earthscan, 2011), p. 43.

2. Kate Fletcher and Lynda Grose, *Fashion & Sustainability: Design for Change* (London: Laurence King, 2012), p. 12.

3. Jacky Watson, *Textiles and the Environment: Special Report no. 2150* (London: The Economist Intelligence Unit, 1991), p. 6.

4. Sandy Black, *Eco-Chic: The Fashion Paradox* (London: Black Dog Publishing, 2008), p. 109.

5. Kate Fletcher, *Sustainable Fashion & Textiles: Design Journeys* (London: Earthscan, 2008), p. 5.

6. Black, *Eco-Chic,* p. 106.

7. Beverly Lemire, *Cotton* (Oxford: Berg, 2011), p. 66.

8. Ibid., p. 40.

9. Elizabeth Wilson, *Adorned in Dreams: Fashion and Modernity* (London: Virago Press, 1985), p. 68.

10. Lemire, *Cotton,* p. 86.

11. Edward C. Bates, "The Story of the Cotton Gin," in Stuart Bruchey (ed.), *Cotton and the Growth of the American Economy: 1790–1860* (May 1890; repr. New York: Harcourt, Brace & World, Inc. 1967), p. 53.

12. Eli Whitney, "Eli Whitney Tells His Father About the Invention," in Stuart Bruchey (ed.), *Cotton and the Growth of the American Economy: 1790–1860* (1793; repr. New York: Harcourt, Brace & World, Inc. 1967), p. 61.

13. Stuart Bruchey (ed.), *Cotton and the Growth of the American Economy: 1790-1860* (New York: Harcourt, Brace & World, Inc. 1967), p. 7.

14. Ibid., p. 13.

15. Martin Bide, "Fiber Sustainability: Green is not Black + White," in Linda Welters and Abby Lillethun (eds), *The Fashion Reader: Second Edition* (Oxford: Berg, 2011), p. 577.

16. T. B. Thorpe, "Cotton and its Cultivation," *Harper's New Monthly Magazine* XLV (February, 1854), vol. VIII, p. 174.

17. Fletcher, *Sustainable Fashion & Textiles,* p. 8.

18. Black, *Eco-Chic,* p. 113.

19. Lynda Grose, "Sustainable Cotton Production," in R. S. Blackburn (ed.), *Sustainable Textiles: Life Cycle and Environmental Impact* (New York: CRC Press, 2009), p. 34.

20. O'Mahoney, "Sustainable Textiles: Nature or Nurture," p. 43.

21. Jozef De Coster, "Green textiles and apparel: environmental impact and strategies for improvement," *Textile Outlook International* 132 (November–December 2007): 145.

22. Grose, "Sustainable Cotton Production," p. 42.

23. Tamsin Blanchard, *Green is the New Black: How to Change the World with Style* (London: Hodder and Stoughton, 2007), p. 40.

24. Grose, "Sustainable Cotton Production," p. 43.

25. Liza Casabona, "Organic Cotton Sales Growing at Retail," *Women's Wear Daily* (June 1, 2010), p. 11.

26. De Coster, "Green textiles and apparel," p. 153.

27. Ibid.

28. Sarah Scaturro, "Eco-tech fashion: rationalizing technology in sustainable fashion," *Fashion Theory* 4(12) (2008): 477.

29. John Patrick, "Color, Magic, and Modern Alchemy," in Leslie Hoffman (ed.), *FutureFashion: White Papers* (New York: Earth Pledge, 2007), p. 178.

30. John Patrick, interview by Colleen Hill, August 7, 2013.

31. "Spring 2009 Ready-to-Wear: Organic by John Patrick," style.com. Available from http://www.style.com/fashionshows/review/S2009RTW-ORGANIC [accessed April 14, 2010].

32. "Profile," Creditex. Available from http://www.creditex.com.pe/ingles/perfil_certificaciones.htm [accessed July 10, 2013].

33. Sandy Black and Stacy Anderson, "Making sustainability fashionable: profile of the Danish fashion company Noir," in *Fashion Practice,* 1(2) (2010): 123.

34. Ibid., p. 124.

35. "Organic Cotton," Illuminati. Available from http://www.noir.dk/illuminati2.php [accessed July 10, 2013].

36. Black, *Eco-Chic,* p. 132.

37. Anne Buck, *Dress in Eighteenth Century England* (New York: Holmes and Meier Publishers, Inc., 1979), p. 186.

38. Ibid., p. 187.

39. Arthur Harrison Cole, *The American Wool Manufacture* (New York: Harper & Row Publishers, 1969), vol. I, p. 53.

40. D. T. Jenkins and K. G. Ponting, *The British Wool Textile Industry, 1770–1914* (London: Heinemann Educational Books, 1982), p. 80.

41. Ibid., p. 151.

42. Esther S. Hochstim, *Women's Attitudes Toward Wool and Other Fibers, no. 153* (Washington, DC: U.S. Department of Agriculture, Agricultural Marketing Service, 1957), p. 20.

43. Ibid., p. 5.

44. Also referenced in Chapter 1, as a reaction against recycled wool.

45. *World Apparel Fibre Consumption Survey* (Rome: Food and Agriculture Organization of the United Nations, 1985), pp. 2–3.

46. "Campaign for Wool." Available from http://www.princeofwales.gov.uk/the-prince-of-wales/initiatives/campaign-wool [accessed July 14, 2013].

47. British Wool Marketing Board, "Wool Statistics." Available from http://www.britishwool.org.uk/pdf/Factsheet4.pdf [accessed April 3, 2013].

48. Paula Simmons, *Turning Wool into a Cottage Industry* (Seattle: Madrona Publishers, 1985), p. 5.

49. Jasmin Malik Chua, "Wool's Carbon Footprint Up to 80% Smaller Than Previously Thought," ecouterre.com. Available from http://www.ecouterre.com/wools-carbon-footprint-up-to-80-smaller-than-previously-thought/ [accessed January 19, 2012].

50. Fletcher, *Sustainable Fashion & Textiles,* p. 10.

51. Bide, "Fiber Sustainability: Green is not Black + White," p. 580.

52. Gail Baugh, "Fibers: Clean and Green Fiber Options," in Janet Hethorn and Connie Ulasewicz (eds), *Sustainable Fashion: Why Now? A Conversation Exploring Issues, Practices, and Possibilities* (New York: Fairchild Books, 2008), p. 331.

53. Jasmin Malik Chua, "Stella McCartney's Latest Bag is Made From the Wool of Her Own Sheep," ecouterre.com. Available from http://www.ecouterre.com/stella-mccartneys-latest-bag-is-made-from-the-wool-of-her-own-sheep/ [accessed March 3, 2013].

54. Lucy Siegle, *To Die For: Is Fashion Wearing Out the World?* (London: Fourth Estate, 2011), p. 163.

55. John W. Roulac, *Hemp Horizons: The Comeback of the World's Most Promising Plant* (White River Junction, VT: Chelsea Green Publishing Company, 1997), p. 30.

56. R. S. Blackburn, *Biodegradable and Sustainable Fibres* (Cambridge: Woodhead, 2005), p. 52.

57. Black, p. 128.

58. Roulac, *Hemp Horizons,* p. 131.

59. Blackburn, *Biodegradable and Sustainable Fibres,* p. 55.

60. Lawrence Serbin, "Hemp Goes Straight," in *FutureFashion White Papers* (New York: Earth Pledge, 2007), p. 48.

61. Ibid., p. 50.

62. Fletcher, *Sustainable Fashion & Textiles,* p. 25.

63. Serbin, "Hemp Goes Straight," p. 47.

64. F. D Lewis, *The Chemistry and Technology of Rayon Manufacture* (Surrey: Love and Malcomson, Ltd., 1961), p. ix.

65. Ibid.

66. Ellen Leopold, "The Manufacture of the Fashion System," in Juliet Ash and Elizabeth Wilson (eds), *Chic Thrills: A Fashion Reader,* (Berkeley: University of California Press, 1993), p. 114.

67. Viscose Company, *The Story of Rayon*, (New York: The Viscose Company, 1929), p. 13.

68. "The Loveliness of Rayon Proclaimed by Drecoll," advertisement. *Vogue* (March 1, 1928), p. 24b.

69. Approx. $13.38 to 54.35 in 2013. Source: United States Department of Labor, Bureau of Labor Statistics, CPI Inflation Calculator. Available from http://www.bls.gov/data/inflation_calculator.htm [accessed].

70. Dilys E. Blum, *Shocking! The Art and Fashion of Elsa Schiaparelli* (Philadelphia: Philadelphia Museum of Art, 2003), p. 34.

71. Textile World, *The Rayon Handbook* (New York: McGraw-Hill, 1939), foreword.

72. Matt Wirz, "The Touch, the Feel—Of Rayon?" *Wall Street Journal* (January 6, 2011),. Available from http://online.wsj.com/article/SB10001424052748703730704576066291209981236.html [accessed May 14, 2013].

73. O'Mahoney, "Sustainable Textiles: Nature or Nurture," p. 47.

74. Black, *Eco-Chic,* p. 148.

75. Todd Copeland, "How Eco-Friendly is Bamboo Fabric, Really?," ecouterre.com. Available from http://www.ecouterre.com/how-eco-friendly-is-bamboo-fabric-really/ [accessed May 14, 2013].

76. O'Mahoney, "Sustainable Textiles: Nature or Nurture," p. 45.

77. Kate Carter, "Pandering to the Green Consumer," *The Guardian* (August 12, 2008). Available from http://www.theguardian.com/lifeandstyle/2008/aug/13/bamboo.fabric [accessed April 13, 2013].

78. "Rayon and Lyocell," IHS Chemical (ihs.com). Available from http://www.ihs.com/products/chemical/planning/ceh/rayon-and-lyocell.aspx [accessed February 2, 2013].

79. Watson, *Textiles and the Environment,* p. 60.

80. Paul Scheider, "The Cotton Brief," *New York Times* (June 20, 1993), p. 11.

81. Blackburn, *Biodegradable and Sustainable Fibres,* p. 168.

82. Leonora Oppenheim, "The TH Interview: Sarah Ratty of Ciel," treehugger.com. Available from http://www.treehugger.com/culture/the-th-interview-sarah-ratty-of-ciel-part-1.html[accessed May 14, 2012]

83. Clarice Louisba Scott, *Women's Dresses and Slips: A Buying Guide* (Washington, DC: U.S. Department of Agriculture, 1940), p. 2.

84. *25 Years of Nylon* (Wilmington, DE: Textile Fibers Dept., E. I. Du Pont de Nemours and Co., 1964), p. 23.

85. Carol J. Salusso, "Nylon," in Valerie Steele (ed.), *Encyclopedia of Clothing and Fashion* (Detroit: Charles Scribner's Sons, 2005), p. 461.

86. Allen C. Cohen, *Nylon, Polyester and Acrylic Fibers: Producers and History of Market Conditions* (New York: Fashion Institute of Technology, Department of Textile Science, 1969), p. 5.

87. Scott, *Women's Dresses and Slips,* p. 5.

88. Bernadine Morris, "Remembering Claire McCardell," *New York Times* (February 20, 1981), p. B4.

89. Kohle Yohannan and Nancy Nolf, *Claire McCardell: Redefining Modernism* (New York: Harry N. Abrams, 1998), p. 112.

90. "Cool as a Summer Shadow" advertisement. *Vogue* (June 1, 1954), p. 9.

91. Esther S. Hochstim, *Women's Opinions of Cotton and Other Fibers in Selected Items of Clothing* (Washington, DC: US Department of Agriculture, Agriculture Marketing Service, 1956), p. i.

92. Davis Jones, "As Washable in December…," *New York Times* (September 28, 1958), p. SMA34.

93. Ibid.

94. Esther S. Hochstim, *Women's Opinions of Cotton and Other Fibers,* p. 21.

95. Salusso, "Nylon," p. 462.

96. David Brunnschweiler and John Hearle (eds), *Polyester: Tomorrow's Ideas and Profits, Fifty Years of Achievement* (Manchester: The Textile Institute, 1993), p. 45.

97. Sidney G. Cooper, *The Textile Industry: Environmental Control and Energy Conservation* (Park Ridge, NJ: Noyes Date Corp., 1978), p. 1.

98. Isadore Barmash, "Polyester Emerges from the Shadow of Nylon," *New York Times* (May 1, 1966), p. 159.

99. M. Mazzaraco, "Di Sant'Angelo's Head," *Women's Wear Daily* (October 16, 1968), p. B2.

100. Lois Winebaum, "The Orientation of Giorgio di Sant'Angelo," *Women's Wear Daily,* (September 9, 1971).

101. US $200 in 1970 was the equivalent of just over $1200 in 2013; US $12 was the equivalent of just over $72. Source: United States Department of Labor, Bureau of Labor Statistics, CPI Inflation Calculator.

102. Fletcher, *Sustainable Fashion & Textiles,* p. 12.

103. Roulac, *Hemp Horizons,* p. 174.

104. ICIS, "Polyester Fiber Market Demand to Drive Global Paraxylene Growth." Available from http://www.icis.com/Articles/2012/03/05/9537632/polyester+fiber+market+demand+to+dri ve+global+paraxylene.html [accessed March 9, 2013].

105. De Coster, "Green textiles and apparel," p. 143.

106. Robin Anson, "Overcoming obstacles to environmental sustainability in the textile and apparel industry," *Textile Outlook International* 161 (April 2013): 8.

107. Lenzing Modal is a type of rayon. It is grown from sustainably harvested beech trees, and its production is carbon dioxide neutral and energy efficient.

108. "Talking Strategy: Andreas Dorner of Lenzing discusses the fibres which will shape the apparel industry in the future," *Global Apparel Markets* 18 (2nd Quarter 2012): 11.

109. Today, cellophane is typically made from petroleum, and its production is not nearly as widespread as it was in the first half of the twentieth century.

110. Dazians fabric store; known for stocking extravagant, theatrical fabrics.

111. "The Dawn of Synthetic Splendor: On with the Passion for Cellophane," *Harper's Bazaar* (April 1934), p. 94.

112. Mary Ann C. Ferro, "Vinyl as Fashion Fabric," in Valerie Steele (ed.), *Encyclopedia of Clothing and Fashion* (Detroit, MI: Charles Scribner's Sons, 2005), p. 400.

113. Mary Quant, *Quant by Quant* (New York: Putnam, 1966), p. 134.

Chapter 4: Textile dyeing

1. M. D. C. Crawford, *The Ways of Fashion* (New York: G. P. Putnam's Sons, 1941), p. 130.

2. Florence Montgomery, *Printed Textiles: English and American Cottons and Linens* (New York: The Viking Press, 1970), p. 287.

3. W. H. Perkin, Esq., F.R.S., "The Aniline or Coal Tar Colours," December 7, 1868, *Cantor Lectures*, Society for the Encouragement of Arts, Manufactures, and Commerce (London: W. Trounce, 1869), p. 4.

4. Perkin, Esq., F.R.S., "The Aniline or Coal Tar Colours," p. 8.

5. Perkin, Esq., F.R.S., "The Aniline or Coal Tar Colours," p. 9.

6. "Colors from Coal Tar," *New York Times* (May 4, 1893), p. 2.

7. "Coal Tar Products Used in Many Ways," *New York Times* (June 7, 1915), p. 5.

8. From Our Own Correspondent, "The Great Exhibition," *New York Times* (July 28, 1862), p. 2.

9. Perkin, Esq., F.R.S., "The Aniline or Coal Tar Colours," p. 3.

10. From Our Own Correspondent, "The Great Exhibition," *New York Times* (July 28, 1862), p. 2.

11. Perkin, Esq., F.R.S., "The Aniline or Coal Tar Colours," p. 3.

12. P. W. J. Bartrip, "How green was my valance?: Environmental arsenic poisoning and the Victorian domestic ideal," *The English Historical Review* 109, no. 433 (September 1994): 895.

13. *The Chicago Medical Times* 4, no. 11 (February 1873): p. 527.

14. Alfred Swaine Taylor M.D., F.R.S., *On Poisons in Relation to Medical Jurisprudence and Medicine: Third Edition* (Philadelphia: Henry C. Lea, 1875), p. 340.

15. J. K. Haywood and H. J. Warner, "Arsenic in Papers and Fabrics," *Bureau of Chemistry-Bulletin No. 86,* (Washington, DC: U.S. Department of Agriculture, 1904), p. 7.

16. Swaine Taylor, ibid., p. 340.

17. "Plenty of Arsenic," *Fraser's Magazine*, reprinted in *New York Times* (February 24, 1878), p. 3.

18. "Arsenic on Paper and Clothing," *New York Times* (April 5, 1891), p. 4.

19. J. K. Haywood and H. J. Warner, "Arsenic in Papers and Fabrics," *Bureau of Chemistry-Bulletin No. 86* (Washington, DC: U.S. Department of Agriculture, 1904), p. 39.

20. Ibid., 40.

21. Waldemar Kaempffert, "German Scientist Links Incidence of Cancer to the Use of Coal Tar Dyes in Food," *New York Times* (September 18, 1949), p. E11.

22. W. H. Perkin, Esq., F.R.S., "Mauve, Magenta, and Some of Their Derivatives," December 14, 1868, *Cantor Lectures*, Society for the Encouragement of Arts, Manufactures, and Commerce (London: W. Trounce, 1869), p. 10.

23. Alice Hamilton, M.A., M.D., *Industrial Poisoning in Making Coal-Tar Dyes and Dye Intermediates* (Washington, DC: U.S. Department of Labor, Bureau of Labor Statistics, April 1921), p. 5.

24. Ibid., p. 7.

25. J. K. Haywood and H. J. Warner, "Arsenic in Papers and Fabrics," p. 39.

26. S. R. Cockett, *Dyeing and Printing* (London: Sir Isaac Pitman & Sons Ltd., 1964), p. 31.

27. Kate Heintz Watson, *Textiles and Clothing* (Chicago: American School of Home Economics, 1911), p. 79.

28. J. W. Slater, *The Manual of Colours & Dye Wares: Their Properties, Applications, Valuation, Impurities, and Sophistication* (London: Lockwood & Co., 1870), p. 144.

29. Rudolf Nietzki, *Chemistry of the Organic Dyestuffs* (London: Gurney & Jackson, 1892), p. 18.

30. Alice Hamilton, M.A., M.D., *Industrial Poisoning in Making Coal-Tar Dyes and Dye Intermediates* (Washington, DC: U.S. Department of Labor, Bureau of Labor Statistics, April 1921), p. 58.

31. Greenpeace, *Toxic Threads: The Big Fashion Stitch-Up* (Amsterdam: Greenpeace International, 2012), p. 24.

32. Bruna de Campos Ventura-Camargo and Maria Aparecida Marin-Morales, "Azo dyes: Characterization and toxicity—a review," *Textiles and Light Industrial Science and Technology (TLIST)* 2, no. 2 (April 2013): 87.

33. Ibid., p. 86.

34. John C. Geyer and William A. Perry, *Textile Waste Treatment and Recovery: A Survey of Present Knowledge Concerning the Treatment and Disposal of Waste Waters Produced in the Textile Industries* (Washington, DC: The Textile Foundation, Inc., 1938), p. 17.

35. Anthony S. Travis, "Poisoned groundwater and contaminated soil: The tribulations and trial of the first major manufacturer of aniline dyes in Basel," *Environmental History* 2, no. 3 (July 1997): 344.

36. Ibid., p. 344, 356.

37. Ibid., p. 351.

38. Rachel Carson, *Silent Spring: Fortieth Anniversary Edition* (Boston and New York: Houghton Mifflin Company, 1962), p. 42.

39. John C. Geyer and William A. Perry, *Textile Waste Treatment and Recovery: A Survey of Present Knowledge Concerning the Treatment and Disposal of Waste Waters Produced in the Textile Industries* (Washington, DC: The Textile Foundation, Inc., 1938), p. 7.

40. Ibid., p. 7.

41. George M. Price, *The Modern Factory: Safety, Sanitation, and Welfare* (New York: Arno, 1969), 285.

42. James D. Gallup, "The Textile Effluent Standards Program in 1977," *Textile Technology/Ecology Interface, 1977*, Environmental Sciences Committee of the American Association of Textile Chemists and Colorists Symposium (Research Triangle Park, NC: AATCC, 1977), p. 39.

43. Marion I. Tobler-Rohr, *Handbook of Sustainable Textile Production* (Oxford; Philadelphia: Woodhead; Cambridge: In association with the Textile Institute, 2011), p. 20.

44. Greenpeace, *Toxic Threads: Polluting Paradise* (Amsterdam: Greenpeace International, 2013), p. 5.

45. Jacky Watson, *Textiles and the Environment* (London: Economist Intelligence Unit, 1991), p. 46.

46. Maria C. Thiry, "Staying alive: Making textiles sustainable," *AATCC Review* (November/December 2011): 27.

47. J. R. Easton, "Key Sustainability Issues in Textile Dyeing," in *Sustainable Textiles: Life Cycle and Environmental Impact*, R. S. Blackburn (ed.) (New York: CRC Press; Cambridge: Woodhead, 2009), p. 139.

48. Ibid., p. 140.

49. Ibid., p. 147.

50. J. N. Chakraborty, *Fundamentals and Practices in Colouration of Textiles* (New Delhi, Cambridge and Oxford: Woodhead Publishing India PVT, Ltd., 2010), p. 382.

51. Ibid., p. 384.

52. John C. Geyer and William A. Perry, *Textile Waste Treatment and Recovery: A Survey of Present Knowledge Concerning the Treatment and Disposal of Waste Waters Produced in the Textile Industries* (Washington, DC: The Textile Foundation, Inc., 1938), p. 21.

53. Chakraborty, *Fundamentals and Practices in Colouration of Textiles*, p. 389.

54. Kate Fletcher, *Sustainable Fashion & Textiles: Design Journeys* (London and Sterling, VA: Earthscan, 2008), p. 52.

55. Cheryl Kolander, "In Defense of Truth and Beauty," in *Future Fashion White Papers* (New York: Earth Pledge, 2007), pp. 168–9.

56. Ibid., p. 170.

57. Ibid., pp. 171–2.

58. India Flint, *Eco Colour: Botanical Dyes for Beautiful Textiles* (Loveland, CO: Interweave, 2008), p. 15.

59. Ibid., p. 89, 91.

60. Kate Brierley, interview by Jennifer Farley Gordon, June 28, 2013.

61. Kristi Ellis and Arthur Friedman, "After the Pakistan Fire: Advancing the CSR Agenda," *Women's Wear Daily*, October 24, 2012. Available from http://www.wwd.com/business-news/business-features/after-the-fire-advancing-the-csr-agenda-6443565 [accessed January 3, 2013].

62. "Silks: Bluesign ® Certified," Eileen Fisher,. Available from http://www.eileenfisher.com/EileenFisherCompany/CompanyGeneralContentPages/SocialConciousness/BlueSign.jsp [accessed August 25, 2013].

63. Holbrook Jackson, *William Morris* (Westport, CT: Greenwood Press, 1971), p. 63.

64. Guillermo de Osma, *Mariano Fortuny: His Life and Work* (New York, Rizzoli, 1980), p. 115.

65. "American Woman Invents Dye from Autumn Leaves," *New York Times* (July 22, 1917), p. 64.

66. Edith O'Neil MacDonald, "Dye Composition," United States Patent Office, No. 1,222,433, (April 10, 1917).

67. India Flint, *Eco Colour: Botanical Dyes for Beautiful Textiles* (Loveland, CO: Interweave, 2008), p. 24.

68. Cheryl Kolander, "In Defense of Truth and Beauty," pp. 172.

69. Anne de la Sayette, "An Introduction to the History, Basic Principles and Practices of Textile Dyeing with Natural Dyes—Large Scale Production Systems and Various Industrial Applications," delivered at *Coloring Fashion: Natural and Synthetic Dyeing in Textiles Today,* Parsons, New York, May 4, 2012.

70. Martin Bide, "Dyeing with Synthetic Dyes," delivered at *Coloring Fashion: Natural and Synthetic Dyeing in Textiles Today,* Parsons, New York, May 4, 2012.

71. Cheryl Kolander, "In Defense of Truth and Beauty," p. 173.

72. Martin Bide, "Dyeing with Synthetic Dyes," delivered at *Coloring Fashion: Natural and Synthetic Dyeing in Textiles Today,* Parsons, New York, May 4, 2012.

73. William McDonough and Michael Braungart, *Cradle to Cradle: Remaking the Way We Make Things* (New York: North Point Press, 2002), p. 42.

74. India Flint, *Eco Colour: Botanical Dyes for Beautiful Textiles* (Loveland, CO: Interweave, 2008), p. 28.

75. "Toxic is So Last Season," Greenpeace. Available from http://www.greenpeace.org/international/en/campaigns/toxics/water/detox/detox-fashion/ [accessed August 31, 2013].

76. Greenpeace, *Toxic Threads: The Big Fashion Stitch-Up* (Amsterdam: Greenpeace International, 2012), p. 6.

77. Jacky Watson, *Textiles and the Environment* (London: Economist Intelligence Unit, 1991), p. 4.

78. A. Sherburne, "Achieving Sustainable Textiles: A Designer's Perspective," in *Sustainable Textiles: Life Cycle and Environmental Impact*, R. S. Blackburn (ed.) (New York: CRC Press; Cambridge: Woodhead, 2009), p. 17.

79. Keith Slater, *The Environmental Impact of Textiles: Production, Processes, and Protection* (Cambridge: Woodhead Publishing, 2000), p. 87.

80. K. Karthikeyan and Bhaarathi Dhurai, "New method of mischarge printing on cotton fabrics using horseradish peroxidase," *AUTEX Research Journal* 11, no. 2 (June 2011): 61.

81. Ibid., p. 62.

82. Melanie Bowles and Ceri Isaac, *Digital Textile Design* (London: Laurence King Publishing, 2009), p. 171.

83. S. V. Kulkarni, C. D. Blackwell et al., *Textile Dyeing Operations: Chemistry, Equipment, Procedures and Environmental Aspects* (Park Ridge, NJ: Noyes Publications, 1986), p. 227.

84. Joanna Kinnersly Taylor, *Dyeing and Screen-Printing on Textiles* (London: A & C Black, 2003), p. 113.

85. S. V. Kulkarni, C. D. Blackwell et al., *Textile Dyeing Operations: Chemistry, Equipment, Procedures and Environmental Aspects*, pp. 55, 61.

86. AirDye® brochure (Colorep®, Inc., n.d.).

87. Costello Tagliapietra and Colorep, Inc., "What is AirDye®?" (Colorep®, Inc., Spring 2010).

88. Maria C. Thiry, "Staying alive: making textiles sustainable," *AATCC Review* (November/December 2011): 27–9.

89. "Colors from Coal Tar," *New York Times* (May 4, 1893), p. 2.

90. François Delamare and Bernard Guineau, *Colors: The Story of Dyes and Pigments* (New York: Harry N. Abrams, 2000), pp. 105, 110.

91. "The Situation in Dyes," *New York Times* (September 8, 1915), p. 14.

92. James Sullivan, *Jeans: A Cultural History of an American Icon* (New York: Gotham Books, 2006), p. 138.

93. Rachel Louise Snyder, *Fugitive Denim: A Moving Story of People and Pants in the Borderless World of Global Trade* (New York: W. W. Norton & Co., 2008), p. 125.

94. Rachel Carson, *Silent Spring: Fortieth Anniversary Edition* (Boston, New York: Houghton Mifflin Company, 1962), p. 6.

95. "The Detox Campaign," Greenpeace. Available from http://www.greenpeace.org/international/en/campaigns/toxics/water/detox/intro/ [accessed August 31, 2013].

96. "Progress and Hurdles on the Road to Detox," Greenpeace. Available from http://www.greenpeace.org/international/en/campaigns/toxics/water/detox/intro/Progress-and-hurdles-on-the-road-to-Detox/ [accessed August 31, 2013].

97. "Greenpeace International's Textile Procurement Policy," Greenpeace. Available from http://www.greenpeace.org/international/en/campaigns/toxics/water/detox/intro/Our-Textile-Policy/ [accessed August 31, 2013].

98. Greenpeace, *Toxic Threads: Polluting Paradise,* pp. 5–6.

99. Ibid., p. 7.

100. "The Detox Campaign," Greenpeace.

101. Greenpeace, *Toxic Threads: The Big Fashion Stitch-Up*, p. 3.

102. Ibid., p. 13.

Chapter 5: Labor practices

1. Philip B. Scranton, "Introduction," in Philip B. Scranton (ed.), *Silk City: Studies in the Paterson Silk Industry, 1860-1890* (Newark: New Jersey Historical Society, 1985), pp. 4, 6.

2. Benita Eisler (ed.), *The Lowell Offering: Writings by New England Mill Women (1840–1845)* (Philadelphia and New York: J. B. Lippincott Company, 1977), pp. 18–19.

3. Steve Dunwell, *The Run of the Mill: A Pictorial Narrative of the Expansion, Dominion, Decline and Enduring Impact of the New England Textile Industry* (Boston: David R. Godine, 1978), pp. 42, 47.

4. Benita Eisler (ed.), *The Lowell Offering: Writings by New England Mill Women (1840–1845)* (Philadelphia and New York: J. B. Lippincott Company, 1977), p. 15.

5. Josephine L. Baker, "A second peep at factory life," *The Lowell Offering* 5 (May 1845): 98.

6. Ibid., p. 99.

7. Benita Eisler (ed.), *The Lowell Offering: Writings by New England Mill Women (1840–1845)* (Philadelphia and New York: J. B. Lippincott Company, 1977), p. 36.

8. Mrs. J. Borden Harriman, "The cotton mill a factor in the development of the south," *Annals of the American Academy of Political and Social Sciences; Supplement: Child Employing Industries* 35 (March 1910): 48.

9. Holland Thompson, *From the Cotton Field to the Cotton Mill: A Study of the Industrial Transition in North Carolina* (New York, London: The Macmillan Company, 1906), p. 271.

10. Ibid., p. 66.

11. D. A. Tompkins, *Cotton Mill, Commercial Features: A Text-Book for the Use of Textiles Schools and Investors* (Charlotte, NC: The Author, 1899), p. 28.

12. Holland Thompson, *From the Cotton Field to the Cotton Mill: A Study of the Industrial Transition in North Carolina* (New York, London: The Macmillan Company, 1906), p. 133.

13. Ibid., p. 151.

14. Victoria Byerly, *Hard Times Cotton Mill Girls: Personal Histories of Womanhood and Poverty in the South* (Ithaca, NY: ILR Press, 1986), p. 7; Steve Dunwell, *The Run of the Mill: A Pictorial Narrative of the Expansion, Dominion, Decline and Enduring Impact of the New England Textile Industry* (Boston: David R. Godine, 1978), p. 147.

15. Holland Thompson, *From the Cotton Field to the Cotton Mill: A Study of the Industrial Transition in North Carolina* (New York and London: The Macmillan Company, 1906), pp. 273, 159.

16. Ibid., 148.

17. Interview with Bertha Miller, in Victoria Byerly, *Hard Times Cotton Mill Girls: Personal Histories of Womanhood and Poverty in the South* (Ithaca, NY: ILR Press, 1986), p. 48.

18. D. A. Tompkins, *Cotton Mill, Commercial Featuers: A Text-Book for the Use of Textiles Schools and Investors*, p. 37.

19. Susan Hall Fleming, "OSHA at 30: Three decades of progress in occupational safety and health," *Job Safety and Health Quarterly* 12, no. 3 (Spring 2001): 4–5.

20. Interview with Clara Thrift, in Victoria Byerly, *Hard Times Cotton Mill Girls: Personal Histories of Womanhood and Poverty in the South* (Ithaca, NY: ILR Press, 1986), p. 117.

21. Steve Dunwell, *The Run of the Mill: A Pictorial Narrative of the Expansion, Dominion, Decline and Enduring Impact of the New England Textile Industry* (Boston: David R. Godine, 1978), p. 14.

22. Holland Thompson, *From the Cotton Field to the Cotton Mill: A Study of the Industrial Transition in North Carolina* (New York, London: The Macmillan Company, 1906), p. 220.

23. Hugh Hindman, *Child Labor: An American History* (Armonk, NY and London: M. E. Sharpe, 2002), p. 158.

24. A. J. McKelway, "The cotton mill: The Herod among industries," *Annals of the Academy of Political and Social Sciences: Supplement: Uniform Child Labor Laws* 38 (July 1911): 44.

25. Holland Thompson, *From the Cotton Field to the Cotton Mill: A Study of the Industrial Transition in North Carolina* (New York, London: The Macmillan Company, 1906), p. 226.

26. Ibid., p. 225.

27. Ibid., p. 131.

28. Al Priddy (Frederic Kenyon Brown), *Through the Mill, the Life of a Mill Boy* (Boston, New York and Chicago: The Pilgrim Press, 1911), pp. 96, 102.

29. Ibid., p.124.

30. Ibid., p. 167.

31. Ibid., pp. 168–9.

32. Ibid., p. 168.

33. Ibid., p. 171.

34. Based on the information provided, it would have been roughly 1905 when Miller started working. Interview with Bertha Miller, in Victoria Byerly, *Hard Times Cotton Mill Girls: Personal Histories of Womanhood and Poverty in the South* (Ithaca, NY: ILR Press, 1986), p. 48.

35. Interview with Bertha Awford Black, in Victoria Byerly, pp. 65, 62.

36. Leonora Beck Ellis, "A study of southern cotton-mill communities. Child labor. The operatives in general," *American Journal of Sociology* 8, no. 5 (March 1903): 624.

37. Jacob A. Riis, *How the Other Half Lives: Studies Among the Tenements of New York* (New York: Hill and Wang, Inc., 1957), p. 2.

38. Abraham Bisno, *Abraham Bisno: Union Pioneer* (Madison: University of Wisconsin Press, 1967), pp. 42, 239.

39. "The Sweat-Shop Problem," *New York Times* (December 17, 1895), p. 4.

40. Jacob A. Riis, *How the Other Half Lives: Studies Among the Tenements of New York* (New York: Hill and Wang, Inc., 1957), p. 89.

41. Abraham Bisno, *Abraham Bisno: Union Pioneer* (Madison: University of Wisconsin Press, 1967), p. 147.

42. Ibid., p. 74.

43. "The Sweatshop Problem," *New York Times* (January 28, 1901), p. 2.

44. Jacob A. Riis, *How the Other Half Lives: Studies Among the Tenements of New York* (New York: Hill and Wang, Inc., 1957), p. 91.

45. "The 'Stanley' Shirt Waist," *Daily True American* (April 10, 1899), p. 3. Available from http://news.google.com/newspapers?id=zIZgAAAAIBAJ&sjid=I3ENAAAAIBAJ&pg=1426,594925&dq=stanley+shirt+waist&hl=en [accessed August 7, 2013]

46. "The Stanley Shirt Waist," *The Evening Argus* (June 22, 1898), p. 5. Available from http://news.google.com/newspapers?id=NDciAAAAIBAJ&sjid=I6sFAAAAIBAJ&pg=6524,3061075&dq=stanley+shirt+waist&hl=en [accessed August 7, 2013].

47. The International Ladies' Garment Workers' Union, "When you go out shopping remember the shirt-waist girl," *The Ladies' Garment Worker* 1, no. 1 (April 1910): 1.

48. "Women Here and There: Their Frills and Fancies," *New York Times* (September 16, 1900), p. 19.

49. Ibid.

50. *Ladies' Garment Worker* 2, no. 4 (April 1911): 6.

51. "141 Men and Girls Die in Waist Factory Fire; Trapped High up in Washington Place Building; Street Strewn with Bodies; Piles of Dead Inside," *New York Times* (March 26,

1911), p. 1; "Doors Were Locked, Say Rescued Girls," *New York Times* (March 27, 1911), p. 3.

52. Edna Woolman Chase, *Always in Vogue* (Garden City, NY: Doubleday, 1954), p. 77.

53. Arthur F. McEvoy, "The Triangle Shirtwaist factory fire of 1911: Social change, industrial accidents, and the evolution of common-sense causality," *Law & Social Inquiry* 20, no. 2 (Spring 1995): 623.

54. Ibid., pp. 627–9.

55. John A. Dyche, "The strike of the ladies' waist makers of New York and its results," *The Ladies' Garment Worker* 1, no. 2 (May 1910): 2.

56. Mary Domsky-Abrams, in an interview by Leon Stein, date unknown. Available from www.ilr. cornell.edu/trianglefire/primary/survivorinterviews/MaryDomskyAbrams.html [accessed July 8, 2013].

57. Arthur F. McEvoy, "The Triangle Shirtwaist factory fire of 1911," p. 631; Leon Stein, *The Triangle Fire: Centennial Edition* (Ithaca and London: ILR Press, 1962, 2011), p. 20.

58. Abraham Bisno, *Abraham Bisno: Union Pioneer* (Madison: University of Wisconsin Press, 1967), p. 124.

59. Max Meyer, "Irresponsibility Wrecked the Protocol," *New York Times* (July 8, 1915), p. 12.

60. Abraham Bisno, *Abraham Bisno: Union Pioneer* (Madison: University of Wisconsin Press, 1967), pp. 210–11.

61. Ladies' Waist and Dress Manufacturers' Association, *Minutes of Conference in re Proposed Amended Protocol in the Dress and Waist Industry Between the Ladies' Waist and Dress Manufacturers' Association and the International Ladies' Garment Workers' Union* (January 1916), p. 12.

62. Joel Seidman, *The Needle Trades* (New York, Toronto: Farrar & Rinehart, Inc., 1942), p. 187.

63. "Richness to Mark Winter Fashions," *New York Times* (September 5, 1933), p. 19.

64. M. D. C. Crawford, *The Ways of Fashion* (New York: G. P. Putnam's Sons, 1941), pp. 102–3.

65. Daniel Lang, "Where the Fashion is Multiplied," *New York Times* (November 5, 1939), p. 121.

66. *Signature of the 450,000*, International Ladies' Garment Workers' Union, 65th Anniversary Convention, Miami Beach, Florida (May 1965), pp. 39, 41, 45.

67. Nan Robertson, "Woman's Refusal to Dress Like Others Gives Seventh Ave. Odd Pricing System," *New York Times* (February 9, 1956), p. 36.

68. David Dubinsky, "Introduction," *Signature of the 450,000*, International Ladies' Garment Workers" Union, 65th Anniversary Convention, Miami Beach, Florida (May 1965), p. 3.

69. M. D. C. Crawford, *The Ways of Fashion* (New York: G. P. Putnam's Sons, 1941), pp. 102–3.

70. Michael Freitag, "New York is Fighting the Spread of Sweatshops," *New York Times* (November 16, 1987), p. A1.

71. "Justice Center in the Eye of the Sweatshop Storm: Building the Union from the Ground Up," *UNITE!* (March/April 1997), p. 8.

72. Stephanie Strom, "A Sweetheart Becomes Suspect: Looking Behind Those Kathie Lee Labels," *New York Times* (June 27, 1996), p. D1.

73. "Sweatshops are Back. Now Slavery is Too." *UNITE!* (September 1995), p. 16.

74. Neil Kearney, "Free Trade Zone Slavery," *Justice* (January 1991), p. 4.

75. "Targeting Sweatshops," *UNITE!* (December 1995), p. 3.

76. "Stop Sweatshop' Campaign Growing," *UNITE!* (January/February 1997), p. 6.

77. Dwight Burton, "…Take Back the 'American Dream,'" *UNITE!* (March/April 1996), p. 17.

78. "Justice Center in the Eye of the Sweatshop Storm: Building the Union from the Ground Up," *UNITE!* (March/April 1997), p. 9.

79. "Mission Statement: We Will Organize Globally," *UNITE!* (July 1995), p. 12.

80. "Three Young Maquila Workers Take on American Retail Giants," *UNITE!* (July 1995), p. 14.

81. Jacob A. Riis, *How the Other Half Lives: Studies Among the Tenements of New York* (New York: Hill and Wang, Inc., 1957), p. 99.

82. U.S. Department of Labor, Bureau of International Labor Affairs, *By the Sweat and Toil of Children: The Use of Child Labor in American Imports Vol. 1* (Washington, DC: The Bureau, 1994–5), p. 16.

83. Nicky Coninck, Martje Theuws, and Pauline Overeem, *Captured by Cotton: Exploited Dalit Girls Produce Garments in India for European and US Markets* (The Netherlands: Centre for Research on Multinational Corporations and India Committee of the Netherlands, May 2011), p. 3.

84. Research Department, International Ladies' Garment Workers' Union, *Conditions in the Women's Garment Industry*, (February 25, 1976), pp. 9, 7; Research Department, International Ladies' Garment Workers' Union, *Conditions in the Women's Garment Industry* (February 23, 1995), p. 7.

85. Arnold J. Karr, "USA: Consumers Say They Will Pay," *Women's Wear Daily* (September 5, 2012). Available from http://www.wwd.com/retail-news/trends-analysis/usa-consumers-say-they-will-pay-6220500 [accessed August 18, 2013].

86. Benjamin Selekman, *The Clothing and Textile Industries in New York and Its Environs, Present Trends and Probable Future Developments* (New York: Regional Plan of New York and its Environs, 1925), p. 23.

87. Joel Seidman, *The Needle Trades* (New York, Toronto: Farrar & Rinehart, Inc., 1942), p. 9.

88. Ibid., p. 52.

89. Benjamin Selekman, *The Clothing and Textile Industries in New York and Its Environs, Present Trends and Probable Future Developments* (New York: Regional Plan of New York and its Environs, 1925), p. 25.

90. Robert B. Reich, "How an American Industry Gets Away With Slave Labor," *New York Times* (August 20, 1995), p. E7.

91. Benjamin Stolberg, *Tailor's Progress: The Story of a Famous Union and the Men Who Made It* (Garden City, NY: Doubleday, Doran and Company, 1944), p. 14.

92. Kelsey Timmerman, *Where Am I Wearing?: A Global Tour to the Countries, Factories, and People That Make Our Clothes* (Hoboken, NJ: John Wiley and Sons, Inc., 2009), p. xiii.

93. Amy DuFault, "Your New T-Shirt Slogan: Spectrum & Ali & Tazreen & Rana," *Ecouterre* (May 30, 2013). Available from http://www.ecouterre.com/can-you-stop-fast-fashion-with-a-t-shirt/ [accessed August 14, 2013].

94. Declan Walsh and Steven Greenhouse, "Inspectors Certified Pakistani Factory as Safe Before Disaster," *New York Times* (September 19, 2012). Available from http://www.nytimes.com/2012/09/20/world/asia/pakistan-factory-passed-inspection-before-fire.html?pagewanted=all&_r=0 [accessed September 21, 2012]; Mahlia S. Lone, "Controversy Goes on Over Pakistan Fire," *Women's Wear Daily* (September 17, 2012).

Available from http://www.wwd.com/markets-news/textiles/controversy-goes-on-over-pakistan-fire-6300031 [accessed January 3, 2013].

95. Declan Walsh and Steven Greenhouse, "Inspectors Certified Pakistani Factory as Safe Before Disaster," *New York Times* (September 19, 2012). Available from http://www.nytimes.com/2012/09/20/world/asia/pakistan-factory-passed-inspection-before-fire.html?pagewanted=all&_r=0 [accessed September 21, 2012].

96. Karyn Monget, "Bangladesh Factory Fire Stirs Action Calls," *Women's Wear Daily* (November 25, 2012). Availiable from http://www.wwd.com/business-news/government-trade/bangladesh-factory-fire-kills-more-than-115-workers-6500524 [accessed January 3, 2014].

97. Julfikar Ali Manik and Jim Yardley, "Building Collapse in Bangladesh Leaves Scores Dead," *New York Times* (April 24, 2013). Available from http://www.nytimes.com/2013/04/25/world/asia/bangladesh-building-collapse.html?pagewanted=all&_r=0/ [accessed August 14, 2013].

98. Judith Thurman, "Rana Plaza Has Happened Before," *The New Yorker* (May 23, 2013). Available from http://www.newyorker.com/online/blogs/books/2013/05/rana-plaza-has-happened-before.html?printable=true&currentPage=all [accessed August 18, 2013].

99. "The Fall of the Pemberton Mill," *London Times,* January 30, 1860. Reprinted in *New York Times* (February 16, 1860), p. 2.

100. "Triangle Fire 90th Anniversary: Demand Global Fairness," *UNITE!* (Spring 2001), p. 3.

101. "Factory Fire in China Takes 80 Lives," *Justice* (September 1991), p. 6.

102. Charles Kernaghan, "Think Tank: Sweatshop Garments Drag All of Us Down," *Women's Wear Daily* (February 5, 2013). Available from http://www.WWD.com/markets-news/markets-features/think-tank-sweatshop-garments-drag-all-of-us-down-6693980 [accessed February 5, 2013].

103. Ibid.

104. Eileen Fisher's "story-telling" includes extensive sustainability-related video content on the company website. Naomi Gross, interview by Jennifer Farley Gordon, July 1, 2013.

105. "An Interview With Jay Mazur: First UNITE President Shares His Vision For the Future," *UNITE!* (September 1995), p. 4.

106. "Major Retailers Still Avoid Responsibility," *UNITE!* (October 1995), p. 3.

107. Arthur Friedman and Kristi Ellis, "Triangle Shirtwaist Factory Fire: The Lessons of History," *Women's Wear Daily* (March 21, 2011), p. 7.

108. *The Apparel Industry Codes of Conduct: A Solution to the International Child Labor Problem?* (Washington, DC: U.S. Department of Labor, Bureau of International Affairs, 1996), pp. 8, v, vi.

109. Kristi Ellis, "ILRF Report Lambasts CSR Effectiveness," *Women's Wear Daily* (December 18, 2012). Available from http://www.wwd.com/business-news/government-trade/ilrf-report-spotlights-dirty-secrets-6546898 [accessed March 1, 2013].

110. *The Apparel Industry Codes of Conduct: A Solution to the International Child Labor Problem?* (Washington, DC: U.S. Department of Labor, Bureau of International Affairs, 1996), p. x.

111. Charles Kernaghan, "Think Tank: Sweatshop Garments Drag All of Us Down," *Women's Wear Daily* (February 5, 2013). Available from http://www.WWD.com/markets-news/markets-features/think-tank-sweatshop-garments-drag-all-of-us-down-6693980 [accessed February 5, 2013].

112. Robert J. S. Ross, *Slaves to Fashion: Poverty and Abuse in the New Sweatshops* (Ann Arbor: The University of Michigan Press, 2007), p. 246.

113. Allen R. Myerson, "In Principle, a Case for More 'Sweatshops,'" *New York Times* (June 22, 1997), p. E5.

114. Kelsey Timmerman, *Where Am I Wearing?: A Global Tour to the Countries, Factories, and People That Make Our Clothes* (Hoboken, NJ: John Wiley and Sons, Inc., 2009), p. 8.

115. Sandy Black, *Eco-Chic: The Fashion Paradox* (London: Black Dog Publishing, 2008), p. 185.

116. Robert J. S. Ross, *Slaves to Fashion: Poverty and Abuse in the New Sweatshops* (Ann Arbor: The University of Michigan Press, 2007), p. 323.

117. Ibid., p. 325.

118. "Appalachia's Poor Sew Fashions for the Rich," *Owosso Argus* (January 5, 1970).

119. Carlos Miele, *Carlos Miele: Coopa-Roca and the Fuxico*, press release, 2010.

120. "The Trade Game: Where in the World is Fast Buck Dress?" *Justice* (January 1993), pp. 10–11.

121. Sass Brown, *Eco Fashion* (London: Laurence King Publishing, 2010), p. 202.

122. "Fair Trade Gains Steam in U.S.," *Women's Wear Daily* (July 15, 2003). Available from http://www.wwd.com/fashion-news/fashion-features/fair-trade-gains-steam-in-u-s-725721 [accessed August 18, 2013].

123. Marc Karimzadeh and Miles Socha, "A New Edun," *Women's Wear Daily* (December 10, 2009), p. 6.

124. "About Edun," Edun. Available from http://edun.com/about [accessed July 1, 2014].

125. Tina Gaudoin, "Mrs. Bono Saves the Day," *The Times* (London, England) (December 2, 2006), p. 49.

126. Larry Rother, "Hondurans in Sweatshop See Opportunity," *New York Times* (July 18, 1996), p. A1.

127. Robert Sullivan, "Power of Commitment: Stream of Consciousness," *Vogue* (March 1, 2005), p. 531.

128. Cecil Beaton, *The Glass of Fashion* (Garden City, NY: Country Life Press, 1954), p. 220.

129. M. D. C. Crawford, *The Ways of Fashion* (New York: G. P. Putnam's Sons, 1941), p. 73.

130. Kirke's original source is Thérèse and Louise Bonney, *A Shopping Guide to Paris* (New York: McBride, 1929). Betty Kirke, *Vionnet* (San Francisco: Chronicle Books, 1998), p. 124.

131. M. D. C. Crawford, *The Ways of Fashion* (New York: G. P. Putnam's Sons, 1941), p. 5, pp. 104–5.

132. "Mediation Board Makes Garage Award," *New York Times* (April 23, 1941), p. 16; "Arbitrators are Named," *New York Times* (October 2, 1948), p. 7.

133. "Max Meyer Dies; Labor Mediator," Special to *New York Times* (February 1, 1953), p. 89.

134. Max Meyer, "Irresponsibility Wrecked the Protocol," *New York Times* (July 8, 1915), p. 12.

135. Alvin Johnson, "Our Industries from the Underside: HURRY UP PLEASE, IT'S TIME," *New York Times* (January 12, 1947), p. BR6.

136. Elizabeth Hawes, *Fashion Is Spinach* (New York: Random House, 1938), p. 30.

137. Ibid., p. 207.

138. Kelsey Timmerman, *Where Am I Wearing?: A Global Tour to the Countries, Factories, and People That Make Our Clothes* (Hoboken, NJ: John Wiley and Sons, Inc., 2009).

139. Florence Kelley, "The consumers' league label," *Bulletin: The Consumers" League of New York* 4, no. 5 (May 1925): 1.

140. Henry Moskowitz, "Prosanis: The Garment Health Label," *Bulletin: The Consumers' League of New York* 4, no. 5 (May 1925), p. 2.

141. "Woman Shopper is Urged to Discourage Sweatshops," *New York Times* (May 10, 1925), p. X20.

142. Mrs. Frederick Nathan, "Real Manufacturer is the Woman Who Goes Shopping," *New York Times* (December 29, 1912), p. 72.

143. "Fashion Show in Interest of Health," *New York Times* (October 25,1925), p. X11.

144. Florence Kelley, "The consumers' league label," p. 2.

145. "Fair Pay Plea Made by Mrs. Roosevelt," *New York Times* (June 20, 1933), p. 21.

146. M. D. C. Crawford, *The Ways of Fashion* (New York: G. P. Putnam's Sons, 1941), p. 183.

147. "Advertising Begun in N.Y. Dress Drive," *New York Times* (August 28, 1941), p. 35.

148. "City Hall Style Show Introduces New Label for New York Creations," *New York Times* (July 8, 1941), p. 21.

149. "A Label and What It Means," *Harper's Bazaar* (September 1,1941), p. 96.

150. Nan Robertson, "Woman's Refusal to Dress Like Others Gives Seventh Ave. Odd Pricing System," *New York Times* (February 9, 1956), p. 36.

Chapter 6: Treatment of animals

1. J. A. Allen, "The present wholesale destruction of bird-life in the United States," *Science* 7, no. 60 (February 26, 1886): 194.

2. Frank M. Chapman, "Birds and Bonnets," *Forest and Stream*, February 25, 1886, p. 84.

3. "For the Woman's Hat," *New York Times* (December 15, 1907), p. 15.

4. "Destruction of birds for millinery purposes," *Science* 7, no. 160 (February 26, 1886): 196.

5. Ibid., p. 197.

6. Ibid., p. 197.

7. Thomas H. Wood & Co. advertisement, *The Millinery Trade Review* 22, no. 7 (July 1897): p. 13.

8. "Cincinnati notes," *The Millinery Trade Review* 22, no. 10 (October 1897): 44.

9. "Notes and news," *The Auk* 11, no. 4 (October 1894): 342.

10. William Dutcher, "Report of the A.O.U. Committee on the protection of North American birds," *The Auk* 20, no. 1 (January 1903): 101; *The Auk* 4, no. 1 (January 1887): 58.

11. "The Audubon Society," *Forest and Stream* 10 (February 11, 1886): 41.

12. "The Audubon Society," *Forest and Stream* 10 (March 18, 1886): 141.

13. Frank Graham, Jr., *The Audubon Ark: A History of the National Audubon Society* (New York: Alfred A. Knopf, 1990), p. 3.

14. Jennifer Price, "Hats Off to Audubon," *Audubon Magazine* (December 2004). Available from http://audubonmagazine.org/features0412/hats.htm [accessed March 2, 2010]; Frank Graham, Jr., *The Audubon Ark: A History of the National Audubon Society* (New York: Alfred A. Knopf, 1990), pp. 15, 18.

15. Allen, ibid., p. 195.

16. "Haphazard Jottings," *Vogue* (June 25, 1896), p. 433.

17. T. Gilbert Pearson, "Birds as a universal appeal," *The Art World* 2, no. 1 (April 1917): 37.

18. "Pleading for the Birds," *New York Times* (January 3, 1900), p. 12.

19. "A Bill for Bird Protection," *Forest and Stream* 10 (February 26, 1886): 84.

20. Allen, ibid., p. 195.

21. Witmer Stone, "Report of the A.O.U. Committee on the protection of North American birds," *The Auk* 16, no. 1 (January 1899): 57–8.

22. Saks and Company, advertisement, *New York Times* (October 5, 1913), p. 5.

23. "Audubon Hats Here," *New York Times* (October 26, 1913), p. XX10.

24. Frank Graham, Jr., *The Audubon Ark: A History of the National Audubon Society* (New York: Alfred A. Knopf, 1990), p. 39.

25. "The Slaughter of the Innocents," *Harper's Bazar* (May 22, 1875), p. 338.

26. "Notes and News," p. 323.

27. "Woman's Cruel Folly," *Vogue* (March 26, 1896), p. xii. Virtually the same text appears in the *New York Times* (March 22, 1896) under the column "Her Point of View."

28. "Answers to Correspondents," *Vogue* (October 11, 1900), p. vi.

29. The figure is as reported by an SPCA chapter in Buffalo, NY, which stated that "one hunter kills 100 in a day, forty to sixty hunters are out in the season." "Spare the Birds," *New York Times* (March 1, 1897), p. 7.

30. Edward Bok, *The Americanization of Edward Bok: The Autobiography of a Dutch Boy Fifty Years Later* (New York: Charles Scribner's Sons, 1920), p. 374.

31. Ibid., pp. 332–3.

32. Ibid., p. 334.

33. Ibid., p. 335.

34. "The Family Scrap Basket: Interesting Bits of Household Fact and Fancy," *Good Housekeeping* (February 5, 1887), p.163.

35. "An appeal to the women of the country in behalf of the birds," *Science* 7, no. 160 (February 26, 1886): 204.

36. "The Slaughter of the Innocents," *Harper's Bazar* (May 22, 1875), p. 338.

37. "Among the Qualities Man Insists Upon…," *Vogue* (July 22, 1897), p. 50.

38. "What She Wears: Ostrich Feather Craze…," *Vogue* (October 31, 1895), p. 282.

39. "Ostrich farms and the trade," *The Millinery Trade Review* 24, no. 6 (June 1899): 63.

40. Ibid.

41. "Concerning Animals," *Vogue* (June 14, 1906), p. ii.

42. *Souvenir Catalogue: Cawston Ostrich Farm* (South Pasadena, CA: Edwin Cawston, 1907–8), p. 5, 20–1. Robin Doughty cites the same remarks which were also printed in the souvenir catalogue from 1906. "Ostrich Farming American Style," *Agricultural History* 47, no. 2 (April 1973): p. 143.

43. *Souvenir Catalogue: Cawston Ostrich Farm* (South Pasadena, CA: Edwin Cawston, 1907–8) pp. 9, 10.

44. Sarah Abrevaya Stein, *Plumes: Ostrich Feathers, Jews, and a Lost World of Global Commerce* (New Haven: Yale University Press, 2008), p. 23.

45. "As to Ostrich Feathers," *New York Times* (October 21, 1917), p. 31.

46. Some examples include: Charles W. Farmer, "Killing, Eating, and Wearing Birds," *New York Times* (May 13, 1900), p. 21; Thomas Upp, "Bright Plumaged Birds," *New York Times* (July

10, 1913), p. 6; Herbert Syrett, "Plumage Saves Birds," *New York Times* (September 13, 1913), p. 10.

47. "The trade," *The Millinery Trade Review* 22, no. 4 (April 1897): 10.

48. Audubon Society biographer Frank Graham, Jr. observed the "certain irony" in this name choice as well. *The Audubon Ark: A History of the National Audubon Society* (New York: Alfred A. Knopf, 1990), p. 10.

49. *The Millinery Trade Review* 22, no. 8 (August 1897): p. 30.

50. This represents the point of view of milliners in the Washington, DC areas as reported by the A.O.U.'s William Dutcher. "Report of the A.O.U. Committee on protection of North American birds," *The Auk* 15, no. 1 (January 1898), p. 95.

51. "For the Woman's Hat," *New York Times* (December 15, 1907), p. 15.

52. "Topics of the Times," *New York Times* (June 2, 1913), p. 6.

53. "Chat," *The Millinery Trade Review* 24, no. 9 (September 1899): 66.

54. "Chat," p. 66; "The truth at last," *The Millinery Trade Review* 24, no. 10 (October 1899): 27.

55. Robin W. Doughty, "Concern for fashionable feathers," *Forest History* 16, no. 2 (July 1972): 9.

56. Robin W. Doughty, *Feather Fashions and Bird Preservation: A Study in Nature Protection* (Berkeley, Los Angeles and London: University of California Press, 1975), p. 67.

57. "Mass meeting of feather workers," *The Millinery Trade Review* 25, no. 5 (May 1900): p. 48.

58. Walter Goodfellow, F.Z.S., M.B.O.U., "The Bird-of-Paradise," *Feathers and Facts: A Reply to the Feather-Trade, and Review of Facts with Reference to the Persecution of Birds for their Plumage* (London: The Royal Society for the Protection of Birds, April 1911), p. 68.

59. "The trade," p.10.

60. "The trade," *The Millinery Trade Review* 22, no. 9 (September 1897): 10.

61. "Woman's Barbarous Dress: The Milliners Protest They Should Not Bear all the Blame," *The Millinery Trade Review*, reprinted in New *York Times* (May 9, 1886), p. 14.

62. "Poor man," *The Millinery Trade Review* 24, no. 4 (April 1899): 25.

63. *New York Times* (April 24, 1910), p. 12.

64. "New York millinery," *The Millinery Trade Review* 22, no. 12 (December 1897): 13.

65. This term is drawn from a letter to the *Boston Transcript* from feather importer Henry Brown and reprinted in the *Millinery Trade Review*. He claimed that the overwhelming majority of wings and birds were "made." "Trade and sentiment," *The Millinery Trade Review* 25, no. 1 (January 1900): 108.

66. T. S. Palmer, *Legislation for the Protection of Birds Other Than Game Birds* (Washington, DC: Government Printing Office, 1900), p. 52.

67. G.O. Shields, "The Slaughter of Birds," *New York Times* (April 27, 1900), p. 8.

68. "Birds saved by the trade: a concession to sentiment," *The Millinery Trade Review* 25, no. 5 (May 1900): 13.

69. "Scientific Notes and News," *Science* 11, no. 284 (June 8, 1900): p. 916.

70. "True friends of the birds," *The Millinery Trade Review* 25, no. 6 (June 1900): 52.

71. "Notes and news," *The Auk* 17, no. 3 (July 1900): 324.

72. "Women Here and There—Their Frills and Fancies," *New York Times* (September 16, 1900), p. 19.

73. "In the Business World: Millinery Trade at War," *New York Times* (November 15, 1903), p. 24.

74. Robin W. Doughty, *Feather Fashions and Bird Preservation: A Study in Nature Protection* (Berkeley, Los Angeles and London: University of California Press, 1975), p. 115.

75. "In the Business World: Won't Attack the Birds Laws," *New York Times* (January 24, 1904), p. 24.

76. Robin W. Doughty, *Feather Fashions and Bird Preservation: A Study in Nature Protection* (Berkeley, Los Angeles and London: University of California Press, 1975), pp. 125–6.

77. C.C. Shayne, "C.C. Shayne's New Fur Fashions," catalog (New York: n.d., c. 1880s), p. 1.

78. "Science: Pampered Rodent," *Time* (April 28, 1947), online archive.

79. Agnes C. Laut, *The Fur Trade of America* (New York: The Macmillan Company, 1921), p. vii.

80. "Concerning Animals," *Vogue* (May 1, 1910), pp. 56, 58; Arthur Samet, *Oddly Enough: From Animal Land to Furtown* (New York: Fur Education Society, 1938), pp. 56–7.

81. C.C. Shayne, "C.C. Shayne's New Fur Fashions," catalog (New York: n.d., c. 1880s), p. 2.

82. "Fur and Near-Fur," *Vogue* (October 15, 1913), p. 92.

83. "Cruelty to Animals," *New York Times* (July 24, 1873), p. 8.

84. "Hints for Fur Buyers," *New York Times* (January 18, 1891), p. 11.

85. Edna Woolman Chase, *Always in Vogue* (Garden City, New York: Doubleday & Company, Inc., 1954), p. 34.

86. Ibid., p. 36.

87. "Josephine Redding," Voguepedia. Available from www.vogue.com/voguepedia/Josephine_Redding [accessed September 2, 2013].

88. *Vogue* (October 12,1899), p. 226.

89. A Repentant Sinner, "Furs and Their Wearers: A Lady's Confession," in Sidney Trist (ed.) *The Animals' Friend* (London: George Bell & Sons, 1896–7), p. 64.

90. "Hints for Fur Buyers," *New York Times* (January 18, 1891), p. 11.

91. Ibid.

92. Ibid.

93. "Fashion: What She Wears: The Extent to Which Fur is to Be Used—Various Muff Models—Barbaric Sumptuousness of Opera Cloaks—Cloak of White Moiré Flowered With Tulips and Nasturtiums—Shawl-Shape Wrap," *Vogue* (November 18,1897), p. 332.

94. Ibid.

95. "Hints for Fur Buyers," *New York Times* (January 18, 1891), p. 11.

96. "Pure Fur Law Demanded to Protect Women and Merchants," *New York Times* (December 14, 1913), X10.

97. "New Styles in Furs," *New York Times* (December 17, 1916), p. X2.

98. *American Album of Fur Novelties* (New York: American Fashion Co., Wm. P. Ahnelt, April 1919) p. 15.

99. Text translated by Robert Warren. Felix Jungmann et Cie (ed.), *Les Belles Fourrures* (Paris: A. Colmer et Cie, September 1913), plate 1.

100. Ibid., plate 5.

101. "Fashion: The Verdicts of the Paris Openings," *Vogue* (October 1, 1916), pp. 44–5.

102. *The Year Book of the Fur Industry* (New York: Ready Reference Publishing Co., 1926), p. 3.

103. Ibid., p. 11.

104. Lois Long, "On and Off the Avenue," *The New Yorker* (October 16, 1926), p. 46.

105. Ibid.

106. "Paris is Wrapped Up in its New Winter Furs," *Vogue* (December 1, 1921), p. 43.

107. *American Album of Fur Novelties*, p. 15.

108. Janet Duer, "The American woman and dress," *Art & Life* 10, no. 6 (June 1919): 329.

109. Agnes C. Laut, *The Fur Trade of America* (New York: The Macmillan Company, 1921), p. 25.

110. Edward Breck, Ph.D., "Letters to the Editor: Use of Steel Traps," *New York Times* (August 23, 1925), p. X10.

111. "20,000,000 Animals Tortured in Traps," *New York Times* (October 24, 1923), p. 12.

112. Agnes C. Laut, *The Fur Trade of America* (New York: The Macmillan Company, 1921), p. vi.

113. Ibid., p. 40.

114. Laut, p. 29.

115. *The Year Book of the Fur Industry* (New York: Ready Reference Publishing Co., 1926), p. 19.

116. Frank G. Ashbrook, "Safeguarding the Raw Fur Supply," in *The Year Book of the Fur Industry* (New York: Ready Reference Publishing Co., 1926), p. 23.

117. Ibid., pp. 23, 25.

118. Frank G. Ashbrook, p. 25.

119. Ibid.

120. "Wear no fur of animal killed inhumanely, Mrs. Fiske urges," *The Milwaukee Journal* (April 1, 1920), 10.

121. "Mrs. Fiske Exposes Trapper Cruelties," *Berkeley Daily Gazette* (June 15, 1925), p. 6.

122. "Wear no fur of animal killed inhumanely, Mrs. Fiske urges," *The Milwaukee Journal* (April 1, 1920), p. 10.

123. "Mrs. Fiske Exposes Trapper Cruelties," *Berkeley Daily Gazette* (June, 15 1925), p. 6.

124. Minnie Maddern Fiske, "What a deformed thief this fashion is," *Ladies' Home Journal* (September 1921), 113.

125. "Mrs. Fiske as Friend of Animals," *New York Times* (May 18, 1919), p. 53.

126. "Topics of the Times," *New York Times* (December 1, 1924), p. 16.

127. Agnes C. Laut, *The Fur Trade of America* (New York: The Macmillan Company, 1921), p. viii.

128. Robert G. Hodgson, *The A.B.C. of Fur Farming* (Ontario: Fur Trade Journal of Canada, 1967), p. 7.

129. "Made in America: Fur Coats by the Millions; New Colours, Dyed or Bred," *Vogue* (February 1, 1951), p. 235.

130. "Curious Farming," *New York Times* (April 22, 1866), p. 4.

131. "Animals: Fur Week," *Time* (November 13, 1933), online archive.

132. Lois J. Fenske and Dwight E. Robinson, "The flight from fur: a study of technological innovation in a luxury market," *Dress* 10 (1984): 27.

133. Frank G. Ashbrook, *Furs: Glamorous and Practical* (New York: D. Van Nostrand Company, Inc., 1954), p. 27.

134. Nan Robertson, "Color in Fur: Some Natural and Some Borrowed," *New York Times* (October 7, 1955), p. 28.

135. "Furs, Profits, Foreign Trade: New King of Beasts," *Time* (January 31, 1944), online archive.

136. Christian Dior, *The Little Dictionary of Fashion* (New York: Abrams, 2007), p. 77.

137. Cedric Larson, "Terms of the fur industry," *American Speech* 24, no. 2 (April 1949): 97–8.

138. "How to Buy a Fur Coat," *Vogue* (October 1, 1959), p. 191.

139. *The Lady Wants Mink*, prod. and dir. William A. Seiter, A Republic Picture, 1953, DVD.

140. "Fur: The Latest Thing," *Time* (December 29, 1952), online archive.

141. *The Lady Wants Mink*, prod. and dir. William A. Seiter, A Republic Picture, 1953, DVD.

142. "How to Buy a Mink Coat," *Vogue* (August 15, 1961), p. 78.

143. "Fur: The Latest Thing," *Time* (December 29, 1952), online archive.

144. Angela Taylor, "Furriers Venture Forth Into Miniskirt and Pants World," *New York Times* (June 16, 1967), p. FS47.

145. "Fashion: Fun Furs," *Time* (October 22, 1965), online archive.

146. Caren Goldberg, "Fur is Better on the Real Owner," *New York Times* (November 10, 1985), p. CN34.

147. Kathy Larkin, "Fur-Weather Forecast," *New York* (November 20, 1978), p. 115.

148. "Environment: Mink Yes, Tiger No," *Time*, August 31, 1970, online archive; "Traffic in Savagery," *New York Times* (September 19, 1968), p. 46.

149. "Fashion: After Mink, What?" *Time* (October 5, 1962), online archive.

150. Angela Taylor, "Fur Coats: Facing Extinction at Conservationists' Hand?," *New York Times* (December 30, 1969), p. 28.

151. Ibid.

152. William G. Conway, "Biologist's Despair," *New York Times* (November 2, 1969), p. SM37.

153. "A Vogue Editorial: Furs, Fashion, and Conservation," *Vogue* (September 1, 1970), p. 144.

154. "Fur: A New Species," *Harper's Bazaar* (August 1970), p. 106.

155. Ibid., p. 111.

156. *Harper's Bazaar* (August 1970), pp. 142–7.

157. Isadore Barmash, "Trouble-Coated Fur Industry," *New York Times* (March 26, 1972), p. F1.

158. Ibid.

159. Angela Taylor, "Fur Coats: Facing Extinction at Conservationists' Hand?" *New York Times* (December 30, 1969), p. 28.

160. Angela Taylor, "Bringing Fashion to Fur," *New York Times* (September 19, 1976), p. 211.

161. Toni Kosover, "Fur Rides High on Fashion," *New York Times* (November 21, 1976), p. 125.

162. Barbara Ettore, "Furriers Worry About Their Boom," *New York Times* (December 10, 1978), p. F11.

163. Although the press treated the youthful consumer as something of a new phenomenon, it was not the first time fur buying had skewed toward a younger generation. According to "Modern Living: The Year of the Fur," in *Time* (December 15, 1967), by the end of the 1960s, many buyers of minks were middle class or working women in their twenties.

164. Kirk Johnson, "Fur Sales Boom—And So Do Imports," *New York Times* (April 7, 1985), p. F8.

165. Judy Bloomfield, "Fur Set to Fly; Industry Plans to Fight Back," *Women's Wear Daily* (June 27, 1989), p. 1; Kim Foltz, "Fur Industry Assails Critics in National Campaign," *New York Times* (December 4, 1989), p. D11.

166. *The Fur Trade Library: Answers* (International Fur Trade Federation, 1985), p. 34.

167. C.C. Shayne, "C.C. Shayne's New Fur Fashions," catalog (New York: n.d., c. 1880s), p. 1.

168. Woody Hochswender, "As the Image of Furs Suffers, So Does Profit," *New York Times* (March 14, 1989), p. A1.

169. Lisa Belkin, "For Thriving Furriers, Protesters Pose Threat," *New York Times* (December 17, 1985), D1.

170. John B. Hinge, "Fur Industry, Under Fire, Shows Its Claws," *Wall Street Journal* (January 3, 1991), p. B5.

171. Valerie Gladstone, "Buying a Fur Coat in an Age of Animal-Rights Protestors," *New York Times* (December 22, 1991), Ll2.

172. Yona Zeldis McDonough, "Sisters Under the Skin," *New York Times* (April 2, 1988), p. 23.

173. "All About PETA," People for the Ethical Treatment of Animals. Available from http://www.peta.org/about/learn-about-peta/default.aspx [accessed September 2, 2013].

174. Dirk Johnson, "Some View Battle in Snow Country As Turning Point in War Over Fur," Special to the *New York Times* (February 12, 1990), p. A18.

175. Arthur Samet, *Oddly Enough: From Animal Land to Furtown* (New York: Fur Education Society, 1938), p. 196.

176. Gunnar Joergensen (ed.), *Mink Production* (Hilleroed, Denmark: Scientifur, 1985), p. 186.

177. Katherine Bishop, "From the Shop to Lab to Farm, Animal Rights Battle is Felt," Special to the *New York Times* (January 14, 1989), p. 1.

178. Dan Mathews, *Committed* (New York: Atria Books, 2007), p. 5.

179. Trip Gabriel, "Fur Protesters Interrupt Shows, but Barely," *New York Times* (February 11, 2000), p. A1.

180. Stacy Perman, "Anti-fur groups set fall offensive," *Women's Wear Daily* (November 23, 1992), p. 2.

181. Woody Hochswender, "Patterns," *New York Times* (May 14, 1991), p. B7.

182. "Calvin Decides to Shed his Fur Coat Collection," *Women's Wear Daily* (February 11, 1994), p. 2.

183. Alisha Davis, "Road Kill on the Runway," *Newsweek* (February 21, 2000), p. 53.

184. Nadine Brozan, "Chronicle," *New York Times* (December 20, 1996), p. B5.

185. Jennifer Steinhauer, "Fur is Coming Out of the Fashion Industry's Closet," *New York Times* (October 1, 1997), p. A1.

186. Anna Wintour, "Letter from the Editor: Cultural Conflicts," *Vogue* (May 1998), p. 58.

187. Teri Agins, "Boss Talk: Pulling Fashion's Strings; *Vogue* Editor Anna Wintour is Arbiter, Adviser, Kingmaker; 'I Like the Fun and the Fancy," *Wall Street Journal* (September 16, 2003), p. B1.

188. Sarah Ferguson, "Strike a Pose," *New York* (November 7, 1994), p. 64.

189. Eric Wilson, "PETA to Sponsor Show," *Women's Wear Daily* (January 29, 2002), p. 2.

190. Elizabeth Holmes, "Less Paint, More Parties—PETA Tames Its Fur Furor; Comes Off the Picket Line to Cozy Up to Fashion Insiders," *Wall Street Journal* (March 10, 2011), p. D1.

191. Constance C. R. White, "Blass Pullout Alarms Industry," *Women's Wear Daily* (January 31, 1989), P. 13.

192. "Background," Origin Assured. Available from http://www.originassured.com/index.php/initiative/ [accessed September 2, 2013].

193. John Sorenson, "Ethical fashion and the exploitation of nonhuman animals," *Critical Studies in Fashion & Beauty* 2, no.s 1–2 (2011): 154.

194. Sally Beatty, "Weekend Journal: Fall Fashion: The Big Cover-up," *Wall Street Journal* (September 3, 2004), p. W1.

195. "Silence on the Lambs," *New York Times* (February 27, 1994), p. SM16.

196. Quoted text appears on p. 144. John Sorenson, 142–4, 147.

197. "The Leather Industry," PETA.org. Available from http://www.peta.org/issues/animals-used-for-clothing/leather-industry.aspx [accessed September 2, 2013].

198. Thomas C. Thorstensen, *Practical Leather Technology: Third Edition* (Florida: Robert E. Krieger Publishing Company, Inc.), p. 138.

199. Richard Daniels, MCGI, FSLTC, *Back to Basics: The Environment* (Liverpool: World Trades Publishing, 2004), p. 9.

200. Maria Ricapito, "Waste Not: Recycled Fur," *New York Times* (November 22, 1998), p. ST5.

201. John Sorenson, "Ethical Fashion and the Exploitation of Nonhuman Animals," *Critical Studies in Fashion & Beauty* 2, no.s 1–2 (2011): 141–2.

202. "Organic Wool Fact Sheet," *Organic Trade Association,* http://www.ota.com/organic/woolfactsheet.html [accessed February 28, 2014].

203. Chioma Nnadi, "Hide & Seek," *Vogue* (November 2011), p. 174.

204. "Retailing Fur Flies Again," *Time* (December 29,1975), online archive.

205. John Sorenson, "Ethical Fashion and the Exploitation of Nonhuman Animals," *Critical Studies in Fashion & Beauty* 2, no.s 1–2 (2011): 152.

206. Ibid., 151.

207. Nancy Hass, "Teaching the Leather Crowd How to Stray from the Herd," *New York Times* (March 19, 2000), p. ST1.

208. John Sorenson, 139–40.

209. Ibid., 139.

210. Ibid., 141.

211. Thomas Hainschwang and Laurence Leggio, "The characterization of tortoise shell and its imitations," *Gems & Gemology* (Spring 2006): 36, 38.

212. "Status of trade in hawksbill turtles," Convention on International Trade in Endangered Species of Wild Fauna and Flora (CITES). Available from http://www.cites.org/eng/prog/hbt/bg/trade_status.shtml [accessed April 8, 2013].

213. *Ivory: An International History and Illustrated Survey* (New York: Abrams, 1987), p. 19.

214. Ashish Kumar Sen, "African Officials Seek U.S. Drones to Fight Elephant Poachers," *Washington Times* (July 31, 2013). Available from http://www.washingtontimes.com/news/2013/jul/31/elephants-rhinos-lions-and-drones-tanzania-conside/ [accessed August 24, 2013].

215. Clifford Warwick, "Reptiles—Misunderstood, Mistreated, and Mass-Marketed," in International Wildlife Coalition (ed.), *Skinned* (North Falmouth, MA: International Wildlife Coalition, 1988), p. 143.

216. Ismat Tahseen, "Fashion Can Be Cold-blooded; Is What National Award-winning Actor Raveena Tandon-Thadani Wants to Convey as She Decries Using Animal Skin for Style," *Daily News & Analysis* (September 13, 2010). *Gale Power Search* [accessed July 16, 2012].

217. "Denounce Wearing of Bird Feathers," *New York Times* (October 23, 1923), p. 12.

218. Frank G. Ashbrook, *Furs: Glamorous and Practical* (New York: D. Van Nostrand Company, Inc., 1954), p. 33.

219. "Fake Fur, Very Much at Home," *Vogue* (October 15, 1949), p. 75.

220. "Fake Fur Becomes a Novelty Fabric," *New York Times* (September 13, 1950), p. 42.

221. Virginia Pope, "Patterns of the Times: Fashioned for Fake Furs," *New York Times* (November 13, 1950), p. 24.

222. Herbert Koshetz, "Imitation Fur is Flying High as Fabric for Women's Coats," *New York Times* (June 17, 1964), p. 59.

223. "Demand for Fake Leather," *New York Times* (September 1, 1968), p. F7,

224. Isadore Barmash, "Young Won't Think Mink; Furs Slump," *New York Times* (September 21, 1969), p. F1.

225. The advertisement asserted that at the time of printing roughly 590 tigers existed. "Advertisement: E. F. Timme & Sons, Inc." *Vogue* (July 1, 1970), p. 14.

226. "Environment: The Vanishing World of Trapper Joe Delia," *Time* (July 27, 1970), online archive.

227. Isadore Barmash, "New York to Stage Its First World Fair for Furs Next Year," *New York Times* (February 9, 1978), p. D1.

228. Constance C.R. White, "Fake Furs Staging a Comeback," *Women's Wear Daily* (July 21, 1988), p. 6.

229. Anne-Marie Schiro, "Fake Furs are Saving More Skins," *New York Times* (September 5, 1989), p. B7.

230. Linda Wells, "Imitation of Life," *New York Times* (November 1, 1987), p. SM62.

231. Stacy Perman, "The Fur is Flying," *Women's Wear Daily* (April 19, 1994), p. 6.

Conclusion

1. "Profile," Isoude.com. Available from http://www.isoude.com/profile [accessed June 28, 2013].

2. St. John the Divine is a late nineteenth-century cathedral located in the Morningside Heights neighborhood of Manhattan, New York.

SELECT BIBLIOGRAPHY

A Lady (1874), *How to Dress on £15 a Year,* London: George Routledge and Sons.

Anson, R. (2012), "Can the shift of textile and clothing production to Asia be reversed?" *Textile Outlook International* (159): 4–9.

—(2013), "Overcoming obstacles to environmental sustainability in the textile and apparel industry," *Textile Outlook International* (161): 4–11.

Arnold, J. (1977), *Patterns of Fashion: Englishwomen's Dresses and Their Construction, c. 1660-1860,* London: Macmillan.

—(1989), "The Cut and Construction of Women's Clothes in the Eighteenth Century," in J. Starobinski, *Revolution in Fashion: European Clothing, 1715-1815,* New York: Abbeville Press.

—(1999), "'The Lady's Economical Assistant' of 1808," in B. Burman (ed.), *The Culture of Sewing: Gender, Consumption and Home Dressmaking,* Oxford: Berg.

Aspelund, K. (2009), *Fashioning Society: A Hundred Years of Haute Couture by Six Designers,* New York: Fairchild Books.

Barmash, I. (1966), "Polyester Emerges from the Shadow of Nylon," *New York Times,* 1 May.

Bartrip, P. W. J. (1994), "How green was my valance?: Environmental arsenic poisoning and the Victorian domestic ideal," *The English Historical Review* 109 (433): 891–913.

Baumgarten, L. (2001), "Altered historical clothing," *Dress,* 25.

Beard, N. (2008), "The branding of ethical fashion and the consumer: A luxury niche or mass-market reality?" *Fashion Theory,* 12(4): 447–68.

Bide, M. (2011), "Fiber Sustainability: Green is not Black + White," in L. Welters and A. Lillethun (eds), *The Fashion Reader: Second Edition,* Oxford: Berg.

Bisno, A. (1967), *Abraham Bisno: Union Pioneer,* Madison: University of Wisconsin Press.

Black, S. (2008), *Eco-Chic: The Fashion Paradox,* London: Black Dog Publishing.

Black, S. and Anderson, S. (2010), "Making sustainability fashionable: Profile of the Danish fashion company Noir," *Fashion Practice,* 2(1): 121–8.

Blackburn, R. S. (ed.) (2009), *Sustainable Textiles: Life Cycle and Environmental Impact,* New York: CRC Press.

Blanchard, T. (2007), *Green is the New Black: How to Change the World with Style,* London: Hodder and Stoughton.

Blom, P. (2004), *Enlightening the World: Encyclopédie, The Book That Changed the Course of History,* New York: Palgrave Macmillan.

Board of Trade by the Minister of Information (1943), *Make Do and Mend,* repr., Sevenoaks, Kent: Sabrestorm Publishing, 2007.

Bok, E. (1920), *The Americanization of Edward Bok: The Autobiography of a Dutch Boy Fifty Years Later,* New York: Charles Scribner's Sons, 1920.

Brown, S. (2010), *Eco Fashion,* London: Laurence King Publishing.

Bruchey, S. (ed.) (1967), *Cotton and the Growth of the American Economy, 1790-1860,* New York: Harcourt, Brace & World, Inc.

Brunnschweiler, D. and Hearle, J. (eds) (1993), *Polyester: Tomorrow's Ideas and Profits, Fifty Years of Achievement,* Manchester: The Textile Institute.

Buck, A. (1979), *Dress in Eighteenth-Century England,* New York: Holmes and Meier Publications, Inc.

Burman, B. (ed.) (1999), *The Culture of Sewing: Gender, Consumption and Home Dressmaking,* Oxford: Berg.

Burnham, D. K. (1973), *Cut my Cote,* Toronto: Royal Ontario Museum.

Butterick, H. G. (1924), *Principles of Clothing Selection,* New York: Macmillan.

Byerly, V. (1986), *Hard Times Cotton Mill Girls: Personal Histories of Womanhood and Poverty in the South,* Ithaca, NY: ILR Press.

Carson, R. (1962), *Silent Spring: Fortieth Anniversary Edition,* Boston and New York: Houghton Mifflin Company.

Cater, K. (2008), "Pandering to the Green Consumer," *The Guardian,* 12 August.

Chakraborty, J. N. (2010), *Fundamentals and Practices in Colouration of Textiles,* New Delhi, Cambridge and Oxford: Woodhead Publishing India.

Chanin, N. (2012), *Alabama Studio Sewing + Design: A Guide to Hand-Sewing an Alabama Chanin Wardrobe,* New York: Stewart, Tabori & Chang.

Chase, E. W. (1954), *Always in Vogue,* Garden City, NY: Doubleday.

Clark, H. (2008), 'SLOW + FASHION—an oxymoron—or a promise for the future…?' *Fashion Theory: The Journal of Dress, Body & Culture,* 12(4): 427–46.

Cockett, S. R. (1964), *Dyeing and Printing,* London: Sir Isaac Pitman & Sons Ltd.

Cole, A. H. (1969), *The American Wool Manufacture,* New York: Harper & Row Publishers.

Cooper, G. R. (1968), *The Invention of the Sewing Machine,* Washington, DC: The Smithsonian Institution Press.

Cooper, S. G. (1978), *The Textile Industry: Environmental Control and Energy Conservation,* Park Ridge, NJ: Noyes Date Corp.

Craik, J. (2009), *Fashion: The Key Concepts,* Oxford: Berg.

Crawford, M. D. C. (1941), *The Ways of Fashion,* New York: G. P. Putnam's Sons.

Daniels, R. (2004), *Back to Basics: The Environment,* Liverpool: World Trades Publishing.

De Coster, J. (2007), 'Green textiles and apparel: Environmental impact and strategies for improvement,' *Textile Outlook International,* 132: 143–64.

Debo, K. and Verhelst, B. (2008), *Maison Martin Margiela '20': The Exhibition,* Antwerp: MoMu Fashion Museum.

Delamare, F. and Guineau, B. (2000), *Colors: The Story of Dyes and Pigments,* New York: Harry N. Abrams.

Diesenhouse, S. (1994) "Polyester Becomes Environmentally Correct," *New York Times,* February 20.

Doughty, R. W. (1975), *Feather Fashions and Bird Preservation: A Study in Nature Protection,* Berkeley, Los Angeles and London: University of California Press.

Dunwell, S. (1978), *The Run of the Mill: A Pictorial Narrative of the Expansion, Dominion, Decline and Enduring Impact of the New England Textile Industry,* Boston: David R. Godine.

Dyeing, Remodeling, Budgets (1931), Scranton, PA: The Woman's Institute of Domestic Arts and Sciences.

Eisler, B. (ed.) (1977), *The Lowell Offering: Writings by New England Mill Women (1840–1845),* Philadelphia and New York: J. B. Lippincott Company.

Esquevin, C. (2008), *Adrian: Silver Screen to Custom Label,* New York: The Monacelli Press.

Essinger, J. (2007), *Jacquard's Web: How a Hand-loom Led to the Birth of the Information Age,* Oxford: Oxford University Press.

Evans, C. (1998), "The golden dustman: A critical evaluation of the work of Martin Margiela and a review of Martin Margiela: exhibition (9/4/1615)," *Fashion Theory: The Journal of Dress, Body & Culture,* 2(1): 73–93.

Ferro, M. (2005), "Vinyl as Fashion Fabric," in V. Steele (ed.), *Encyclopedia of Clothing and Fashion,* Detroit, MI: Charles Scribner's Sons.

Fletcher, K. (2008), *Sustainable Fashion & Textiles: Design Journeys,* London: Earthscan.

Fletcher, K. and Grose, L. (2012), *Fashion & Sustainability: Design for Change,* London: Laurence King.

Flint, I. (2008), *Eco Colour: Botanical Dyes for Beautiful Textiles,* Loveland, CO: Interweave.

Funaro, D. (1976), *The Yestermorrow Clothes Book: How to Remodel Secondhand Clothes,* Radner, PA: Chilton Book Co.

The Fur Trade Library: Answers (1985), International Fur Trade Federation.

Geyer, J. C. and Perry, W. A. (1938), *Textile Waste Treatment and Recovery: A Survey of Present Knowledge Concerning the Treatment and Disposal of Waste Waters Produced in the Textile Industries,* Washington, DC: The Textile Foundation, Inc.

Ginsburg, M. (1980), "Rags to riches: The second-hand clothes trade 1700–1978," *Costume,* 14: 121–35.

Graham Jr., F. (1990), *The Audubon Ark: A History of the National Audubon Society,* New York: Alfred A. Knopf.

Greenpeace (2012), *Toxic Threads: The Big Fashion Stitch-Up,* Amsterdam: Greenpeace International.

—(2013), *Toxic Threads: Polluting Paradise,* Amsterdam: Greenpeace International.

Gwilt, A. and Rissanen, T. (eds) (2011), *Shaping Sustainable Fashion: Changing the Way We Make and Use Clothes,* London: Earthscan.

Hamilton, A. (1921), *Industrial Poisoning in Making Coal-Tar Dyes and Dye Intermediates,* Washington, DC: U.S. Department of Labor, Bureau of Labor Statistics.

Hansen, K. (2005), "Secondhand Clothes, Anthropology of," in V. Steele (ed.), *Encyclopedia of Clothing and Fashion,* Detroit, MI: Charles Scribner's Sons.

Hanson, M. and Cox Crews, P. (eds) (2009), *American Quilts in the Modern Age, 1870-1940,* Lincoln, NE: University of Nebraska Press.

Hart, A. and North, S. (2008), *Historical Fashion in Detail: The 17th and 18th Centuries,* London: V&A Publications.

Hawes, E. (1938), *Fashion Is Spinach,* New York: Random House.

Hawley, J., Sullivan, P., and Kyung-Kim, Y. (2005), "Recycled Textiles," in V. Steele (ed.), *Encyclopedia of Clothing and Fashion,* Detroit, MI: Charles Scribner's Sons.

Hemmings, J. (2009), "Rebecca Earley Upcycles Style," *Fiberarts,* January/February: 38–41.

Hethorn, J. and Ulasewicz, C. (eds) (2008), *Sustainable Fashion: Why Now? A Conversation Exploring Issues, Practices, and Possibilities,* New York: Fairchild Books.

Hindman, H. (2002), *Child Labor: An American History,* Armonk, NY and London: M. E. Sharpe.

Hochstim, E. S. (1957), *Women's Attitudes Toward Wool and Other Fibers, no. 153,* Washington, DC: U.S. Department of Agriculture, Agricultural Marketing Service.

Jenkins, D. T. and Ponting, K. G. (1982), *The British Wool Textile Industry, 1770-1914,* London: Heinemann Educational Books.

Jones, D. (1958), "As Washable in December…," *New York Times,* 28 September.

Jubb, S. (1860), *The History of the Shoddy Trade: Its Rise, Progress, and Present Position,* London: Houlston and Wright.

Kibel, J. F. (1998), "Pulp Fashion: The History of Patented Paper Clothing," master's thesis, Fashion Institute of Technology.

Kidwell, C. (1974), *Suiting Everyone: The Democratization of Clothing in America.* Washington, DC: Smithsonian Institution Press.

Kirke, B. (1998), *Vionnet,* San Francisco: Chronicle Books.

Kolander, C. (2007), "In Defense of Truth and Beauty," in L. Hoffman (ed.), *FutureFashion: White Papers,* New York: Earth Pledge.

Kulkarni, S. V. and Blackwell, C. D. et al. (1986), *Textile Dyeing Operations: Chemistry, Equipment, Procedures and Environmental Aspects,* Park Ridge, NJ: Noyes Publications.

Laut, A. C. (1921), *The Fur Trade of America,* New York: The Macmillan Company.

Lemire, B. (2009), "Developing Consumerism and the Ready-made Clothing Trade in Britain, 1750–1800," in P. McNeil (ed.), *Fashion: Critical and Primary Sources,* Oxford: Berg, 2: 241–65.

—(2011), *Cotton,* Oxford: Berg.

Leopold, E. (1993), "The Manufacture of the Fashion System," in J. Ash and E. Wilson (eds), *Chic Thrills: A Fashion Reader,* Berkeley: University of California Press.

Leung, C. (2005), "Reflections on 'meta design' with Mary Ping," *Fashion Projects* (1).

Lewis, F. D. (1961), *The Chemistry and Technology of Rayon Manufacture*, Surrey: Love and Malcomson Ltd.

Marsden, R. (1903), *Cotton Spinning: Its Development, Principles, and Practice,* London: George Bell and Sons.

Marshik, C. (2011), "Smart Clothes at Low Prices," in I. Parkins and E. M. Sheehan (eds), *Cultures of Femininity in Modern Fashion,* Durham, NH: University of New Hampshire Press.

Martin, R. (2003), "Energy and Economy, Measure and Magic," in J. S. Major (ed.), *Yeohlee: Work,* Peleus Press.

Maskiell, M. (2009), "Consuming Kashmir: Shawls and Empires, 1500–2000," in P. McNeil (ed.), *Fashion: Critical and Primary Sources,* Oxford: Berg, 3: 207–40.

Mathews, D. (2007), *Committed,* New York: Atria Books.

McDonough, W. and Braungart, M. (2002), *Cradle to Cradle: Remaking the Way We Make Things,* New York: North Point Press.

McEvoy, A. F. (1995), "The Triangle Shirtwaist factory fire of 1911: Social change, industrial accidents, and the evolution of common-sense causality," *Law & Social Inquiry* 20 (2): 621–51.

McMorris, P. (1984), *Crazy Quilts,* New York: E. P. Dutton.

McRobbie, A. (ed.) (1988), *Zoot Suits and Secondhand Dresses, an Anthology of Fashion and Music,* Boston: Unwin Hyman.

Menkes, S. (1993), "The Shock of the Old," *New York Times,* March 21.

Milinaire, C. and Troy, C. (1975), *Cheap Chic,* New York, Harmony Books.

Montgomery, F. (1970), *Printed Textiles: English and American Cottons and Linens*, New York: The Viking Press.

Nemy, E. (1970), "Those Vintage Dresses That Defy the Whimsies of Fashion," *New York Times,* January 9.

Nieto-Galan, A. (2001), *Colouring Textiles: A History of Natural Dyestuffs in Industrial Europe,* Dordrecht, Boston and London: Kluwer Academic Publishers.

Packard, V. (1960), *The Waste Makers,* New York: David McKay and Company, Inc.

Palmer, A. (2001), *Couture & Commerce: The Transatlantic Fashion Trade in the 1950s,* Vancouver: UBC Press.

Palmer, A. and Clark, H. (eds) (2005), *Old Clothes, New Looks: Second-Hand Fashion,* Oxford: Berg.

Palmer, T. S. (1900), *Legislation for the Protection of Birds Other Than Game Birds*, Washington, DC: Government Printing Office.

Parkins, I. and Sheehan, E. (eds) (2011), *Cultures of Femininity in Modern Fashion*, Durham, NH: University of New Hampshire Press.

Parton, J. (1867), *History of the Sewing Machine,* repr. New York: International Ladies' Garment Workers' Union, 1967.

Patrick, J. (2007), "Color, Magic, and Modern Alchemy," in L. Hoffman (ed.), *FutureFashion: White Papers,* New York: Earth Pledge.

Perkin, W. H. (1869), "The Aniline or Coal Tar Colours," *Cantor Lectures*, London: W. Trounce.

—(1869), "Mauve, Magenta, and Some of Their Derivatives," *Cantor Lectures*, London: W. Trounce.

Posselt, E. A. (1888), *The Jacquard Machine Analyzed and Explained,* Philadelphia: Dando Printing and Publishing Company.

Priddy, A. (F. K. Brown) (1911), *Through the Mill, the Life of a Mill Boy*, Boston, New York and Chicago: The Pilgrim Press.

Riis, J. (1957), *How the Other Half Lives: Studies Among the Tenements of New York*, New York: Hill and Wang, Inc.

Ritter, J. G. and Feather, B. (1990), "Practices, procedures, and attitudes toward clothing maintenance: 1850–1860 and 1900–1910," *Dress*, 17: 156–68.

Roshco, B. (1963), *The Rag Race: How New York and Paris Run the Breakneck Business of Dressing American Women*, New York: Funk & Wagnalls.

Ross, R. J. S. (2007), *Slaves to Fashion: Poverty and Abuse in the New Sweatshops*, Ann Arbor: The University of Michigan Press.

Roulac, J. W. (1997), *Hemp Horizons: The Comeback of the World's Most Promising Plant,* White River Junction, VT: Chelsea Green Publishing Company.

Rourke, M. (1992), "An Activist Autumn: Paris Defines Trendy Issues in Statements of Black and White," *Los Angeles Times,* March 23.

Sanderson, E. (1997), "Nearly new: The second-hand clothing trade in eighteenth-century Edinburgh," *Costume*, 31: 38–48.

Scaturro, S. "Eco-tech fashion: Rationalizing technology in sustainable fashion," *Fashion Theory*, 12(4): 469–88.

Schneider, P. (1993), "The Cotton Brief," *New York Times,* June 20.

Scott, C. L. (1940), *Women's Dresses and Slips: A Buying Guide,* Washington, DC: US Department of Agriculture.

Seidman, J. (1942), *The Needle Trades*, New York, Toronto: Farrar & Rinehart, Inc.

Selekman, B. (1925), *The Clothing and Textile Industries in New York and Its Environs, Present Trends and Probable Future Development,* New York: Regional Plan of New York and its Environs.

Serbin, L. (2007), "Hemp Goes Straight," in *FutureFashion White Papers,* New York: Earth Pledge.

Siegle, L. (2011), *To Die For: Is Fashion Wearing Out the World?,* London: Fourth Estate.

Simmons, P. (1985), *Turning Wool into a Cottage Industry,* Seattle: Madrona Publishers.

Slater, K. (2000), *The Environmental Impact of Textiles: Production, Processes, and Protection*, Cambridge: Woodhead Publishing.

Soohoo, P. (2004), "Fashions for Victory: Innovation, Improvisation & Innovation in American Women's Fashion, 1940–1946," master's thesis, Fashion Institute of Technology.

Sorenson, J. (2011), "Ethical fashion and the exploitation of nonhuman animals," *Critical Studies in Fashion & Beauty,* 2 (1–2): 139–64.

Spool Thread Company (1943), *Make and Mend for Victory,* New York, Spool Thread Company.

Stein, S. A. (2008), *Plumes: Ostrich Feathers, Jews, and a Lost World of Global Commerce,* New Haven: Yale University Press, 2008.

Stevens, R. and Iwamoto Wada, Y. (eds) (1996), *The Kimono Inspiration: Art and Art-to-Wear in America,* Washington, DC: The Textile Museum.

Stolberg, B. (1944), *Tailor's Progress: The Story of a Famous Union and the Men Who Made It,* Garden City, NY: Doubleday, Doran and Company.

"Style Inspiration Seen in Rag Bag and 'Make-Do Fashions' Prove Chic" (1943), *New York Times,* April 29.

Synder, R. L. (2008), *Fugitive Denim: A Moving Story of People and Pants in the Borderless World of Global Trade,* New York: W. W. Norton & Co.

"The Sweat-Shop Problem" (1895), *New York Times*, December 17.

"Talking Strategy: Andreas Dorner of Lenzing discusses the fibres which will shape the apparel industry in the future," (2012), *Global Apparel Markets,* 18: 4–14.

Taylor, A. (1966), "Fashions to Buy, Wear and Then Throw Away," *New York Times,* August 19.

—(1967), "An East Side Boutique Dedicated to Disposability," *New York Times,* June 10.

—(1970), "There's Something New at Altman's: Shop That Has Authentic Old Clothes," *New York Times,* July 9.

—(1971), "For One-of-a-Kind Fashions," *New York Times,* July 26.

Terkel, S. (2000), *Hard Times,* New York: The New Press.

Textile World (1939), *The Rayon Handbook,* New York: McGraw-Hill.

Thomas, D. (2007), *Deluxe: How Luxury Lost Its Luster,* New York: Penguin Press.

Thompson, H. (1899), *From the Cotton Field to the Cotton Mill: A Study of the Industrial Transition in North Carolina*, New York and London: The Macmillan Company.

Timmerman, K. (2009), *Where Am I Wearing?: A Global Tour to the Countries, Factories, and People That Make Our Clothes*, Hoboken, NJ: John Wiley and Sons, Inc.

Tobler-Rohr, M. I. (2011), *Handbook of Sustainable Textile Production*, Oxford, Philadelphia: Woodhead and Cambridge: In association with the Textile Institute.

Tompkins, D. A. (1899), *Cotton Mill, Commercial Features: a Text-Book for the Use of Textiles Schools and Investors*, Charlotte, NC: The Author.

Travis, A. S. (1997), "Poisoned groundwater and contaminated soil: The tribulations and trial of the first major manufacturer of aniline dyes in Basel," *Environmental History* 2 (3): 343–65.

U.S. Department of Labor (1994–5), *By the Sweat and Toil of Children: The Use of Child Labor in American Imports Vol. 1*, Washington, DC: The Bureau of International Affairs.

—(1996), *The Apparel Industry Codes of Conduct: A Solution to the International Child Labor Problem?* Washington, DC: U.S. Department of Labor, Bureau of International Affairs.

Viscose Company (1929), *The Story of Rayon*, New York: The Viscose Company.

Watson, J. (1991), *Textiles and the Environment: Special Report no. 2150*, London: The Economist Intelligence Unit.

Weiss, E. (1981), *Secondhand Super Shopper: Buying More, Spending Less, Living Better*, New York: M. Evans.

Wetherill, L. (2009) "Consumer Behavior, Textiles and Dress in the Late Seventeenth and Early Eighteenth Centuries," in McNeil, P. (ed.), *Fashion: Critical and Primary Sources*, Oxford: Berg, 2: 159–75.

Wilson, E. (1987), *Adorned in Dreams: Fashion and Modernity*, Berkeley: University of California Press.

Wirz, M. (2011), "The Touch, the Feel—Of Rayon?," *Wall Street Journal*, 6 January.

Women's Home Companion Readers (1948), *Women's Clothing: A Survey of Selection, Sewing and Spending*, New York: Crowell-Collier Publication Company.

World Apparel Fibre Consumption Survey (1985), Rome: Food and Agriculture Organization of the United Nations.

The Year Book of the Fur Industry (1926), New York: Ready Reference Publishing Co.

GLOSSARY

Aigrette the feather of an egret or white heron, used as millinery trimming during the late nineteenth and early twentieth centuries.

Aniline dyes synthetic chemical dyes, derived from coal tar.

Cooperative (or collective) a group of artisans, usually involved in the handcrafting or production of goods, often found in impoverished areas.

Cruelty-free any material that is not derived from or does not harm an animal through its production; this category encompasses all synthetic or manmade fibers.

Dye effluent the waste, primarily liquid, generated during the dyeing process.

Fair trade a supportive, ongoing trade relationship in which trading partners are provided with just treatment, wages and/or compensation.

Fast fashion trend-driven clothing that is made as cheaply and quickly as possible, and that is intended for wear a small number of times before disposal.

Greenwashing the incorporation of a marginal amount of sustainable practice into a business model, usually implemented by large organizations in an attempt to enhance their public image.

Manmade fibers fibers that are chemically produced from natural polymers. Common manmade fibers include acetate and rayon.

Mordant a substance or material used as a dye fixative.

Natural fibers fibers that are derived from plants (such as cotton and linen) or animals (such as silk and wool).

Post-consumer waste refuse consisting of consumer products that have been disposed of at the end of their lifecycles.

Pre-consumer waste refuse resulting from the processing and manufacture of a consumer product; in fashion production, this refers to materials such as scrap fabric.

Recycled textiles fibers that have been fully reprocessed and converted into new fabrics.

Repurposed clothing garments that were heavily altered, or entirely refashioned from existing garments or textiles.

Secondhand clothing garments re-distributed to new owners, usually through being given away, or through resale at a secondhand shop or market.

Slow fashion a method of clothing production that centers on transparent production models, the use of local resources and economies, and the creation of high-quality goods with greater value and longer lives.

Sweatshop any working environment in which production of goods is done through violation of any aspect of fair labor, whether that is wages, hours, or conditions of work; the word is derived from the manufacturing chain in which a contractor, or "sweater" is the middleman between manufacturer and "sweated" employee.

Synthetic fibers fibers that are chemically produced from artificial polymers. Common synthetic fibers include acrylic, nylon and polyester.

Upcycling the technique of transforming unwanted materials into products of equal—or usually higher—value.

Zero waste a method of clothing design and production that results in minimal refuse, particularly focused on the elimination of scrap fabric.

INDEX

Page references in italics denote a figure

Printed in Great Britain
by Amazon

19007953R00149